ETHICS
and the
AUSTRALIAN
NEWS MEDIA

ETHICS

and the

AUSTRALIAN NEWS MEDIA

JOHN HURST
Deakin University

and

SALLY A. WHITE
Royal Melbourne Institute of Technology

M

First published 1994 by
MACMILLAN EDUCATION AUSTRALIA PTY LTD
107 Moray Street, South Melbourne 3205

Associated companies and representatives
throughout the world

National Library of Australia
cataloguing in publication data

Hurst, John, 1934–,
    Ethics and the Australian news media.

    Bibliography.
    Includes index.
    ISBN 0 7329 1940 1.
    ISBN 0 7329 1939 8 (pbk.).

    1. Journalistic ethics — Australia. 2. Mass media — Australia —
    Moral and ethical aspects. I. White, Sally, A. II. Title.

174.9097

Typeset in Palatino and Times
by Typeset Gallery, Malaysia

Printed in Hong Kong

Cover design by Raoul Diche
Cover photograph courtesy of News Ltd
Index by Michael Wood

Contents

Acknowledgements

My thanks are due to the library staff of Deakin University, the University of Melbourne and the State Library of Victoria for their assistance with research; to the many people who responded in writing or in interviews to questions about the news media, and to my daughter Elizabeth and good friends Peter Ross and Elaine Lloyd, for their encouragement. Nor should I forget a patient and thoughtful editor, Jenni Coombs, for piloting this book through its final passage to publication.

J.H.

Many people helped bring this book to fruition, either through discussion and argument that helped to clarify my thoughts or in research assistance. Particular thanks go to the ever-helpful editorial library staff at *The Age*, to the diligent and enthusiastic Carol Abbott and Cheryl Brander of the RMIT Communications Studies Department and, above all, to Ranald Macdonald for his inspirational and persistent championing of ethical journalism over many years. I am grateful to Michael Gawenda for permission to use his article from *The Age* on the Bendigo jail siege, to Georgina Griffin for giving access to her research material for her final year project in the BA (Journalism) at RMIT, and to Michael Wood for his indexing expertise. This book is dedicated to the memory of my mother, Mollie Allen, whose loving and sound criticism was deeply missed.

S.A.W.

Introduction

Complaints about media performance are not new. For every champion of the press — such as American James Madison who said that freedom of the press was 'the only effectual guardian of every other right' — there is a detractor, such as the 18th century English political journalist William Cobbett, who likened journalists to a parcel of toads which, when disturbed by a brickbat, 'turned on their backs . . . showing their nasty white bellies, and all croaking out their alarm, and emitting their poisonous matter'. Journalists have also been called jackals, sharks, reptiles, liars, whores and ratbags. In contemporary Australia, criticism is sometimes less colourful but no less trenchant. Australia journalists are 'huge and fearsome mastiffs'.[1] They are motivated by self-aggrandisement, self-promotion and ego.[2] They are 'obsessed with a sense of power, the power to sneer and smear'.[3] Their stories are 'absolute manufactured garbage written without regard for the truth'.[4]

Behind all the name-calling is the idea that journalists behave dishonourably and unethically. Of course, unkind names, of themselves, should not deter journalists from doing their job but allegations of unethical conduct are damaging because they hit at the credibility and integrity of the media's product. Many media professionals would rightly argue that it is not the duty of the media to win friends but rather to seek out and reveal the misdeeds, cant and impropriety of people and institutions within society. At the same time, however, the media must be sufficiently popular, commercially, to ensure their continued existence in a world in which the demands for people's attention grow increasingly clamorous. This dilemma has a profound effect on the ways in which the media operate; its effects and the tensions it creates are one of the main themes of this book.

Opinion poll surveys testify to public distrust and dissatisfaction with media performance with disturbing regularity. A Time-Morgan poll in mid-1993 awarded Australian newspaper journalists an ethics and honesty rating of 8 per cent, well behind that given to politicians. The only surveyed occupation to receive a lower score than journalism was selling used cars.[5] Equally significant for the practice of journalism is the perception that journalists do not care much about accuracy, a basic tenet of good journalism. An earlier Gallup Poll in 1988 had given journalists an ethics rating of 9 per cent; it also found that three-quarters of the Australians surveyed thought that 'stories were often inaccurate'.[6]

The Australian Centre for Independent Journalism in Sydney tried to determine just how often metropolitan daily newspapers got stories wrong. The research team's general finding was that although Australian newspapers made more errors than they admitted in published corrections, they were performing better than their North American counterparts.[7] However, the survey showed about half of all articles contained at least one error[8] and when prominent people were asked to nominate mistakes in stories about themselves, 77 per cent said there was an average of one or two errors in each story.[9]

The findings of specific research make uncomfortable reading for Australian journalists. However, most public criticism of media performance in Australia is more generalised and tends to fall into several broad categories. Some critics are mainly concerned with the country's high level of concentration in media ownership with the implications that has for a narrowing in the diversity of news and opinion. Others are more concerned about intrusions into people's privacy, the perceived hectoring of interviewees by journalists, and an apparent cynical disregard for the rights and sensibilities of others in the quest for improved ratings or boosted circulation.

A third general category of criticism is that the process of news gathering and dissemination in all media — print and broadcast — distorts the reality of Australian life. Such critics argue that women are almost invisible as news makers; young people get a bad press; ethnic minorities are ignored or treated insensitively. A second thread of the complaint about distorted reality is that the media exaggerate or sensationalise the nature of events to make their stories more commercially appealing. Some people also worry that the accuracy and truth of stories are compromised by advertising pressures or the interlocking commercial interests and political allegiances of proprietors and senior media executives.

Yet another complaint is that the technical demands of television and, to a lesser extent, radio mean the gap between entertainment and information is growing ever narrower while, in newspaper pages, opinion masquerades as objective truth.

Concern about standards in Australian journalism has been voiced for more than 130 years. As Clem Lloyd notes in his history of the Australian Journalists Association (AJA) (now the AJA section of the Media, Entertainment and Arts Alliance): 'There were frequent calls to raise the professional status of journalism, to give journalists a better education, to inculcate in them finely attuned senses of honour and respectability.'[10] The *Victorian Review* in the 1860s proposed a university education for journalists as an antidote to the 'ignorance and puerility [that] disfigure the columns of a large section of the newspaper press'.[11] The maintenance of standards was a prime motivation behind the formation of the AJA; yet it was the proprietors who, in 1927, first articulated some principles of ethical journalism. The New South Wales Country Press Association gave its member newspapers a copy of a 15-point code of ethics which included 'provisions for fair play, respect for privacy . . . truthful reporting, elimination of the sensational and salacious'.[12]

Despite a decade of discussion among the journalists, it was not until the 1944 federal conference of the AJA that the union adopted a uniform eight-point code. The code of ethics, which was incorporated into the union's constitution and rules, drew hostile comment from the employers. Rupert Henderson, general manager of *The Sydney Morning Herald*, gave voice to a sentiment that remains deeply entrenched in most media managements today. He said that 'the maintenance of ethical standards is a matter between newspapers and their readers . . . Newspapers will conduct their newspapers in accordance with the standards which have established their reputation . . . They are not willing to surrender or to share their responsibility in the control of what is, to them, a great trust'.[13] Henderson's vigorous defence of the freedom of newspaper managements to conduct business as they saw fit is invariably echoed whenever the role of the Australian news media is debated.

Certainly the adoption of the code of ethics did not still public criticism of journalists' conduct. Calls for change continued to surface intermittently, usually in response to a news event in which the media were deemed to have behaved improperly. Some of the ideas for change caused more ripples than others. Understandably, whenever representatives of governments murmured that the media had to improve their performance, the industry closed ranks in defence of the principle of media independence. Occasionally, a threat of intervention triggered action. In 1975, a discussion paper emanating from the office of the federal Minister for the Media proposed the formation of a press council to deal with complaints against the press.

The AJA had supported the idea of such self-regulation since its 1955 federal conference had urged the various AJA branches to consult with state governments and proprietors with a view to setting up state press councils, based on the British Press Council model.[14] Maverick publisher Ranald Macdonald of David Syme & Co. Limited had advocated the idea too, but it was the government discussion paper that galvanised the Australian Newspaper Council to set up the Australian Press Council in 1976.

The Press Council formulated a statement which laid down two broad principles to which it was committed. They were that the freedom of the press to publish was the freedom of the public to be informed and that such a freedom entailed obligations towards the people. The Press Council further outlined 11 general propositions — covering accuracy, honesty, fairness and candour — that would guide its judgements about a newspaper's conduct. Several of the propositions draw directly on clauses of the AJA code of ethics, a document praised by Laurence Street QC, later Governor of New South Wales, as embodying the three basic ingredients of all professional ethics, 'namely the ingredients of honesty, fairness and due responsibility'.[15] A draft code of practice, developed by the Federation of

Australian Television Stations to cover television news and current affairs programs and issued for comment in early 1993, picked up the themes of fairness, accuracy, impartiality and sensitivity to privacy and taste. Yet the Australian public, and its news makers, remain unconvinced that the self-regulatory mechanisms of the Australian media are doing the job.

It is clear that, to win the public trust needed to secure the news media's functions in a democracy, the media can no longer resort to restating traditional catchcries about a free press or the need for accuracy and fairness. They must re-evaluate the substance of those catchcries and re-examine their own operations and the nature of the implicit contract they make with their audiences. They must decide on the parameters of right conduct in a changing world and ask whether the existing mechanisms to ensure right conduct are genuinely effective or mere smokescreens. In other words, they must pay much more visible attention to the ethics of their business. They must open themselves willingly to more debate about the principles and application of media ethics and revise their entrenched positions when necessary. We hope that this book — by identifying the values and principles operating within the news media and examining specific cases that demonstrate how constraints put pressure on sound ethical decision making — can contribute to that debate.

Principles and Present Practice

In 1965 the Australian Journalists Association (AJA) published a book called *The Journalist's Craft*. It was a useful text, designed to explain to young journalists the basic workings of newspapers and to introduce the fundamental requirements of the craft of reporting. Nowhere in it does the word 'ethics' appear. Nearly 30 years later, the Australian Senate's Standing Committee on Legal and Constitutional Affairs called for submissions to an inquiry into the rights and obligations of the media. Its terms of reference included journalistic ethics and any matters relevant to the standards and quality of reportage.

What happened in the intervening decades that shifted attention from the nuts and bolts of news gathering to an evaluation of the right conduct of the news gatherers? There are many possible causes. One is that the information age brought with it a realisation that buying and selling information had a much more overtly commercial aspect than had been apparent in the past. Competition had become fiercer, both between media and within the separate sectors of print, television and radio, while the costs of running large media enterprises had become daunting. Mere survival increased the possibility of conflict of interest as news organisations diversified into owning airlines, land development companies or the theatres of London's West End. The increasing internationalisation of the media — foreshadowed by Canadian communications pundit Marshall McLuhan in his phrase 'the global village' — may have contributed to a more critical approach to the media's functions. Certainly the new nations that emerged as the old empires crumbled were vociferous in their calls for different ways to describe the media's role and to guide journalistic practice. At the same time, the development of communications technologies brought war and civil protest into people's living rooms in real time, which raised new ethical problems.

Another less media-specific reason may have been a reaction to the painful experience of the 1980s, dubbed the Decade of Greed, in which deregulation had caused pain and social dislocation and the shell-shocked publics in Western countries began to demand a return to principle. The calls for ethics to be included in the curricula of business, law, medical and journalism schools were an expression of community concern about the excesses of the immediate past. Yet worries about ethical behaviour in the press had been voiced earlier in response to the 20th century's rapid change and secularisation. Following the turmoil of World War I, new institutions openly competed with the established duality of Church and State for power over people's attitudes. Among them was the press, which had grown mightily in popular influence over the preceding half century, helped by the technological innovations of the telegraph and the linotype machine.

This book tries to elucidate the problems that arise when the interests of the news media conflict, or appear to conflict, with the interests of the community in which they operate. Such elucidation, however, has to be grounded in an understanding of some basic philosophic concepts and a knowledge of the organisational environment of the Australian media. It must be said at the outset that a discussion of media ethics is bedevilled by the overlapping of ethics and the law. In any society, many aspects of right conduct are enshrined in law; others are not. Thus a breach of ethics may entail a civil or criminal offence, but not necessarily. In Australia, the media have no special rights and few privileges under law. Similarly, they have no special duties imposed upon them, except those in the electronic media that stem from the general broadcast licensing system. Yet the debate about media functions and behaviour is couched in words such as 'responsibility', 'duty' and 'rights'. Unfortunately, these words often have distinctly different meanings in law and ethics, which are either unrecognised or undifferentiated in the media debate.

Another overlap occurs when people regard good manners as a measure of right conduct. Right conduct is much more than etiquette, even if the consideration for others that lies behind good manners is one of the values that underpins ethical behaviour. Unfortunately, members of the public expend much critical energy on the bad manners of a television or radio journalist who hectors an interviewee and point to such behaviour as evidence of declining ethical standards, when it is merely embarrassing, irritating or counter-productive.

When the New South Wales Country Press Association published Australia's first media ethics code in 1927, it was not far behind the trend in the United States. It was during the 1920s that the US press began to codify the principles that applied to the profession. But, as American writer John Hulteng notes, these early statements of principle 'tended to be couched in general terms, leaving the specific application of these broad strokes to the individual judgments of the men and women who had to make the decisions and call the shots out on the streets or at the newsroom desks'.[1]

The general nature of statements of journalistic ethical principles causes conflict between news professionals and members of the public. To a member of the public, intrusion into privacy can be seen as unethical conduct, irrespective of the status of the person whose privacy has been violated. To a journalist, intrusions are often ethically justified because a particular case appeals to the more potent principle of the public's right to know.

It is not surprising that debates about media ethics become heated. Ethics — or 'the philosophic study of morality'[2] — has preoccupied philosophers for centuries, from Confucius in China 2500 years ago or Aristotle 100 years later in Greece to John Stuart Mill in 19th century Britain or the 20th century American philosopher, John Rawls. Philosophic discussions about definitions and applications are intricate, rigorous and, to the lay person, often incomprehensible. Yet the desire to pinpoint what constitutes right conduct is fundamental to the human quest to build societies in which people can live harmoniously with one another. Indeed, it is fair to say that a consideration of the interests and well-being of others is built into most moral concepts to a greater or lesser degree.

Nearly everyone is a philosopher of sorts. We have beliefs and make judgements about all manner of things: the existence of God, the morality of big business, the behaviour of noisy school children on public transport, pornography, capital punishment, genetic engineering, the nature of fair play in sport. But most of us discuss such topics in isolation from underlying ethical principles. We seldom spend time to determine whether there is general agreement on the laws that govern behaviour and, if we did so, would find that general agreement is rare.

Lack of agreement is particularly prevalent in diverse, multicultural societies such as Australia's. During the 1980s, Gallup International embarked on a huge global values study. The findings demonstrated that many formerly accepted codes of behaviour could no longer be seen as universally applicable. One of the survey questions sought to determine how many people believed that the quintessential code of the Judeo-Christian tradition, the Ten Commandments, still applied personally to them. A mere 28 per cent of Australians thought the commandment to keep the Sabbath holy applied to them; 75 per cent believed they should not commit adultery and 91 per cent said the first commandment, which instructs 'Thou shalt not kill', applied fully to them.[3] It follows that a discussion on the rightness of Sunday trading, divorce law reform or compulsory military service cannot proceed in Australia on the assumption that the parties to the argument agree on the fundamental rules of behaviour, even if they can agree that characteristics such as honesty and fairness are desirable.

American philosopher Fred Feldman contends that the most common method of conducting an ethical discussion is 'nontheoretic'. People attempt to develop and defend their positions on important moral issues without explicit appeal to general moral principles.

> Most of us hold at least a fairly ragged assortment of moral views. We believe that certain kinds of action are morally right. We believe that certain kinds are morally wrong. And we just don't know what to think about several other kinds. Yet when we are asked to give reasons, we are often somewhat confused at the outset. When we think about one issue,

we tend to support our view by appeal to one principle. When we think about another issue, we defend our position by appeal to a different principle. Unfortunately, it often happens that the principles to which we have appealed are inconsistent.[4]

Much debate on ethics in the Australian media suffers from such a non-theoretical approach. Public outcry about a particular instance of media behaviour concentrates on that case alone. In their defence, the news media call on what they regard as accepted general principles, such as the importance of maintaining confidentiality of sources, the public's right to know or full disclosure of relevant facts. But there is little continuing discussion within the industry about the apparent contradiction between, for instance, maintaining confidentiality and full disclosure. And the public remains unconvinced that the media have the authority to determine for themselves what is right conduct.

It is true that debate about media ethics is made more complicated by the conception of the news media as having two functions that have to be reconciled. The noted media analyst Professor Henry Mayer called it the Janus view.[5] The Janus view holds that the media have both business and public utility aspects.

In Australia, the media are businesses, run for profit. Even those ostensibly non-profit sectors — such as the Australian Broadcasting Corporation and SBS — need audiences to survive. In recent years, these government-funded broadcasters have been under pressure to become at least partly self-funding. At the same time, democratic tradition gives the news media a social function of informing citizens about the events that occur and the ideas that circulate in a specific community and in the world at large. The two imperatives — to succeed as a business and to inform the public — do sometimes conflict. Moreover, there is occasionally a sharp division within the news industry itself, let alone among the public, about what should be the predominant nature of the product. Mayer pointed to the intractable problem that no one can agree on what should be the relative stress laid on the two functions when he asked: 'Is it 50–50 social–commercial or 25–75?'.[6]

The dual nature of the media also means that the groups that must be considered in reaching an ethical decision are diverse. Journalists have obligations and duties to the media company for whom they work, reflecting the fact that they are part of a business. They have responsibilities to the community in which they operate and upon whom, indirectly, they depend for their livelihood. They have responsibilities towards the news makers and the consumers of news. And they have moral duties to themselves as individual members of their society. Many of the difficulties in making ethical decisions arise from these multiple duties and loyalties. Each journalist is, in effect, three people: an employee, a professional and an ordinary human being.

Yet it is possible for journalists to reach consistently ethical decisions. When journalists argue that ethical conduct has to be dictated solely by the differences between situations, they do themselves and their craft a disservice. Lurching from situation to situation, from day to day, is hardly a tactic designed to inspire the confidence and respect of the public. American journalist John C. Merrill, discussing a trend towards 'situation ethics', noted that the pragmatic advice of the Florentine diplomat, Niccolo Machiavelli, to his Renaissance prince was a type of situation ethics. Machiavelli had said a ruler should not depart from what was morally right if he could observe the right path, but should know how to adopt the bad if necessary. Merrill commented, somewhat acidly:

> Journalists like to point out Machiavellianism in others (especially in government officials), but they themselves very often operate under this variant of situation ethics. They usually contend they believe in absolutes (such as giving their audiences all the pertinent facts or not changing or distorting quotes from a source), yet they depart from these principles when they think that 'in this special case' it is reasonable to do so. They normally talk about their belief in 'letting the people know' but they determine innumerable exceptions to this principle — times when they will not (because of the circumstances of the special situation) let the people know. And, of course, they are not very interested in letting the people know that they are not knowing.[7]

The appeal to situation ethics often appears to be a screen, hastily erected after the event, to justify what journalists do when fired by the excitement of the chase for a good story. Rejecting situation ethics, however, does not mean rejecting the fact that the elements of a given situation do affect the way a journalist will decide to behave.

American ethicists Clifford C. Christians, Kim B. Rotzoll and Mark Fackler are convinced that cogent moral reasoning is possible, despite the complexities of news gathering. They, like Feldman and other contemporary philosophers, suggest that case-by-case, or 'non-theoretic', discussion is a barren exercise. They write: 'Those who care about ethics in the media can learn to analyze the stages of decision making, focus on the real levels of conflict, and make defensible ethical decisions'.[8] They advocate the use of the Potter Box, a guide to methods of reasoning devised by an American theologian, Dr Ralph Potter. The Potter Box has four interlinked corners, or points at which one must define and evaluate the elements contained in a given ethical situation. First, one must define the facts; then one must identify the personal values that are brought to bear; next one must distinguish the relevant moral principle; and, finally, one must decide where one's loyalties lie. Once these steps are taken, one can make an ethically consistent judgement.[9]

The Potter Box process makes ethical reasoning sound like doing a simple four-step; however, as Christians, Rotzoll and Fackler point out, each point requires rigorous attention to detail and a willingness to put aside personal bias or unexamined prejudice. Equally important, they make it clear that the judgements made in any one case can be entirely different but just as ethically defensible.[10] The Potter Box is not used explicitly in this book, but we assume that the identification of facts, values, principles and loyalties is essential for consistency in ethical decision making.

Key Philosophic Concepts

No study of moral issues, even at a lay level, can proceed without introducing some key concepts. Talk about right conduct by journalists often centres around words such as 'good', 'bad', 'rights', 'duties' and 'obligations'. Yet such terms are not specific to media ethics. They are the building blocks of reasoning in moral philosophy.

Value

The idea of value, or the goodness or badness of something, is a basic one in philosophic discourse. As the North American philosophers Michael Bayles and Kenneth Henley explain: 'The fundamental principle of right conduct is that good is to be done and promoted and evil is to be avoided'.[11] But, unfortunately, ethical theorists often differ on those things that are intrinsically good. Some contend that knowledge, friendship, life itself, are intrinsic goods. Others have held that rationality is the only general human good while others say pleasure is the only real good. Bayles and Henley argue that what is 'understood as constituting a good human life varies from society to society and even from person to person, but that variation lies within a set of limits determined by human nature'.[12] In other words, while they concede that there may be legitimate differences of behaviour between cultures, certain universal values underpin right human conduct.

Bayles and Henley assert that there are three main sorts of thinking about moral questions: subjectivism, scepticism and relativism. They dismiss the subjectivist approach, which holds that moral judgements are simply expressions of personal opinion, because '[m]oral principles aim to resolve disputes about how everyone ought to act; mere personal preferences do not address such matters'.[13] They have little time for scepticism because it states that moral judgements can never be known to be true. For Bayles and Henley, scepticism has 'no role in practical disputes because it removes the basis for discussion and guidance'.[14] Relativism, especially the sub-branch of social relativism, gets equally short shrift. Bayles and Henley sum up social relativism thus:

> Social relativism places society in the role of absolute moral authority . . . moral judgments are relative to the society in which they are made. The judgment that abortion is wrong will be true if made in a society in which that is the prevalent belief, and the judgment that abortion is permissible will be true in a society which shares that belief. For the social relativists, the sentence, 'It is wrong to hold human beings in slavery,' is neither true nor false unless some assumption is made concerning the society in which the judgment is made.[15]

Social relativism has more application to media ethics than scepticism or subjectivism as the news media are dependent on the society in which they operate. But it is still not helpful in determining right conduct because the significance of news events, and the media product itself, so often transcend national boundaries, and because journalists must move across borders. The long-standing tensions between Australian news media and the Indonesian government are just one example of the inability of social relativism to resolve the difficulties of reporting across cultures. Bayles and Henley further point to the problem that social relativism cannot accommodate moral dissent within a society.[16] Yet Western news media regard the airing of dissent as an important task. But, in dismissing social relativism as an approach, we should not forget that dominant social beliefs do have a strong impact on the formation of an individual's moral beliefs.

In Australian society, goods that are generally believed to be important (even if they are not always upheld) are fairness, honesty, respect for the rights of other people and keeping one's word. The media have identified three other goods that apply specifically, although not exclusively, to their profession. They are accuracy, full disclosure and respect for the needs of the community as an entity. These seven goods, or principles of conduct, lie at the heart of much of the detailed discussion in this book.

Rights

A second important concept in philosophic reasoning is that of rights. Political philosophers in particular have long grappled with determining the rights to which citizens are entitled. In 17th century England, John Locke argued that individuals had natural rights to the preservation of life, liberty, health and possessions and the right to punish those who did evil.[17] In the American Declaration of Independence, Thomas Jefferson listed the inalienable rights as 'life, liberty and the pursuit of happiness'. But, as with so much philosophy, the problem lies less in deciding an individual's rights than in drawing the boundaries between the rights of the individual living with other individuals in a society. The great American jurist Oliver Wendell Holmes is credited with making defining the bounds of individual rights seem simple when he supposedly remarked: 'My right to fling out my arm ends where your nose begins'. Unfortunately, it is not as easy as that. As Bayles and Henley point out, 'moral problems often involve conflicts between individuals, each of whom has a right that deserves some respect'.[18]

Some theorists make a distinction between positive and negative rights. Many commonly recognised rights are negative ones that require only that individuals do not interfere with the rights of others. Yet, as Bayles and Henley note, it is the extent of positive rights that cause most controversy in ethical theory. This is particularly true in media debates because some positive rights, such as the right to freedom of expression and the public right to know, are the very stuff of news gathering and dissemination.

There is, however, one negative right that gets frequent mention in debates on media ethics. It is the individual's right to privacy, to be left alone. The right to privacy may guarantee absence of intrusion upon a person's seclusion, the public disclosure of embarrassing private facts, publicity that puts individuals in a false light, and appropriation of a person's name or likeness for personal advantage.[19] Increasingly, on a crowded planet where information technology is highly sophisticated and social institutions are complex, the right to privacy is moving out of the realms of moral philosophy and into the rule of law. And, during that transition, it causes much friction.

Obligations and Duties

The third essential concept in moral philosophy is that of obligation and duty, which is allied to the idea of a moral wrong. Fred Feldman maintains that moral evaluations of actions generally fall into one of three categories.[20] An act may be obligatory in that failing to do it would be improper. The largest category of human actions comprises those that are permissible. Permissible acts are right to do but the failure to do them is not wrong. Choosing to do a permissible act, such as risking one's life to save another person, often earns praise. Failure to do so does not bring condemnation. However, some actions are expressly forbidden. To do them is to do a moral wrong.

All ethical theories include some account of values, obligations and rights although they may give different relative weighting to the three elements. Those theories that give priority to values are called teleological, from the Greek word, *telos*, meaning 'goal'. In such theories, the values are the desired result of applying obligations and rights. The rightness of conduct is judged in terms of the end values; so the familiar phrase 'the end justifies the means' is a crude teleological statement. Other theories place greater importance on obligations, or on what one must do, irrespective of the effects of the action. These are called deontological, from the Greek, *deon*, meaning 'that which is binding'.

Schools of Philosophic Thought

Phrases such as 'the public interest', 'freedom of the press' and 'the public right to know' have a timeless ring. They are used so often than it seems they have been part of philosophic debate for centuries. But historians of the press can point to the relative youth of freedom of the press. While information exchange has characterised all human societies, even prehistoric ones, the phenomenon of the Western press was not possible until Johann Gutenberg's re-invention of printing in the 15th century. And it took several more centuries before a form of news packaging, which modern readers would recognise as mass circulation newspapers, evolved. The evolution of a Western-style press that was able to challenge the authority of governments went hand in hand with developments in philosophic thinking. A brief look at the principal families of ethical thinking is useful if we are to understand how some of the ideas about the role of the modern Western media evolved.

Western philosophy began with the Greeks who were deeply concerned with ideas of goodness and righteousness. One of the pre-eminent Greek philosophers was Aristotle (384 BC to 322 BC) who proposed a *natural law* theory in which actions should be directed towards goals.[21] A central idea in Aristotelian ethics was the Golden Mean. The commonly held interpretation of the Golden Mean states that moral behaviour should stand midway in the scale between extremes so that right conduct would, for instance, be neither recklessly generous nor parsimonious but somewhere in the middle. Many Christian philosophers, such as Thomas Aquinas in the 13th century, were attracted to natural law theory because it proposed that humans had special dignity and special freedoms and each human life was uniquely valuable.[22]

The 17th century saw the rise of theories of *natural rights*, which had special significance for the development of the press. Natural rights theories threw over the natural law idea that human beings were social by nature, asserting instead that the prime moral characteristic of humans was the liberty of the individual. This liberty was independent of the laws and customs of society and transcended society.[23] The effect of such ideas on theories of social organisation and modern Western democracy was profound. Natural rights theory held that any authority over individuals, including the authority of governments, could only be justified through the existence of a social contract into which individuals entered freely. Natural rights significantly influenced the Founding Fathers who drafted the United States Constitution and its first ten amendments which constitute the country's Bill of Rights. As the Declaration of Independence put it, governments derive 'their just powers from the consent of the governed'. Natural rights theory directly affected contemporary ideas about press rights because the First Amendment says that government shall make no law 'abridging the freedom of speech, or of the press'.

The emphasis that natural rights theorists placed on individualist and self-interested rationality as the key to right conduct was reassessed by the next important school of ethical thought, *Kantianism*, whose main proponent was the 18th century German philosopher, Immanuel Kant. Kant's work is dense, but in essence he proposed that in assessing moral worth all one had to look at was good will, or the ability 'to act solely from duty and for the sake of duty'.[24] By asserting good will, he dispensed with the idea of self-interest inherent in natural rights theory. It was Kant who introduced the notion of the categorical imperative which dictates that a certain action must be done, whatever its results. For instance, one keeps a promise not because one fears being regarded as untrustworthy but because promises must be kept. Although many dismiss Kantian ethics, it is important to recognise that he made a strong differentiation between the individual decision, which for him was the genuine moral one, and the socially imposed decision.

A modern spin-off from Kantianism is the theory of *contractarianism*. One of this school's main advocates is American philosopher John Rawls. Rawls maintains people can identify the principles of right conduct by evoking what he calls 'the veil of ignorance'. The veil presupposes that rational people, if given the general facts of a situation, can decide what are the principles that should be acknowledged and followed. But, in Rawls's theory, important information is hidden behind the veil. The people make their decision notionally ignorant of what part they have to play in the situation. For example, in deciding the right conduct about an instance of media intrusion into grief, those who decide should ignore the knowledge that they are a reporter, a news editor or the grieving person. Only by putting one's self-interest and facts about oneself to one side can genuinely right conduct be determined. A less sophisticated expression of the idea is putting oneself in someone else's shoes.

Around the same time that Kant was refining his ideas in the German town of Konisberg, the English philosopher Jeremy Bentham was formulating the theory of *utilitarianism*. Utilitarianism aimed to create as great a balance of good over bad as possible, and conceded only one intrinsic good, happiness, and one intrinsic bad, unhappiness.[25] It was a consequentialist philosophy in that the consequences of an act were what determined the act's moral rightness or wrongness. Utilitarianism had a strong effect in 19th century Britain when John Stuart Mill elaborated on Bentham's original idea. It influenced the significant electoral and penal reforms of the time. The phrase, 'the greatest good for the greatest number', although an over-simplification of utilitarianism, sums up the common understanding of the theory.

Later philosophers identified two sub-branches of the theory. *Act utilitarianism* is when the net utility (or the balance of happiness over unhappiness) is calculated for the individual acts themselves. *Rule utilitarianism* is more indirect; in it, the rightness or wrongness of conduct is judged by whether the acts conform to certain rules, which in turn are judged by their net utility.

A quick overview of the main strands of ethical reasoning shows that current debates on the media's role and conduct draw from various schools of thought. Critics of media performance use utilitarian arguments to put the view that community rights, or the good of the many, should not be ignored by individual journalists or media executives intent on presenting conflict and sensation. And, the individual rights advocated by the natural rights theorists are called into service when the media invade privacy or bully interviewees.

On the other hand, the media defend themselves against intervention by government by appealing to the libertarian ideals of the natural rights school. Interestingly, the freedom of the press is used as an argument against restraints placed on the media as competitive businesses and as a defender against the improper use of power by other social institutions. For instance, in 1981 at the Victorian Government Inquiry into the Ownership of the Press, known as the Norris Inquiry, Australian publishers used freedom of the press to argue against government control of newspaper takeovers. And Australian media history is littered with examples of appeals against the pre-publication restraint imposed by the D-notice system and fear of the country's defamation laws. These appeals seek to protect the content of the news media rather than their business organisation.

As Fred Feldman points out, utilitarianism is natural and intuitive for many people.[26] It is particularly seductive for those, such as the media and politicians who, in their different ways, claim to speak for others. Thus the media frequently call on the public interest or the public's right to know to defend their actions. In doing so, they shift the concept of rights from individual rights to institutional rights, even if those are exercised on behalf of individual members of society.

The Public Right to Know

As we have seen, the press's capacity to argue for a new right of freedom was both enhanced by, and part of, the radical shifts in philosophic thinking of the Age of Enlightenment when authoritarian regimes in Europe were challenged.

Other new rights have evolved more recently. The most notable, which is frequently aired in debates about media conduct, is the idea of the public right to know. But there is no legal right to know although the public may have a need to know, sometimes about matters which the authorities deliberately and legally withhold.

The American media commentator Everette Dennis maintains that the public right to know is a journalistic invention of the 1950s when journalists in the United States became increasingly thwarted by bureaucrats standing between the media and government information.[27] The Freedom of Information (FOI) movement both in the United States and Australia found its justification in the public right to know. The initial demands for more open government and greater access to public records and government decision making were, as Dennis acknowledges, necessary and desirable. They reinforced the part of the media's role that is dedicated to the maintenance of an informed citizenry. However, critics claim the public right to know is often pushed too far. While some aim to protect the very government activity that should be scrutinised, many are concerned with a more vexed area of ethical debate. They are concerned when the media insist on access to information about private individuals or seek to report events, such as crimes or sieges in progress, on the basis of the newly articulated right.

We will argue in this book that the legitimate defence of the public right to know is, to its detriment, sometimes called upon to justify those media actions dictated solely by competitive pressures. The quest for healthy circulation figures breeds a powerful desire to scoop the opposition or to publish a story with sensational impact that titillates readers. The immediacy of some news gathering techniques can compound the problem by leaving too little time for the reflection needed to reach a consistent ethical decision. Some dramatic and vivid stories — such as terrorist activity and crime — have a public interest dimension and the public is entitled to know what has happened. However, it is possible to delay publication or broadcast so that other ethical considerations are taken into account without compromising the principle of the public's right to information. The news media need to define more rigorously the boundaries of the public right to know.

The Public Interest

The public interest is another pervasive term used in media debates. It is, however, poorly defined. Few books about the media attempt a definition. The Statement of Principles of the Australian Press Council states that it will give 'first and dominant consideration to what it perceives to be the public interest' but goes on to acknowledge that the term is a matter of subjective judgement.[28] The council's British counterpart, the Press Complaints Commission (formerly the British Press Council), is more definite although not comprehensive. In its code of practice, it identifies four aspects of the public interest: detecting or exposing crime or serious misdemeanour, detecting or exposing seriously anti-social conduct, protecting public health and safety and preventing the public from being misled by some statement or action of an individual or organisation.[29]

Anyone who tries to understand how the media use the term 'public interest' is hard-pressed to find consistency. At times it seems public interest simply applies to any story that is interesting and appeals to the curiosity of the audience. At others, the term has much more gravity. It is invoked when the rights of the community, and individuals within that community, are under threat. It is here that public interest is closely connected to the perceived function of the news media as an important part of the democratic process.

The public interest is an essential ingredient in many ethical decisions. But it is vital that the term is clearly enunciated and universally applied. We argue that the media devalue a very real defence by appealing to the public interest when the matter under discussion is essentially one that falls into the category of 'interest to the public'. The essential distinction between matters of public interest — or those matters the public need to know in order to exercise their rights and duties as citizens — and matters of simple public curiosity must be remembered when trying to reach a sound ethical decision. The Australian Press Council, in a 1992 submission to a parliamentary committee on the protection of confidential personal and commercial information, made the distinction when it talked of 'publication . . . in the public interest, being a matter of serious concern or benefit to the public, and not something merely of interest to the public'.[30] The phrase 'matter of serious concern' is useful but is still imprecise.

Just what is in the public interest? The role and performance of the institutions of government policy making and implementation are obviously areas about which the public should be informed. Governments, whether national, state or local, are directly accountable to the citizens who elect them and pay for them; their policies and actions must generally be open to scrutiny. By governments, we mean their executive, administrative and judicial arms. Thus the doings of elected representatives, public servants and some private organisations, such as contractors who work for governments, fall within the ambit of public interest.

Yet it is not only governments that are accountable to the public, although their accountability is most obvious. Businesses — whether large or small, public or private — are accountable to their various stakeholders. The stakeholders may be direct ones: employees, shareholders and customers. These stakeholders have a legitimate interest in knowing whether the business is generally being run honestly and competently. Indeed, the law requires considerable disclosure of the activities of public companies, without insisting on detailed publication of material that may be, at any given time, commercially sensitive. Other stakeholders may be indirect ones, such as the members of the community in which a company does business. So the people who live near a factory that has inadequate waste disposal practices or beside farmland being sprayed with pesticides have a legitimate interest in the activities of the factory and farm.

Similarly organisations that seek membership and funds from the general public are accountable to that public. For instance, the activities of churches, unions, political parties, charities and sporting clubs all fall within the public interest category.

Yet not everything that a publicly accountable institution does should be reported. Very occasionally, it is permissible to withhold — for a time — information that could damage national security or endanger the lives of individuals or threaten the liberty, security and rights of individuals. The operative phrase here is 'for a time'. Once the danger is past, the media should be permitted, or even obliged, to report and analyse the event.

On a broader scale, the media should reveal political, economic or social trends because those trends will clearly affect society's members, to a greater or lesser degree. It may not, however, be in the public interest to concentrate on individual case examples of those trends where the private rights of individuals may be infringed.

The media's functions, as we have seen, are multiple. They should report events; equally, it is in the public interest that they should not only report social trends but operate as opinion leaders, in the sense that they initiate investigation of, and debate about, those trends. Yet the opinion-leader function brings with it accusations of bias and unfairness. There is no question that the media have just as much right to hold opinions and to advocate action as other social institutions. However, the media's right to express an opinion is slightly different from other groups' rights because they also have the role of providing a forum for discussion. To convey their own picture of the society, institutions rely on the media to transmit their messages. These pictures can be divergent, often antagonistic. People in the media have a role as citizens to make their fellow citizens aware, not only of facts but of the various interpretations of those facts. It goes against the public interest — and the tenets of professional journalism — for the media to ignore their public forum function. However, in arguing that the news media should provide forums for public discussion, it is impractical to assert that everything everyone wants to say must be reported.

It is in the public interest to show things as they are. But, paradoxically, there is a powerful argument that it may also be in the public interest to conceal some realities if they are grossly offensive to prevailing standards of morality and taste or are likely to encourage grossly destructive and damaging actions against individuals. This perennial problem often arises in discussions about the news media's treatment of war, disaster and crime. It is, however, possible to argue with ethical consistency that, while the media should not sanitise the dreadful realities of war, famine, violence or disaster, they should not make a habit of recording these horrors in intimate detail when the only reason for such treatment is the sensational nature of the imagery.

As noted earlier, there are many items carried in the news media that do not appeal to any of the public interest criteria outlined above. Their function is to entertain, to engage the attention or imagination, to trigger an emotional response, to start people talking, or simply to pass the time agreeably. These items are a perfectly legitimate component of news. As part of a news package, they aim to capture audiences and retain them. And to the extent that they affect a news product's popularity, they actually enable the media to perform the public interest role. But when it comes to weighing the various values, principles and loyalties that come into play when journalists and news media managers have to decide what is right conduct in news gathering and presentation, the entertainment items fall into a very different category from items in the public interest.

Australia's Self-regulatory Environment

The growing demands for improved ethical standards among Australian journalists have focused attention on the existing mechanisms for monitoring conduct. In the early 1990s some newspapers responded to the public disquiet by publishing details of where readers could lodge complaints against press conduct. Changes to the Australian Broadcasting Act in 1992 put the onus on the television industry to regulate itself by requiring it to formulate codes of practice, one of which covered news and current affairs programs. The Australian Press Council decided to seek to publicise its activities more widely[31] and to travel to the various states to conduct its business. The journalists' section of the Media, Entertainment and Arts Alliance decided to review the structure of the judiciary committees which police the journalists' code of ethics.

But the flurry of sensitivity to criticism left the self-regulatory environment of Australian news media ethics little changed. Just what are those mechanisms? How do they operate and what is their power?

The Media, Entertainment and Arts Alliance Code of Ethics

The oldest form of self-regulation by journalists is the judiciary system of the journalists' section of the Media, Entertainment and Arts Alliance (MEAA). The AJA section administers the 10-point code of ethics. An earlier eight-point version of the code had been adopted by the AJA federal council in 1944. The original code was incorporated into the union's constitution and rule book, giving it 'the disciplinary functions of a professional association, such as the Australian Medical Association, or the Bar Councils'.[32] The 1984 revisions to the code laid more stress on privacy matters and areas of potential discrimination such as gender, race, sexual preference, religious belief, marital status and physical or mental disability. Perhaps more important was the addition of a preamble, which articulated for the first time the context in which the clauses of the code were to be judged. It reads: 'Respect for truth and the public's right to information are the over-riding principles for all journalists'.[33]

Each Australian state has an AJA judiciary committee, comprising elected union members. Any person can lodge a complaint against any member of the union for conduct that falls under any of the code's clauses. Traditionally, a high proportion of Australia's journalists working in newspapers, magazines, radio and television are union members; however, as numerous critics of the code have pointed out, many of those responsible for news decisions escape judgement. Editors and some senior editorial executives, such as news editors, chief sub-editors and chiefs-of-staff, are exempt from union membership and so cannot be called to defend their decisions.

Judiciary committee hearings are held in private and adjudications rarely published in detail. The system does, however, have punitive powers. If found guilty, journalists may be censured, fined or, in the worst case, expelled from the union.

In 1993 the MEAA decided to review the journalists' code yet again and appointed a seven-member group to look at several aspects, particularly whether adjudications should be published and the composition of the judiciary committees be expanded to include public representatives.

The Australian Press Council

The Australian Press Council held its first meeting in July 1976 although it did not adjudicate its first complaint until some months later. When first established, the council comprised six publishers' representatives, three elected AJA representatives, an independent chairman who nominated three other public representatives. The AJA withdrew its representation in 1987 and the council was restructured. In 1993, when the House of Representatives Select Committee on the Print Media recommended a further restructuring to include equal representation from the public, the publishers and the AJA,[34] the council had 21 members. There were eight public members including the chairman, 10 publishers' representatives — drawn from metropolitan, suburban and country newspapers and the news agency Australian Associated Press — two independent journalists and one editorial member.

The Press Council is industry-funded and its declared responsibility is 'preserving the freedom of the press within Australia and ensuring the maintenance of the highest journalistic standards, while at the same time serving as a forum to which anyone may take a complaint concerning the press'.[35] It has no power to punish those publications that it finds have failed to meet its standards. Its authority rests solely on moral suasion or, as the council puts it, 'the willingness of publishers and editors to respect the Council's views, to adhere voluntarily to ethical standards and to admit mistakes publicly'.[36]

One important difference between the AJA judiciary system and the council is that the council hears complaints against the publication, not against individual journalists. There are no exempt categories: editors, chiefs-of-staff and other editorial executives are held as responsible as the journalist who may have written an offending item.

The council requires that complainants take their objections to the newspaper or periodical concerned and try to have the matter resolved. If they are still aggrieved, they may complain in writing to the council within three months of the offending publication. The council, however, is not prepared to act as a stalking horse for possible legal action in matters that may be seen as defamatory. So complainants must sign a waiver of the right to such action before the council will hear the complaint.

Not all complaints lodged with the council go to adjudication by its complaints committee; some are settled by mediation with the council secretary acting as go-between, others are withdrawn, some deemed inappropriate. In the year ended 30 June 1992, for instance, 85 complaints out of 481 were disposed of by adjudication.[37]

Broadcast Media Regulation

The broadcast industry in Australia has always been subject to a much greater measure of government regulation than its print counterpart. Governments had the power to regulate ownership and access to broadcasting through the licensing system and to direct content and presentation by requiring set levels of Australian programming, news, advertising, children's programs and so on.

Initially, the different treatment for broadcasting was justified by the assertion that the airwaves were a scarce public resource that had to be allocated and indirectly controlled by government on behalf of the public. Technological advances have rendered this argument less persuasive, but regulation continues despite the 1992 changes to national broadcasting legislation. The *Broadcasting Services Act 1992* — which replaced the Australian Broadcasting Tribunal with the Australian Broadcasting Authority (ABA) — had a deregulatory emphasis. It gave broadcasters the opportunity to self-regulate the content of much of their programming by setting up a system of codes of practice to be registered by the ABA.

The commercial television peak body, the Federation of Australian Commercial Television Stations (FACTS), developed six codes. Journalists are directly affected by three: the basic code, the news and current affairs programs code and the complaints code. The news and current affairs code was similar to previous mandatory standards that required accuracy and fairness, but it included a new provision, which brought it into line with the journalists' code and Press Council principles. The provision prohibits 'the portrayal of individuals or groups in a negative light by placing gratuitous emphasis on race, nationality, religion, colour, country of origin, gender, sexual preference, marital status or intellectual or physical disability'.[38]

All commercial television stations and the Special Broadcasting Service signed the codes, which were registered in mid-1993. The codes contain no penalties for lack of compliance because the Act empowers the ABA to fine stations up to $2 million for offences and to lay down mandatory standards if it believes the self-regulatory codes are 'not operating to provide appropriate community safeguards'.[39]

Viewers who wish to complain about a television news and current affairs item must complain in writing to the station within 30 days of the broadcast. The station is obliged to respond in writing and to make 'every reasonable effort to resolve promptly complaints . . . except where a complaint is clearly frivolous, vexatious or an abuse of the Code process'.[40] If still unsatisfied, the complainant can go either directly to the ABA or the station will forward the matter to the chairman of FACTS. Each station must report details of any complaints to FACTS which will then lodge a summary with the ABA. The code also requires FACTS to publish an annual report, outlining the number and the substance of all complaints and the outcome of the ones referred to its chairman.

Just as the AJA code and the Press Council have drawn criticism, so too have the television codes. Media commentator Paul Chadwick pointed, among other things, to the news code's narrow focus: 'Its focus is on what goes on the screen. Self-regulation by journalists must also pay attention to off-screen matters such as intrusions into grief (whether or not the person agrees to an interview or it is aired), conflicts of interest and confidentiality of sources.'[41]

Under the new legislation, commercial radio, too, had to develop codes of practice for registration with the ABA. Like its television counterpart, the Federation of Australian Radio Broadcasters (FARB) used the previous standards as a bench-mark. The code relating to news and current affairs seeks

- to promote accuracy and fairness;
- to distinguish between fact and opinion;

- to avoid presenting news in such a way that it creates public panic or unnecessary distress;
- to correct substantial errors of fact;
- to avoid misrepresentation of viewpoints;
- to ensure balanced presentation of viewpoints on controversial issues of public importance; and
- to protect individuals against unwarranted intrusions into privacy.[42]

At the same time, FARB issued two sets of guidelines, dealing with the portrayal of women and indigenous Australians in radio programs. The guidelines did not need ABA registration.

The FARB complaints procedure is less formal than that of either television or the press, for both complainant and radio station. Listeners can complain either in writing, or orally during normal office hours. The station must ensure that complaints 'will be conscientiously considered, investigated if necessary, and responded to as soon as practicable'[43] although no actual procedures of investigation are outlined. Dissatisfied listeners may then complain to the ABA. A member radio broadcaster must keep records of the complaints and the station's response and send a summary of those records to FARB for forwarding to the ABA; non-member stations forward their summaries direct. As with the self-regulation of television, there are no outsiders involved in the judgement of whether any part of the codes has been breached.

The Australian Broadcasting Corporation (ABC) differs from the commercial radio and television stations in that it has both a charter and separate legislation that impose special responsibilities. For instance, under the *Australian Broadcasting Corporation Act 1983*, the corporation is legally required to provide an independent news service and its editorial independence in all programming is guaranteed. Further, it is specifically charged with making programming decisions on behalf of the Australian people and is accountable to parliament. However, it still comes within the ambit of the ABA because people unhappy about the ABC's complaints procedure can go to the authority.

Like its commercial rivals, the ABC has developed codes of practice that set rules about violent or discriminatory broadcasting and prescribe ideals of accuracy, impartiality and balance for news and current affairs programs. The news code requires correction of demonstrable errors and, in a departure from the commercial codes, singles out the protection of journalists' sources for special attention. Editorial staff 'will not be obliged to disclose confidential sources which they are entitled to protect at all times'.[44]

People may complain to the ABC orally or in writing; but, if they want the ABC to respond they must complain in writing. The code requires the corporation to make 'every reasonable effort to resolve complaints . . . except where a complaint is clearly frivolous, vexatious or not made in good faith' (see Appendix 3). The commercial television stations also believe they have the capacity to judge the motivations of a complaint but the ABC differs from them in having an Independent Complaints Review Panel that reviews allegations of serious bias, lack of balance or unfair treatment. The panel acts as a first court of appeal if the original complaint has not been resolved to the complainant's satisfaction.

On the face of it, Australia has enough mechanisms to ensure that the news media fulfil their responsibilities adequately and ethically. The various codes and statements of principle articulate eloquently the importance of accuracy, fairness, honesty, openness, keeping one's word, respect for the individual and respect for the needs of the community in news gathering and dissemination. But, as we noted in the introduction, Australian news makers and Australian audiences do not appear convinced that the articulation of values is sufficient to ensure ethical conduct. The following chapters in this book examine the specific constraints and conflicting loyalties and principles that come into play when journalists go about their multifaceted job of informing and entertaining the public.

Respect for Truth: Fact Plus Fairness

In 1872, 25-year-old C. P. Scott became editor of a regional English newspaper, *The Manchester Guardian*. Scott gave the paper an international reputation and the newspaper fraternity a number of maxims. He believed vehemently in the rigid separation of fact from comment. 'Comments are free, but facts are sacred', he wrote. The newspaper's 'purest office is the gathering of News. At the peril of its soul it must see that the supply is not tainted.'[1] Scott's words became a rallying call for later generations of journalists whenever critics accused them of a range of misdemeanours from bad taste to peddling falsehoods. The duty of the journalist was to present the facts, however unpalatable they may be.

The trouble is that facts may be sacred, but they do not necessarily convey a true picture. While journalists often defend themselves against allegations of unethical practice by saying they just want to reveal the facts, the process of news gathering and presentation means that facts are selected, weighted and often discarded in the production of any news story. The celebrated British journalist James Cameron acknowledged the process of manipulation and interpretation inherent in the journalist's task when he said: 'Facts are boring. It's what you make of them that matters.'[2] C. P. Scott would have been appalled.

What the news media make of facts is a continuing source of discussion, analysis and occasional vituperation. Allegations of bias, inaccuracy and unfair reporting abound. For instance, bias and inaccurate reporting were the most frequent cause for complaints to the Australian Press Council in the early 1980s and unfair treatment accounted for one-seventh of all complaints received in the year ending June 1992. Submissions to Royal Commissions and government inquiries often claim bias; journalists have gone on strike over bias and readers have called for buyer boycotts of allegedly biased publications. Yet accuracy, fairness and impartiality are key words in all Australian self-regulatory codes of practice and the journalists' code says respect for truth is one of the two overriding principles of journalism. Why does the rhetoric of journalism seem to be at such odds with the practice? There are several reasons, most of which stem from the contradictions inherent in a craft that, on the one hand, puts great store on verifiable, objective fact but, on the other, gains its authority from interpreting the significance of events and processes within society.

When we discuss the role and responsibilities of the news media in reflecting reality — which is essentially what we do when grappling with the difficult concepts of bias and fairness — several related but distinct issues come into play. One is the notion of objectivity as a working principle for journalism. Is objectivity possible, or even desirable? Another is the relationship of fact to truth. A news story may be accurate in every factual detail but fundamentally untruthful because it has omitted other, equally accurate, material. Then there are the problems of the most accurate way to measure fair and balanced coverage and the most effective way to achieve it. Is the simple measurement of airtime or column centimetres a meaningful gauge of balance? Must balance be achieved within a single news item or can it be fairly achieved over time? How far must a journalist go in verifying the accuracy of statements or assertions put forward by news makers? Yet another issue is the degree to which the news media should be bound to report conflicting opinion or give the right of reply. Does a news outlet have to give space to opinions with which it disagrees? Or must it give equal prominence to a single issue candidate in an election campaign as it does to the major parties? Is it practical always to separate fact from comment and speculation? Is it ethical for the news media knowingly to publish opinion, either their own or others', that is based on untruths or inaccuracies? Equally important in the bias debate is the notion that the mass news media in Western society will inevitably support the political and economic status quo because they are an essential part of the existing dominant power structure. Can those who advocate social change ever get a fair hearing from an institution that has a vested interest in maintaining current social structures? Is there an ethical distinction between unconscious bias and deliberate bias?

There are probably no clear-cut answers because, in all of these questions, we are really dealing with the way the media and the public perceive the world. One person's balance is another's bias.

Objectivity

A former editor of *The Herald* in Melbourne and the Sydney *Daily Telegraph*, Syd Deamer, once gave an aspiring political reporter the following advice:

> There is no such thing as a good objective journalist. If you are not sensitive enough to feel for your subject, to have a point of view, to suffer joy or agony or sympathy about a story you are covering, you will never be a good journalist. Don't strive to be objective, strive to be fair.[3]

Deamer's denial of objectivity points to one of the most vexed issues in journalism.

For several decades from the period immediately after World War I, objectivity was regarded as a professional ideal. Being objective was equated with being fair and unprejudiced. *The Washington Post's* Alan Barth wrote in 1950 that 'the tradition of objectivity is one of the principal glories of American journalism'.[4] But the concept was to become a rod with which to beat the industry as critics used a perceived lack of objectivity as evidence of poor conduct. Just as scientific thinkers had earlier begun to challenge the idea of value-free scientific observation, so too did journalists begin to realise that the presence of an observer alters the nature of an event and that detached observation was not synonymous with objectivity.

To some degree the argument about objectivity is a semantic one. Yet, as the American journalism academic John C. Merrill observed, many journalists and lay people still use the term with approval. Merrill contends that an objective report would match reality and tell the truth, the whole truth and nothing but the truth. But the ideal is impossible, he says.

> No reporter knows the truth; no reporter can write a story which can match reality . . . The story, in other words, is never what it purports to be; it is always much bigger than its verbal image.
>
> All reporters, in addition to being limited in their objectivity by the weakness of language, are also conditioned by experience, by physical state, by education, and many other factors. They do not come to their stories as blank sheets of paper on which the reality of events is to be written. They may want to be unprejudiced, balanced, thorough, and completely honest in their reporting, but they simply cannot be.[5]

If Merrill believes, like Syd Deamer, that there is no such thing as a good objective journalist, his colleague Everette Dennis disagrees. For Dennis, objectivity is simply a method and style of presenting information. Its early proponents were men like C. P. Scott. They sought — somewhat simplistically Dennis contends — to separate fact from opinion, to present an emotionally detached view of events and to strive for fairness and balance by giving both sides an opportunity to put their views so that the public could decide. Dennis argues that when the restrictions of the traditional 'inverted pyramid' style of reporting — which organises information in descending order of importance — came under attack in the 1960s and 1970s from new journalistic styles, the support for objectivity crumbled. He believes, however, the goal is worth a second look. Reporting techniques borrowed from new styles of journalism could help make journalism better and more reliable; 'impartiality is not beyond the capabilities of the modern journalist if procedures are followed providing for systematic decisions'.[6]

It is obvious that objectivity is too troublesome a word to be of much help in judging the right conduct of journalists. It is interesting to note that no self-regulatory code in Australia uses the term, preferring the less ambiguous and less ambitious 'fairness' and 'impartiality'. But the concept does serve to remind us that, while journalists are private individuals who bring their own value systems and beliefs to their job, there is an implied obligation for the news media to present the full spectrum of fact and opinion, untarnished by personal interest.

Bias is a Four-Letter Word

In Australian debates about media performance, bias is invariably used pejoratively. Its connotations are of deliberate and sustained distortion of the truth by omission, sensationalism and exaggeration or management tampering with journalists' stories. It would seem there is no such thing as good bias. The softer synonyms of 'inclination', 'proclivity' or 'tilt' are never used. To borrow the slogan of a group of disaffected Melbourne *Herald Sun* readers, bias is bad news.

Yet it can be legitimately argued that the greatest amount of bias in the news media is unconscious bias, dictated by perceptions of prevailing values in the community. 'When the media [argue] in favor of law and order, [their] bias is a reflection of attitudes among the overwhelming majority of readers, viewers and listeners.'[7] A second form of bias arises from the market orientation of any given media outlet. A periodical targeted to business executives, for example, is unlikely to give much coverage to the activities of motor bike enthusiasts; when it occasionally does run an item about bikers, the coverage is likely to reflect the views of the majority of its readership. The magazine is biased against bikers but no one is likely to fuss much.

A third type of unconscious bias — and one of particular importance to journalists concerned about right conduct because of its connection to the loyalties that govern action — arises from the acculturation that occurs in all newsrooms. After a time, the journalist accepts the particular news values of the organisation and loses the impetus to take a personal stance. As one journalist told media analyst Patricia Edgar:

> I knew what I could write and get away with, and I knew what I couldn't write, and so obviously I didn't; I've never in my journalistic career beaten my head against a wall. There was no point in writing material for the news organization which was not going to get in. I don't think that's censoring, it's just a sensible attitude to a job, that's providing the editor with what he wants.[8]

The acculturation bias is probably the non-deliberate bias that journalists find most difficult to resist because they want to be part of the group; they want to be able to use the first person plural pronoun which indicates they belong to a significant institution, so they say 'that's not our kind of story'. The acculturation process and the selection of news to suit a particular market are the indirect cause of critical media analysis that holds that mass media organisations marginalise minorities, do a poor job of reflecting social reality and are inevitably slanted towards big business. But, despite these critics, acculturation bias is not a reliable indicator of personal ethical weakness.

A former journalist and Tasmanian Premier, Harry Holgate, identified yet another type of unintentional bias, which he believed was responsible for many complaints about political reporting. It was unintentional bias, based on error of fact. Unless refuted quickly, such errors could be perpetuated for an inordinate period.[9] Bias based on error of fact poses few insurmountable problems of ethics. The good professional journalist will adopt meticulous systems of news gathering and writing aimed at maximum accuracy, thus minimising the risk of bias by error. The constraints of time and the occasional unavailability of news sources who can help verify material make some errors inevitable, however. So long as the news media outlet is willing to correct these inaccuracies promptly, little lasting damage is done to its reputation for impartiality.

Other biases stem from a journalist's own upbringing, education and experience. A reporter brought up in a strict, nonconformist home, for instance, may have an unconscious bias against libertarian atheists or, indeed, a bias in favour of them as a personal rejection of his or her family's values. An urban reporter may be inclined to agree with the city viewpoint on subsidies to farmers more than the rural one, partly because the city attitude is one with which he or she is familiar. Such unconscious biases are natural, and unlikely to bring the journalist before a self-regulatory body on charges of unethical conduct. Conscientious journalists, however, should be mindful that their individual backgrounds do have a tilting effect on the process of weighing what is important in a news story. The only way to minimise the effect of such tilt is for a journalist to be rigorously self-aware and to make a particular effort to understand those news sources and opinions to which he or she is naturally unsympathetic.

Political Reporting

Specific charges of bias usually assert that the bias is deliberate and the majority of accusations relate to political reporting. As American media analyst Edith Efron wrote at the beginning of her analysis of the 1968 US presidential election coverage by the television networks: '"Bias" is a concept which by now has become a loaded codeword — used as automatic invective by people who dislike the networks on political grounds and denied by those who are politically sympathetic to [them] . . .'[10] A former editor of the *The Examiner* in Launceston, Michael Courtney, pointed out that 'in Australia when we talk of political bias the automatic translation is anti-Labor bias'.[11] While Courtney talked of the Labor Party, the allegations of bias are wider and include reportage of the whole labour movement, including organised labour. It is not within the scope of this book to investigate specific charges; that has been done at length elsewhere.[12]

Our discussion centres around issues of moral philosophy, not those of political philosophy. We are investigating the obligations, loyalties and principles that are tested in reporting those events and processes about which there is legitimate division of opinion. No discussion of bias, however, would be complete without reference to cases which illustrate the passion that allegations of politically biased coverage evoke. Each case examined below relates to one of the three groups of players: journalists, management and audience.

The 1975 federal election campaign was arguably the most polarised in Australian post-war history. The dramatic dismissal of the Whitlam Government on 11 November was simply a midway mark in the coverage of political events that had generated strident accusations of media bias against the Labor Party. The accusations were levelled at all media but it was News Limited's *The Australian* that received the bulk of the criticism. Even fellow newspapermen, normally reticent about criticising the performance of their competitors in such tricky areas as bias, found fault with the national daily's coverage. Greg Taylor was editor of *The Age* when he recalled, two years after the event, the rival coverage:

> I believe they were slanting the news and they were doing it so obviously. Let's say that I'd been on *The Australian* in '75 and taken it into my head to slant news, I hope I wouldn't have been nearly as obvious as they were. It was just so obvious

it was ridiculous and of course it became widely known that journalists were being pushed into certain directions.[13]

News Limited journalists became sufficiently concerned about the tampering with their copy that, with the support of 75 of their colleagues, three journalists who were also officials of the journalists' union wrote to their ultimate boss, Rupert Murdoch, on 2 November alleging that their professional integrity was being compromised. The letter accepted that management had the right to set political guidelines for its papers but objected to the way in which the guidelines were being applied. Receiving no reply to the first letter, they sent another to which they got an immediate reply that did nothing to assuage their concerns.

On 5 December Rupert Murdoch was interviewed on *A Current Affair* by Michael Schildberger. Schildberger asked: 'Why are you running such a campaign against Labor?' Murdoch's reply was predictable. 'Well, we run newspapers. I wouldn't say they were running any more campaigns than anyone else. We have opinions, we express those opinions, we report the news. When we report news that people don't like they say it is biased, but that always happens from both sides.' In answer to the next question he said: 'we have gone to great lengths to keep the bias out of it and keep a fair and equal reporting, particularly in *The Australian*, where there are many pages of reports every day, fair and equal to both parties. It is true that in our editorials we have expressed strong opinions which we believe to be right, but only in our editorial space.'[14]

Three days later, 8 December, journalists at *The Australian* voted overwhelmingly to strike; the next day the Arbitration Commission ordered them to return to work and Murdoch was directed to meet a delegation to discuss bias. It was the first time that Australian journalists had taken strike action over bias, although individual journalists before and since have resigned over their copy being changed or being asked to slant a story.

The difficulty in pinning down the nature of political bias is perhaps best illustrated by another Murdoch interview on *A Current Affair*, conducted two years after the strike. In that interview, Murdoch said of his staff: 'Journalists were showing bias and we cut bias out of their stories, which is a different thing. We cut the bias out and they said that was biased because we cut the bias out.'[15]

The News Limited strike raises the issue of conflicting loyalty. Acting collectively, the journalists decided to put their loyalty to their employer aside in favour of the principle of fair reporting. But what should an individual do if he or she decides that the obligation to the audience to present the news impartially has been compromised? A former editor of *The Age*, Creighton Burns, has recalled that his father, Tam Burns, while working as a journalist during the 1930s often resigned from papers on matters of principle. Fortunately for Burns senior, there were sufficient publications for him to move on to. The choice for contemporary journalists, working in an environment in which media ownership is severely contracted, is much harder.

It is the ultimate test of ethical fortitude for a journalist to resign rather than be party to reports that he or she believes are unfair or misleading; he or she has made the painful choice to put the public interest before self-interest. One less personally damaging tactic may be to request that one's name, or byline, be removed from a story that has been manipulated unfairly. But a refusal to be associated publicly with a misleading story does not meet the aim of playing fair by the reader nor does it necessarily signal that the unbylined story is biased. Indeed, it may well do the opposite as the purpose of bylines is often unclear, particularly to the general public.

A byline on a commentary or feature article traditionally allowed a measure of personal perspective or interpretation by the journalist. The unbylined news report used to indicate a sup-posedly objective piece of news, in which the reporter's judgement played no part. But the almost universal application in Australia since the 1970s of bylines to most news reports, especially those written by staff reporters, has muddied the waters. The absence of a byline may now mean something different. In a content analysis of the 1975 election campaign, for instance, Patricia Edgar noted that *The Australian* published nearly twice as much news without bylines as *The Age* and more than twice as much as the Melbourne Herald and Weekly Times papers, *The Herald* and *The Sun*.[16] Yet it was *The Australian's* coverage that was regarded as being the least objective, the most biased.

News Limited was involved in a second celebrated case of political bias. This time it was the company's *The News* in Adelaide that was accused of bias in its coverage of the 18-day state election in South Australia in the spring of 1979.

In December, the Australian Press Council heard a complaint from J. D. Bennett, the acting secretary of the South Australian branch of the vehicle builders' union and a second complainant, W. Skupch. Bennett complained that *The News* had been biased in that it made no attempt to obtain or report the views of organised labour even though it prominently reported the views of a number of employer bodies; its coverage was also unfairly unbalanced in the publicity it gave to the views of the Liberal Party and party supporters. Skupch criticised the paper's views on political and social issues, including unemployment, industrial development and the economic and social condition of the state. He argued that journalistic fairness dictated that *The News* should have sought out and published the opinions and solutions to complex social problems advanced by the diverse groups in society.

In its adjudication, the council restated several general principles it considered fundamental:

> The council upholds the right of a newspaper to have its own political position; to accept certain beliefs and policies and to reject others; to favour the election of one party and to oppose the election of another. Unless this is accepted, the council cannot see how one could continue to speak meaningfully about the freedom of the Press. If it is accepted, it follows as a fact of life and of human nature that newspapers will often be partisan and biased; and they will appear to be so, especially to those who are committed with equal firmness to different opinions, policies and parties.[17]

But it noted the moral obligation of newspapers, which professed to inform the community about political and social affairs, to present a reasonably comprehensive and accurate account of public issues. It reiterated the idea that papers should strive to make a clear separation of their own editorial viewpoints and their duty to reflect faithfully in news columns the interplay of opinion within the community. It said: 'It is generally agreed that it is ethically illegitimate journalistic practice to employ selective and tendentious reporting in order to manipulate readers' opinions in a direction conformable to the editorial opinion of the newspaper.'[18] The council concluded that readers of *The News* would have been left in no doubt that the paper strongly desired the defeat of the Corcoran Labor Government. But it declined to make a firm ruling in the absence of what it believed was evidence of specific instances of bias. It found that the one specific instance put forward by Skupch of a front-page headline, 'Stop the Job Rot!', did indicate bias, was 'somewhat misleading' and more emotive in language and tone than straightforward reporting would justify.[19]

The following month, the South Australian branch of the ALP appeared before the council complaints committee in Adelaide. It was armed with a detailed analysis of the space allocated to favourable and unfavourable coverage of the two main parties, complaints about four particular articles and about the editorials published throughout the campaign. The council wrote one of its lengthiest adjudications on the complaint and raised several points worth noting.

The ALP presented evidence that *The News* had printed 3314 column centimetres of pro-Liberal and/or anti-Labor copy but only 2070 column centimetres of pro-Labor and/or anti-Liberal copy; it backed up its charge of gross imbalance with figures on the allocation of space of page one and subsequent pages throughout the campaign. Reiterating its stand that newspapers had a right to be partisan, the council found the paper had indeed been intensely partisan and had not disguised the fact that its object was to present the case against the Labor government. The council's duty, it asserted, was 'to determine whether *The News*, in seeking to influence the electorate to vote for a change of government, was culpably guilty of misrepresentation or distortion in presenting the views and actions of the government . . . or whether it failed to fulfil its public duty of informing the public of the policies and arguments of the Labor Party'.[20]

The ALP had made a central issue of disproportion or imbalance in the allocation of space but the council maintained that, while the power to select material of publication could be a power to distort, it could not agree that a demonstration that one party in an election campaign had been given a greater amount of 'favourable' space than others was, in itself, conclusive evidence. 'The views or proposals of other parties may nevertheless have been fairly or adequately conveyed.'[21] The issue was not quantity of coverage, but the content of the material and the adequacy of coverage of dissenting views.

In deciding on the allegations about four particular items, the council found that, in the circumstances, two articles could be taken as affording some evidence of *The News'* partisan stance but not of distortion or falsification. But it found another story and its accompanying headline, '$40 Pay Shock; Government Backs Rise', were unfair reporting. The report said the Labor government had intervened in the Arbitration Commission to support a pay claim by the Metal Trades Federation. The ALP argued that the story and the headline seriously distorted the government's intention and action by ignoring two things: the traditional concept of an ambit claim, in which unions automatically sought more than they could reasonably expect, and the fact that the Arbitration Commission could not make awards — such as the metal trades' ambit claim — that fell outside specified wage-fixation guidelines. The council noted that 'an experienced editor, and especially an experienced industrial reporter, would have had a better understanding of what really was involved [than the article or headline implied] . . . We think it reasonable to expect that the story should have been written in such a way as [to] put the government's intervention more clearly into the context of "ambit claims" and wage-indexation guidelines'.[22] The interesting point here is that the council made a distinction between factual reporting and truthful reporting. The government's intervention and existence of the $40 a week pay claim were facts but, without the background context of the way industrial relations were conducted, the story was not truthful.

Most of the ALP's third complaint — that editorials in *The News* were biased against Labor — was dismissed. The council found the editorials were mainly advocacy of a vote for the Liberals or expressions of the paper's own opinions and judgements. But the council found that the editorial of 24 August was much more open to question. The editorial castigated the Premier for 'an extraordinary tacit admission that he may have to impose [a state] income tax after the poll'.[23] Corcoran was quoted in the same issue of *The News* as denying his intention to introduce a surcharge, a denial also published in that morning's edition of *The Advertiser* along with the Premier's comments that a vote of confidence in Labor would give him greater bargaining power when it came to negotiating with the federal government about new federal–state financial arrangements. The council said:

> It seems to us that this editorial seeks to gain an unfair advantage by somewhat distorting the thrust or emphasis of Mr Corcoran's reported statement. It fails to do justice to Mr Corcoran's stress on his opposition to the introduction of State surcharges. As for the admission being an 'extraordinary' one . . . State surcharges forced by Commonwealth pressure was at the time regarded as being a real and discussable public issue by Premiers other than Mr Corcoran. Thus we do not consider this editorial to be a fair and responsible comment on what was a responsible statement by the Premier.[24]

The council's ruling precipitated News Limited's withdrawal from the organisation for several years, a significant enough response in itself. But equally significant was the articulation of an important obligation. The press was free to be partisan and to argue its point of view forcibly; but, in building that case, it was unethical if it did not lay out for public scrutiny the relevant facts, even if some may lessen the potency of its case. The adjudication in *The News* case was consistent with the council's earlier statement on bias in which it said: 'A newspaper has a right to take sides on any issue, but it does not have the right to resort to distortion or dishonesty to advocate such a cause'.[25]

The final example of political bias allegations occurred in Victoria in the dying days of the Kirner Labor Government. It involved the Herald and Weekly Times Limited publications, the *Herald Sun* and *Sunday Herald Sun*. The Herald group had been taken over by News Limited in December 1986, the first major move in a cascade of media ownership changes over the next few years. In 1990 the original Herald and Weekly Times papers, *The Herald* and *The Sun News-Pictorial*, were merged and long-time Murdoch executive Piers Akerman was appointed editor-in-chief. Most in the Victorian ALP and Victorian Trades Hall Council regarded Akerman as a monster, far worse than anything previously encountered at the company's Flinders Street headquarters even though the old Herald group had never been a friend of Labor. Not all Labor politicians agreed. Jim Kennan, who was later briefly to become the Opposition Leader after the Labor government's defeat, rejected the idea of a *Herald Sun* campaign to get rid of the Kirner government. He told a House of Representatives inquiry: 'There have been examples that we have felt have been anti-government or unfair reporting in that paper, and other examples that have not been.'[26] But Kennan's attitude was atypical. Allegations of unfair reporting came thick and fast and by July 1992 Labor supporters had called a public meeting to protest against the Flinders Street bias. The *Herald Sun* did not report the meeting which set up a 'Bias is Bad News' committee to monitor the paper's coverage. The committee compiled a 32-page dossier comparing *Herald Sun* coverage of education, employment and other political issues with that of other publications. It suggested Labor supporters boycott the publication and lodged several complaints with the Australian Press Council.

One of the stories the committee chose to compare demonstrates how methods of presentation of facts can alter the tone and thrust of a story, resulting in at least the appearance of bias. In February *The Bulletin* published the results of its regular public opinion polls on the approval ratings of political leaders, conducted for the magazine by AGM–McNair pollsters. In measured language, *The Bulletin* wrote:

> While still ahead of Jeff Kennett, Joan Kirner's approval rating has dropped five points over the last survey period to 41%. According to The Bulletin Poll, the Victorian Labor premier's approval rating is now only slightly higher [than] her disapproval rating (36%) which also fell over the survey period — down three points . . .
>
> However, opposition leader Kennett can take little comfort from the latest Bulletin survey. His approval rating fell four points to 23%, although disapproval also fell — down seven points to 43%.
>
> Overall, Kirner's lead in approval declined one point, from 19 to 18. She remains strongly preferred as premier, leading Kennett by 55% to 41%.[27]

The tone of the *Herald Sun* interpretation of the figures was racier. Its page-one story, headlined 'Poll Batters Kirner Hopes', began thus:

> The personal popularity of the Premier, Mrs Kirner, has taken a dive, according to a major opinion poll.
>
> The AGM–McNair poll, which was compiled for *The Bulletin*, showed the Premier's personal approval rating slumped five points last month to 41 per cent.
>
> And in a further blow, the poll showed Victorians appear to be changing the way they think about the Opposition Leader, Mr Kennett.
>
> Mr Kennett's personal rating continued its roller-coaster ride with a four-point drop to 23 per cent.
>
> But the number of people who disapproved of his handling of the Liberal leadership showed signs of a dramatic turnaround with a seven-point improvement in one month.[28]

Nowhere did the story mention that Kirner remained preferred premier. The difference between Kirner's five-point 'dive' in approval and Kennett's four-point 'drop' is marginal and many would say it does not justify the difference in prominence or language choice. But some journalists would argue that tabloid language is by its nature more vivid than other publications and the word choice is simply a characteristic of tabloid journalism rather than an indicator of bias.

Several reporters at the *Herald Sun*, however, had concerns about the paper's coverage of political matters. Its chief political reporter in Canberra, Peter Wilson, resigned following the publication of a front-page story on 15 June under the heading 'I'll Create 2 Mil Jobs — Hewson'. The story carried the byline of a Melbourne-based reporter, Derek Ballantine, and its first two paragraphs read:

> A daring plan to create two million jobs by the end of the decade was unveiled yesterday by the Opposition Leader, Dr Hewson.
>
> He vowed to scrap payroll tax, introduce a youth wage, fast-track mining developments and abolish penalty rates that were holding back tourism.[29]

Wilson reportedly told Akerman that the paper should make it clear that the Hewson jobs plan had previously been spelled out in the job creation section of the federal Opposition's Fightback! election package released the preceding year. No such clarification was forthcoming. When news of Wilson's departure became public, he kept his counsel. He told Mark Skulley of *The Sydney Morning Herald*: 'I did not talk to the press or comment to the press. I'm still not. This is a personal matter of principle'.[30] Akerman said he saw no problem with the Hewson story; it had originated in an article offered by Hewson but had carried a journalist's byline because it had been substantially reworked. The Prime Minister, Paul Keating, had asked for space to have a similar piece published which had been run in full as an open letter on the inside pages with a front-page pointer.[31]

Akerman went part of the way towards countering criticism by providing the Prime Minister with a right of reply. But several questions remain. Was the addition of a byline of a reporter a deliberate attempt to obscure the fact that the material emanated directly from the Leader of the Opposition without being subject to professional, and supposedly impartial, scrutiny? Was presenting Hewson's jobs plan as a new one a distortion stemming from bias? It certainly was not accurate. How open was the *Herald Sun* in giving its readers relevant information upon which to gauge the truth of its reporting as opposed to its accuracy?

The three cases illustrate several points about bias in political reporting. Journalists are faced with hard choices if they believe their work is being deliberately altered to distort the situation. There is distinct difference in advocating an opinion vigorously and doing so without disclosing all relevant information. Language and presentation of material — both in its ordering and omission — can gravely misrepresent the true position. But, most of all, the cases show that allegations about bias can never be resolved to the satisfaction of all parties. Yet that reality does not absolve journalists from reflecting on their own political prejudices and curbing or declaring them when necessary, or from upholding the principle that full disclosure of all relevant facts and a fair representation of divergent opinion is a vital part of the news media's public responsibility. If one of the important principles that journalists hold dear is respect for the needs of the community as a whole, then the journalist is bound to support full and balanced coverage of divergent political opinion.

Fair Treatment in News and Comment

Political bias is unfair reporting writ large. It denies the public a capacity to choose based on the understanding of the relevant facts and issues. There are, however, other aspects of news gathering and presentation conduct that may be equally unfair, if not as immediately important to the democratic process.

When discussing fair treatment, it is important to recognise that the notion, when it is applied to news, has two aspects. One is the fair presentation of facts within news reports. Fairness here is about facts and the authority of those facts. Under the journalists' code of ethics, the journalist must 'report and interpret the news with scrupulous honesty by striving to disclose all essential facts and by not suppressing relevant available facts or distorting by wrong or improper emphasis'. Fair presentation of facts requires the journalist to find out those essential facts, check them and present them in a balanced way, and to disclose to the audience his or her source wherever possible. It requires the reporter to be sceptical and to test any allegation made by a source. Here the reporter's duty to the audience is especially weighty because the audience has no sure way of judging the truth or accuracy of any report. It must simply trust the journalist and if that trust is misplaced then media credibility suffers.

If it is a duty to present facts fairly, there must be mechanism whereby errors can be quickly corrected. All the regulatory codes in Australia mention correction of mistakes but most hedge their bets by referring only to 'significant', 'substantial' or 'demonstrable' errors or to those that are 'harmfully inaccurate' or 'damaging to the reputation and interests' of people. Restricting corrective mechanisms to one class of mistakes indicates the impracticality of correcting all the minor errors that creep into news pages or bulletins. It also raises the difficult question of who is to decide what inaccuracy is harmful or significant. And who is ultimately responsible for ensuring correction: the journalist who made the error or editorial management?

The second aspect of fairness is the fair representation of the many diverse views, attitudes and interests circulating in the community about any given issue. Fair representation goes beyond simple verifiable facts and into the realm of opinion and the balanced presentation of opinion. Ensuring fair representation is primarily the responsibility of those in the news media who have charge of the overall shape of the final product, the news executives, rather than the individual journalist.

It is often properly asserted that the news media have every right to their opinion about social and political issues. But those concerned about fair representation also assert that the media's voice should not drown diversity. The public, they maintain, have a right of access to the media so that different voices may be heard.

The right of access is a vexed issue for the media who rightly point to the impracticality of publishing or broadcasting the opinions of everyone who wants to put a point of view. Journalists and media managements assert their right to select what they believe to be important or interesting to their audiences. However, access rights become increasingly significant when the number of media outlets decline. Increasing concentration of ownership of the media poses severe threats to the right of individual members of the public or groups to be heard.[32]

Another point about fairness is the question of to whom must the journalist be fair? The answer is to two very different sets of people: to the news makers themselves and the audience. To some extent the responsibilities to be fair to two parties overlap in that if a specific report is fair to the people and institutions named in it, it will automatically be fair to the audience. But while news makers can recognise the unfairness of a report concerning them, the audience cannot.

Withholding Relevant Facts

No news story can be accurate or truthful if essential facts are missing. Two examples from reports about higher education in Australia make the point.

In the late 1980s, Australian tertiary education institutions became enmeshed in a series of amalgamations of universities and colleges of advanced education. One such proposed merger was that of the Royal Melbourne Institute of Technology (RMIT), the Footscray Institute of Technology and the Western Institute into a new multi-campus university called the Victoria University of Technology (VUT). The new university's chancellor was Creighton Burns, a distinguished journalist and a former editor of *The Age*.

In an analysis of *The Age's* coverage of the amalgamation and RMIT's subsequent withdrawal from the arrangement,[33] the head of the Department of Communication Studies at RMIT, associate professor Jack Clancy, contended the paper's coverage had been biased, and unfair to the oldest and biggest party in the merger, RMIT. Among other examples, Clancy cited a report on 8 March 1991 that created an unfair impression of the institute by omitting essential facts. The story, headlined 'RMIT enrolments too big, say students' and written by one of the paper's two education writers, began: 'The Royal Melbourne Institute of Technology was condemned by its student leaders yesterday for enrolling 900 students more than it can handle'. The facts were accurate — to a point. One student leader, the Students' Representative Council president, Simon Wood, had condemned RMIT's over-enrolment. And the body of the story did acknowledge briefly that over-enrolment had become a national problem.

Another story in *The Age* a month later detailed Victorian enrolments and showed that VUT stood sixth out of nine tertiary institutions with an over-enrolment of 8 per cent, compared to the highest figure of 15 per cent. But, as Clancy pointed out, the RMIT percentage of 7.8 per cent was below the overall VUT figure, a fact omitted in the second article. It is possible that detailed figures were not available when the first story was written but Clancy was justified in noting that it seemed 'reasonable to expect an experienced reporter specialising in tertiary education to be aware that over-enrolment was a phenomenon common among tertiary institutions and no greater than average at RMIT'.[34]

An even more telling case went to the Australian Press Council in 1990. Lawrence Apps, reader in journalism at the University of Queensland, complained about an article in Brisbane's *Sunday Mail*. The article, headlined 'Hard porn slides in media course', said that audio-visual slides showing women being subjected to degrading forms of sexual abuse, including mutilation, were being shown to journalism students, the majority of whom were young women. An editorial in the paper claimed the material came from the underground pornographic industry.

Apps complained, saying the story was inaccurate because it failed to explain the context in which the slides were shown or the purpose of their inclusion in the course. Far from being images from the underground pornography industry, the slides depicted material published in mainstream media, which was the very reason for using them. The audio-visual kit had been prepared by an organisation in San Francisco called Women Against Violence in Pornography and Media and was a standard teaching resource that had been used at the university for the previous three years. The council upheld his complaint, pointing out 'that deliberate omission of relevant facts is as unacceptable as the deliberate publication of false statements'.[35]

Sometimes, of course, it is impossible for reporters to discover all the essential facts. The MEAA/AJA code recognises this when it mentions 'available facts'. But the moral responsibility of reporters is surely to try as hard as possible to get the facts. They fail in their duty to accuracy and fairness if they simply gather easily available facts. If that is all they did, journalists would have little claim to operating in the public interest. The news media would just be a vehicle for the transmission of untested assertions.

Checks and Double Checks

Journalists set great store on accuracy, or so they say. Critics, however, might be forgiven for believing there is sometimes something in the cynical slogan 'Never let the facts stand in the way of a good story'. If accuracy is essential for good journalism, then journalists should practice systematic checking methods to ensure their stories are as accurate as humanly possible. Occasionally, however, the desire to publish a 'meaty' story, competitive pressures or lazy habits result in stories that are unfair because they are inaccurate.

In its adjudication number 28, the Press Council censured *The Weekend Australian* and the Perth *Sunday Times* for publishing an article 'containing incorrect allegations of fact without first taking reasonable steps to check their accuracy'.[36] The offending article made several allegations about the West Australian branch of the Australian Labor Party: that the party's national executive might intervene in the affairs of the branch which had a $70 000 federal election debt; that scrutineers' reports claimed that hundreds of ballot papers in the electorate of Swan had been defaced; and that 'as a result of the branch's first-past-the-post system of internal elections, the left-wing had secured the State's two positions on the [party's] National Executive'.[37]

After hearing witnesses in Perth, the council found that there was nothing on the national executive agenda that could lead to federal intervention, that the branch debt was only $40 000, that the ballot paper allegation was not substantiated and that the branch did not have a first-past-the-post internal election system. The article's author told the council he had received the information in good faith from informants of whose reliability he was satisfied and that he had tried unsuccessfully to check the facts with other people. After writing the story on the Friday, he had telephoned his head office in Sydney for instructions on whether to hold the story until the next week but had been told to submit the article as it was.

The council found that neither of the two papers had published anything that acknowledged the inaccuracies in the article although the rival *Daily News* had carried denials in its Monday edition. It noted that 'the allegations were of such a kind as to be easily checked by enquiries from officials of the party and from other people . . . The author, by seeking instructions from his Sydney office, plainly recognised that there was some risk of inaccuracy in letting the article go forward without further probing of the facts. The papers must accept responsibility for the decision to take that risk. It should have been realised at once that harm might well be caused to the branch if any of the statements in the article should prove to be untrue, and yet for the sake of early publication the obvious need for checking the facts was deliberately foregone [sic]'.[38]

What was the reporter's ethical responsibility in this case? The council saw no grounds for questioning his integrity or motives. Yet why did he write an unchecked version in the first place? Why, if he was concerned about the story's possible inaccuracies, did he not tell his superiors he was unable to file it? He would not have won favour for refusing to write an inaccurate story but that may be the price of ethical strength. The defence of unquestioningly obeying the instructions of one's superiors rarely holds up. An individual cannot expect others to make ethical decisions on his or her behalf.

Another early Press Council decision demonstrates how laziness and lack of checking can promulgate untruths. The *Sunday Observer* in Melbourne published an article in November 1980 which claimed the Governor-General and the Victorian Premier could be charged with taking part in an illegal lottery. The two men had attended a fund-raising banquet in which a diamond was placed in a mango sorbet as a prize in a lucky dip. In fact, the Raffles and Bingo Permits Board was satisfied that the lottery was legal.

The paper said the basis of the story came from a press release issued by a member of parliament. The council found the explanation unacceptable. '[The] conduct of the paper in sensationally suggesting that the Governor-General and the Premier could be charged with taking part in an illegal lottery was unexcusable.'[39] The simple act of checking with the permits board would have been fair to the Governor-General and the Premier; but it would have meant the end of a startling story.

Sensationalism and Exaggeration

One of the most frequent complaints about media behaviour is that of sensationalism. It is a charge that often rings true. The unrelenting pressure to bring out a product that arrests the audience's attention can weaken the ethical resolve of most journalists. When a so-called slow news day comes along, it is very tempting to spice up a lacklustre story with a dash of hyperbole, or downright invention.

Former editor Michael Courtney recalled the days in the early 1950s when he was a young reporter on *The Sun* in Melbourne and sightings of flying saucers were all the rage. He and his colleagues would create fictitious people who claimed to have seen the mysterious objects.[40] Such yarns made good reading but that is all they were: yarns. And they must have misled, particularly because they were published in a newspaper that laid claim to greater integrity. Today stories that trumpet that Elvis Presley is alive on Mars or that aliens ate someone's baby are recognised for what they are by all but the most gullible. They are fiction, entertainment, and have nothing to do with journalism. They cannot even aspire to the description of 'infotainment'.

These days, sensationalism in the news media is more pernicious and harder to detect than the outright fabrication. Information is gathered from different sources, facts are not checked, separate incidents are blended into a single item. The end result looks like the truth but it often is misleading, damaging and unfair. Take the complicated case of the Bomaderry Tigers, one of the Press Council's first adjudications.

In the mid-1970s, the New South Wales' south coast boasted two sporting teams, both known as the Bomaderry Tigers. The Bomaderry Australian Rules Football Club complained to the council about two front-page articles, one in the *South Coast Register* published in Nowra and the other in Sydney's *Sunday Mirror*. The *Register* had devoted its report to what it described in a banner headline as the 'disgraceful behaviour' of the Tigers at the test cricket match in Adelaide and at the Eden Fishermen's Club. The paper said that the football Tigers — who should have been giving the local cricket star, Ian Davis, support in his bid for a test century — had cat-called him all day, yelled obscenities and compared him unfavourably to another Nowra cricketer. Because the Bomaderry Tigers emblem had been clearly seen during telecasts of the test, the other set of Tigers had been embarrassed. The report then described various forms of bad behaviour by the football Tigers which had occurred at the Eden club and which had resulted in a letter of admonishment by the Eden Fishermen's Club being sent to the non-football Tigers. 'If this is the behaviour of grown men of your club the Board wishes to point out that they will not be welcome to visit our Club again,' the fishermen said sternly.

The council found the whole incident somewhat confusing. Accounts of what happened conflicted but it seemed clear that the unruly barrackers at the test match were not all Tigers. Only one person was a football Tiger but he 'had displayed the emblem in such a way as to make it appear that the persons he was with belonged to a club of that name. In the circumstances', the council found, 'the assumption that those persons were members of the Bomaderry Tigers was understandable.'[41] It also found that, bearing in mind the normal conduct of groups of spectators at test matches, it was an overstatement to brand the behaviour as 'disgraceful'. The *Register's* linking of the two incidents had given a wrong impression of consistently bad behaviour. But one gains the impression that the council was not unduly concerned about the incident, even though it upheld the complaint against the local paper.

The council's stronger censure was reserved for the *Sunday Mirror*. The metropolitan paper took up the story four days after its publication in Nowra, putting the Eden episode first and embellishing it significantly. The story read, in part:

A premiership football team has been barred from a leading south coast social club for life for allegedly fondling waitresses and stripping on the dance floor.

The burly footballers — let loose by their wives after a grand final win — hurled four-letter words at officials who told them to stop their loutish behaviour.

Club supervisors were forced to close the club an hour early when they could not control the footballers.[42]

The council determined the only justification for reporting a life ban was the Eden Fishermen's Club letter, there was no justification at all for the allegations about fondling waitresses and the fact that one man took off his shirt was hardly enough to justify claims of stripping on the dance floor. It found that the complainant Tigers had been responsible for some regrettable behaviour at Eden but the *Sunday Mirror's* headline and the statement that followed it were serious overstatement. 'The report as a whole had been a piece of unfair sensationalism.'[43]

The Right of Reply

A number of Press Council decisions support the idea that the press has an obligation to air divergent views in a community, even if a paper disagrees with those views. So fairness in the news media, at least in Australian terms, is not only about the fair presentation of facts but about people being given a fair go to put their point of view.

David Bowman in his book *The Captive Press* maintains that:

Newspapers do not reflect society, or the world, but odd bits of it, and being controlled by the dominant forces in society, newspapers reflect and reinforce the view of those forces. This limitation is of far greater significance than the constrictions placed on the press by law, inhibiting as some of those are.[44]

Yet it would seem that, in order to defend the news media's special claim to be a vital part of democratic debate, there is acceptance by most Australian self-regulatory bodies that the range of opinion about social and political issues should be allowed expression.

Interestingly, neither the Press Council principles nor the MEAA journalists' code spell out the need to publish diverse views. The broadcast media codes do. The Federation of Australian Radio Broadcasters' codes says broadcasters should ensure 'reasonable opportunities are given to present significant views when dealing with issues of public importance' and the television code says that current affairs programs 'must represent viewpoints fairly'. The ABC code requires programs to achieve balance by seeking to present 'as far as possible principal relevant viewpoints on matters of importance'. It adds the rider that such balance does not have to be reached within a single program or news bulletin but should be achieved within 'a reasonable period of time'.

An explanation of the broadcast media's greater sensitivity in this matter may be the traditional view that the airwaves were a finite resource, a view since superseded by technological advance. But the scarcity argument used to be powerful indeed, and was the justification for government regulation of broadcast media in Western democracies. In the United States the inhibitory effect on public debate caused by the allocation of broadcast licences led the Federal Communications Commission to oblige broadcasters to uphold the Fairness Doctrine which requires that conflicting points of view be represented fairly.

The Press Council, while the need to allow diverse views is not articulated in its principles, made its stance clear early in its history. In its second year it released a statement on bias. 'A newspaper which claims to provide a general news service has full freedom of editorial comment, but it has a public duty to provide fair news reports of matters of public controversy.'[45] It is important to note the implied distinction that the council made between those publications that provided a general news service and those that did not. Special interest publications, presumably, have no public duty to provide fair reports or open their pages to dissenting opinion.

The size of a publication is irrelevant; small regional or suburban papers with restricted circulation are the same as large metropolitan dailies. If they provide general news, certain rules apply, according to the council. The case of the bishop's 'letter' illustrates two aspects of fairness.[46] In 1979 the council heard a complaint against the *St. George and Sutherland Shire Leader* in New South Wales, claiming that material that purported to be a Letter to the Editor was in fact the edited extracts of a radio broadcast by the Anglican Bishop of Wollongong. The bishop had said that under God's standards homosexuality was expressly forbidden. The complainant asserted the paper had rejected his attempts to put a contrary view; the paper's rejoinder was that it did not propose to allow itself to be used for propaganda supporting homosexual causes.

In its adjudication No. 57, the council found against the paper on two grounds and censured it for 'an act of suppression and intolerance which should not be excused'. 'The reading public is entitled', it said, 'to an accurate presentation of the material in a newspaper. To present material as a Letter to the Editor, when it is not, is against the best interests of the reading public.' The council continued:

> Although the Bishop did not complain about the way his talk was treated, the material was printed as a letter without his knowledge or consent.
>
> Such treatment of sensitive material may lead the public to assume that the editorial views of a newspaper are receiving unsolicited support from influential figures in the community when this may not be the case.
>
> The Letters to the Editor of any newspaper are an important part of the activities of a newspaper which purports to serve the general public. The public should be able to accept that the integrity of such an item is beyond reproach.
>
> The second reason . . . was that the newspaper refused a reasonable right of reply to views contrary to those expressed by Bishop Short. This action clearly is a rejection of the duty which newspapers have to respect the right of the general reader to be informed of the arguments on each side of a public debate.
>
> The Letters to the Editor column is a valuable forum for such debate.[47]

The *St. George and Sutherland Shire Leader* had a bad day that day at the council's hearing. Adjudication No. 58 also found the paper had been less than fair, this time in its characterisation of a local residents' action group. The complaint related to an editorial entitled 'Who Backs the Nuclear Fear?'. The editorial discussed a petition against the proposed installation of a third nuclear reactor at the Lucas Heights research establishment and painted the residents' action group as dupes of communist propaganda, a view to which it held stoutly at the council hearing. Attempts by the group and various individual members to get space for a reply had been refused. The council in upholding the complaint noted that 'a newspaper is under a strong obligation as a matter of ordinary fairness to hold its columns open to a reasonable reply'.[48]

Another case in which the council reasserted the principle that people should be given the opportunity to reply to allegations in editorials, as opposed to news reports, came up late in 1986. On 18 June, *The Sydney Morning Herald* published a trenchant editorial stating that the ABC was pervaded by a public service culture that meant too many of its employees had primary regard for their positions rather than the product. The ABC Staff Union immediately sent a reply by courier denying the allegation. The letter was not published.

The editor defended the paper's right to express its views but the council said that right was not at issue. 'What is in issue is the paper's refusal to allow the representative body of ABC staff to reply to the paper's criticism of its members.'[49] When the complaint finally reached the council's complaints committee, the paper's representative conceded that the letter should have been published and failure to do so was an oversight. The admission did not prevent the council from upholding the complaint.

Adopting Other People's Words

The evolution of a sophisticated public relations industry in Australia over the past 50 years or so has resulted in a practice which can, if misused by journalists, mislead audiences. And the journalist who misleads the public is being unfair to that public and betraying a trust.

Public relations practitioners are information managers, just as journalists are information managers of a kind. Public relations professionals arrange information on behalf of their clients in order to manage the relationship between an organisation and its publics. Journalists arrange it on behalf of a general or specific audience. Naturally, and quite properly, a public relations practitioner's first loyalty is to the client. So long as they do not lie, public relations practitioners act ethically in presenting a client in the best possible light even if such presentation necessitates omitting critical material. Journalists, by contrast, are committed to presenting the full picture if they can and, as we have noted earlier in this chapter, are bound to test any information they gather. Their first loyalty is to the audience.

Every day dozens of media releases pour into newsrooms around the country. They come from lobby groups, companies, political parties, individuals, charities and a host of other organisations. Many are well written, clear and concise. They contain information that can be both important and interesting. They look for all the world like a regular news story. But they present, of course, only one side of the picture. Media releases can provide the raw material for news stories. It is when they provide the whole story that ethical concerns arise.

A Sydney public relations practitioner, Jim Macnamara, has argued that media analysts have obscured the important role of public relations in framing the agenda for public discourse by concentrating on the traditional mass media.[50] In a study of the influence of public relations on media content, Macnamara said claims by some public relations practitioners that they write or supply most of the news published or broadcast were exaggerated. He continued:

> However, claims by editors and journalists that they diligently research and report stories objectively, relying primarily on their own initiative, are equally untrue in many instances . . .
>
> Many media consumers are unknowingly reading press releases every day in both the popular and quality press, obscured behind a veil of complicity between journalists and public relations practitioners. The programs broadcast by the electronic media are also heavily influenced by public relations in a range of ways.[51]

Macnamara surveyed 417 Australian journalists and tracked the usage of 150 releases issued by 27 companies. He found that 70 per cent of journalists admitted to using PR material. More than half said they extracted quotes from releases and 20 per cent said they sometimes or often used PR material in full. The usage of such material was higher in trade, specialist, suburban and regional media, although releases were also used extensively in major national, state and metropolitan media. A single release, on average, was used five times and one was used 69 times.[52]

When PR material is used in the news media and not flagged as such, the audience is gulled into believing that the material has been processed by an independent journalist. That is not the case. Frequently the misrepresentation is compounded because the reporter's byline appears on the story when in fact he or she may have written only the lead paragraph or two.

Such conduct is grossly unethical. Adopting the form of someone else's work and passing it off as one's own is plagiarism. Academics have had their careers ended and students have been expelled for similar deceit. But, if the extent of the practice is any guide, the Australian news media seem to see little morally wrong with it. The Herald and Weekly Times Limited in Melbourne, however, said, in its professional practice policy adopted in

November 1993, that plagiarism was unacceptable. The policy also decreed that reporters and contributors had a responsibility to identify to their editorial supervisors any material that was ostensibly the retyping of publicity material.

Journalists, particularly those in publications with small staffs and lots of space to fill, say that it is impractical to check out everything in a release. The material is often of considerable relevance to the audience. But the news media cannot have it both ways. If independent scrutiny is the hallmark of professionalism in journalism, then it must be honoured. Of course, there are times when a fact cannot be tested or an opinion balanced but it is no difficult or time-consuming task to indicate to the audience, by correct attribution, that is the case. There are no times when the wholesale theft of someone else's words — even if that person has given tacit approval for their use by issuing a release — is ethically justified.

Adopting another's words as one's own is not confined to the use of public relations material. On 6 September 1991 *The Age* in Melbourne carried an editorial, headed 'Why two good men have left "The Age"'. The editorial outlined the reasons for the resignations of two journalists: a Sydney-based finance writer, John Sevior, and a former Australian Journalist of The Year, Peter Smark.

Sevior's resignation was triggered by a segment on the ABC's *Media Watch* program which showed the text of an article from the *Financial Times* in London relating to the British economy beside that of an article by Sevior about the Australian economy. The two were virtually the same. Sevior tendered his resignation to *The Age* editor, Michael Smith, who issued a memo to staff saying:

> John has been an excellent, diligent reporter in his time at *The Age*.
>
> I accept his assurance that the lapse was out of character and had not happened before.
>
> However the breach was so serious that it could not be tolerated on a newspaper that demands the highest standards from others in the community.[53]

Shortly after Sevior's resignation, *The Age* learned that the previous March Smark had drawn heavily and without attribution on an article from *The Economist* for his column that appeared in both *The Age* and *The Sydney Morning Herald*. When *The*

Economist raised the issue with the Sydney paper, Smark had apologised: 'The crime was,' he wrote in an explanation to the London weekly, 'not to acknowledge the paternity of the piece . . . I ask forgiveness for sloppiness this time.'[54] At the time, Smark's lapse went unpublicised but with Sevior's resignation, the matter flared again and Smark quit *The Age*.

Unfairness manifests itself in diverse ways, as we have seen. It can be called bias, lack of balance, partiality or partisanship. It can be a sin of omission or a sin of commission. Its reasons are many: ignorance, misunderstanding, sloppiness, prejudice, laziness, the pressures of time, and deliberate intention to distort. It can be perpetrated by junior reporters or senior editors. But it is — for those journalists and editorial managers who respect both the rights of the individuals who make news and the need of the community to have access to independently gathered and impartially presented news — always a breach of right conduct.

CHAPTER 3

Victims and Enemies: Gender, Race and Minorities Reporting

The Australian news media suffered something of a sea change in its attitude to the portrayal of women and minority groups in the two decades from the mid-1970s. A working party of the Australian Journalists Association (AJA) drew up guidelines for its members on non-sexist or gender inclusive language in early 1976; the guidelines were not adopted. Yet later the same year, the industry first officially acknowledged gender and minority issues when the Australian Press Council promulgated its statement of principles. One principle asserted that 'the publication of material disparaging or belittling individuals or groups by reference to their sex, race, nationality, religion, colour, country of origin or intellectual or physical disabilities [was] a breach of ethical standards'.[1] Eight years later, the AJA revised its code of ethics to include a clause requiring its members not to place unnecessary emphasis on race, gender, sexual preference, religious belief, marital status and physical or mental disability. In 1986 the Australian Broadcasting Tribunal introduced new program standards for both radio and television which forbade the transmission of broadcasts likely to incite or perpetuate hatred against or gratuitously vilify any person or group on the basis of ethnicity, nationality, race, gender, sexual preference, religion or physical or mental disability. By 1993, the shift of attitude was so great that the Herald and Weekly Times Limited in Melbourne suggested in its professional practice policy that journalists should avoid membership of clubs and associations with discriminatory policies.[2]

The introduction of guidelines on issues such as gender and race mirrored profound social and political changes in Australian society. The force of the change was seen not only in the emergence of the self-regulatory codes but in the spate of anti-discrimination legislation enacted at state and federal level. As always, the news media were in the difficult position of both mirroring and advancing the changes by reporting and opening themselves as a forum for public debate about the legislative and social shifts. However, if the complaints to the self-regulatory bodies and to various state and federal inquiries on discrimination in Australia are any guide, many citizens believe the practices of the news media in reporting the activities and aspirations of minority groups have not been fundamentally altered even though the written guidelines profess to uphold the principles of equality and fairness.

Criticism of news media performance in these areas falls into two basic categories: the general and the specific. Critics object to both the amount and the thrust of overall coverage. They charge that the views and achievements of women and minority groups are under-represented in the media, that the portrayal of such sectors is often sensationalised, trivialised or stereotyped and that the language and imagery used in reporting perpetuates oppression and suppression. Such reporting is, they say, essentially untruthful and unfair. In particular cases, the charge is that journalists exhibit ignorance or insensitivity to the sensibilities of women or minority groups and to the effects their reporting might have in triggering hurtful repercussions for individuals and groups.

Reporting social transformations is never easy. It is impossible to please all of the public all of the time when the topics are as personal and value-laden as race, sex and religion. The ground shifts continually as pressure for change accelerates, too slowly for some, too fast for others. Such volatility is amply illustrated by the fact that the Press Council principle in relation to gender and race has undergone more modification than any other clause.

When introduced, its wording was unqualified. But the reality of making judgements in an area so subject to personal interpretation forced change in 1992. The qualifying phrase, 'gratuitous emphasis', was added, as was a sentence which tried to balance freedom of expression with anti-discriminatory values: '. . . where it is in the public interest, newspapers may report and express opinions upon events and comments in which such matters are raised'.[3] Although the council continued to make it clear in individual adjudications that discriminatory reporting was an ethical breach, direct reference to ethical standards was dropped.

Social change, however, does demand attention to ethical frameworks and a reassessment of right conduct because values, which have to be factored into ethical decision making, are themselves undergoing change. For Australian journalists, the gender and minorities debates are of particular significance because they force re-evaluation of some professional assumptions about truth, accuracy and the public interest.

Freedom of speech is an individual right that, since the time of the natural rights theorists, has been seen as a protection against state suppression. Yet, as nearly everyone acknowledges, freedom of expression is not absolute. The Australian Press Council expressed the qualification thus: 'A reasonable balance has to be maintained between the fundamental values or liberties of individuals on the one hand and the interests of the public and the State on the other'.[4] Those who fight against discrimination extend the idea by arguing that, when one individual's freedom of expression does harm to another individual's rights to personal security and respect, freedom of expression can be legitimately curtailed. Such arguments are the justification for anti-vilification legislation; but not everyone agrees wholeheartedly. The Press Council submitted to the Western Australian government that proposed amendments to that state's criminal code, aimed at creating offences relating to racial harassment and incitement to racial hatred, should be modified to exempt fair reporting by journalists undertaking their legitimate activities. The council based its call on the belief that 'it would, for example, be in the public interest for the public to know of the statements of public figures even where those may constitute an offence [under the act]'.[5]

The conflict between free speech and controls against discrimination causes apparently irreconcilable problems. The media argue that not only should they be allowed to express their own opinion but that the public interest dictates they are bound to report the views of others about controversial matters even if those views are objectionable or ill-founded. In an adjudication about publication in *The Australian* of two letters about the alleged incapacity of Asians and Africans to control their fertility, the Press Council said: 'It is important that the existence of such views be known; indeed it may on occasion be important to publish them so that they can be answered'.[6] The anti-discrimination advocates, however, maintain that allowing the expression of racist or other discriminatory beliefs implicitly condones such views; allowing public figures to express them, under the guise of objective reporting, is worse because people in the public eye have a more authoritative voice.

The problem is further compounded by the fact that — when discussing gender, religion and ethnicity in a country with an extremely diverse population — the 'public' is not monolithic. When one talks of public interest in relation to political matters, it is easy to define the public. The people whose interests are served encompasses all those affected by policy decisions, whether they are voters or not and whether they engage in the debate or not. But when talking of public interest in relation to gender, the public may be the majority of the population, women. When talking of ethnicity or religion, which particular public's interests are paramount: those of the Aboriginal public or the whole public, those of the Muslims, the Christians or the Jews, those of the Serbs or the Croats? And who determines the composition of the public: the news media, the regulators, the citizens whose lives are not much touched by the issue under discussion or the groups directly affected?

Another complication is the range of sensitivity to any remarks about race, disability or gender. It is extremely difficult to quantify the amount of offence or the potential to hurt that a report or opinion may cause. Satirical comment and cartoons cause particular trouble. Their defining characteristics are overstatement and stereotyping, which are often misinterpreted as the Press Council has frequently pointed out.

The myriad difficulties do not mean, however, that journalists are absolved from identifying the loyalties, the personal values and professional principles that must be weighed in reporting ethically on individuals and groups who are different from them.

Sex and Sexuality

Matters of sex and sexuality pose immense problems for accurate and fair reporting. Everyone has an opinion about them because they are both universal and intensely personal. In Western societies, they are also now issues that are widely discussed in public so the part played by the media in defining gender roles has become part of the debate. Media performance has been subjected to intense scrutiny by social and communication theorists, policy makers, the general public and media workers. The debate embraces all aspects of media, especially advertising and the images of women conveyed in films, television series, popular music and so on, but it has some elements peculiar to the news media.

Scrutiny of the media began with the re-emergence of the women's movement during the late 1960s and early 1970s but, as we have seen, the codes of ethical practice took longer to acknowledge criticisms. The main complaints were that females, although more than half the population, were virtually invisible in the media. When they did appear, it was in a limited range of roles: as mothers, wives or bedmates. They were portrayed as dependent, home-bound, incompetent, weak, objects for sexual gratification, or merely decorative.

In mid-1993 the National Working Party on the Portrayal of Women in the Media — originally set up to look at the images of women in advertising — issued a study of the way women appeared in the news media. The study showed the principal objections of earlier critics still stood. A survey of 34 Australian metropolitan newspapers and television news and current affairs programs found considerable imbalance:

> After reviewing 5,000 television and newspaper print items the study's principal finding was that women do not receive balanced representation in Australian television and news-papers. It also noted that where portrayal is achieved it is pre-dominantly contextually negative.
>
> . . .
>
> The main news stories are rarely about women. Women are seldom asked for comment nor are they well represented as presenters or reporters.
>
> Women are most associated with human interest, leisure

and crime issues and are portrayed mostly as victims, witnesses or random bystanders. They are depicted least of all as main subject, participant or authority figures.[7]

Do such results indicate that the news media are ignoring their responsibility to report the real picture of society? Responding to the study, University of Queensland academic John Henningham was reported as saying it was hard to argue that the media could do more than reflect society; if coverage of women in politics was low, it might be because there were actually very few women in politics.[8] The general manager of the Federation of Australian Commercial Television Stations, Tony Branigan, said the report seemed to ignore the fact that the proportion of female politicians, leading businesswomen and spokeswomen had not yet reached 51 per cent; 'So long as men dominate in these areas, it is inevitable the media must give more attention to males,' he said.[9]

In reporting some areas of social activity, the media are unjustly castigated for doing the job of reporting the society as it still is. Certainly the ratio of women to men in positions of authority in political and big business, for instance, does not match the ratio in the general population. In other areas, the charge of failing to report reality unquestionably stands: sports news is one. One 1993 study[10] pointed out that women's sport attracted 4.2 per cent of coverage in metropolitan and regional newspapers; mixed sport accounted for another 12.1 per cent and less than a third of those reports were devoted to women. Women's sport occupied, on average, 1.2 per cent of the total time allocated to sports coverage by five major television stations. Compare this to sporting participation figures. An Australian Bureau of Statistics study conducted in Victoria in 1992 found more women participated in two out of the ten top sports and in three — tennis, squash and golf — women were more likely than men to be regular participants.[11]

Figures do not tell the whole story, however. The more telling argument about distortion of reality lies in the nature of accepted news practice and what are the characteristics that the journalism profession believes makes news into news, as distinct from information. Murray Masterton found in a 67-nation study that the six news criteria of consequence, proximity, conflict, human interest, novelty and prominence were universally accepted as the dominant characteristics.[12] Human interest stories, while difficult to define precisely, were usually about people who would not ordinarily be newsworthy and often focused on children, pets and other animals.[13] Small wonder that women who feature more prominently in human interest news than in other categories feel they are not being taken seriously. Television journalist Mary Delahunty lamented the tendency for political reporting to be presented in terms of winners and losers: 'It's very much this male adversarial concept all the time'.[14] The higher-than-usual appearance of women as victims of crime may also be attributable to the conflict criterion, for crime reports are quintessential conflict stories.

Journalists put considerable value on the traditional news criteria; it is clear that audiences, or at least large portions of the audiences, do not value them as highly. Although the news media often defend themselves against charges of insensitivity by saying their duty is to report society as it is and their regard for the truth should transcend other values, one can argue that media truth is filtered through the narrow channels of industry-determined news values. Good and positive events may be real, but they are not news. Yet, if truth and fairness are important principles for the journalist should they be compromised by adherence to values that inevitably distort reality?

The difficulties of reporting gender and sexuality issues can be demonstrated by individual cases. One interesting case comes from politics. During 1990, the fairness of the media image of the Victorian Premier, Joan Kirner, was questioned. Just before Kirner took over the top job after the resignation of John Cain, the Melbourne *Truth* published a front page picture showing a plump Kirner in a bathing suit emerging from a swimming pool. The headline read: 'Miss Piggy for Premier?'. The Miss Piggy tag, however, was not a journalistic invention; it had first been used by Kirner's New South Wales Labor colleague, Barrie Unsworth. Another much-used sobriquet, Mother Russia, also came from within her own party.

The cartoonists, however, made much of Kirner's weight and dress-sense. Several cartoons showed her with pointed feet that looked remarkably like trotters; *The Age* caricaturist John Spooner depicted her with rolls of fat around her neck and massive shoulders like an American gridiron player. In one cartoon, the *Herald Sun's* Jeff Hook portrayed her as 'a bloated figure bursting at the seams of a polka dot dress and weighing down the then Prime Minister, Bob Hawke, and the then Treasurer,

Paul Keating'.[15] It was this last cartoon that stirred Kirner to complain of sexist media coverage, saying she was committed to ensuring that women were not reduced to stereotypes: 'I could have ignored the cartoon . . . and said "Oh well, that's how it goes in politics. But that's not how it goes for men".'[16] With cartoonists, however, it does go that way for men. Billy McMahon's ears, Bob Hawke's bouffant hairdo, Paul Keating's predilection for Italian suits were all magnified cruelly. Such depiction may offend but it does treat female and male politicians equally unkindly.

An example of less equal coverage of the new premier was an interview, conducted on Kirner's second day in office and published in *The Sunday Sun* in Melbourne. The 54-paragraph story, except for five paragraphs, was devoted to Kirner as bride, wife, mother, daughter. The headline read 'Scandal and mystery man in Joan's life'; a wedding photo of Kirner was captioned 'Joan Kirner as a 46 kg blushing bride on her wedding day in 1960 . . .'.[17]

The portrayal of a new state leader as a blushing bride stereotype is surely belittling. However, many would argue that, while it does reflect poorly on the media's understanding of changed standards of acceptability, it is thoughtless rather than sinister. It rates in the same category as the Western Australian headlines that had Australia's first female premier, Carmen Lawrence, 'stirring the coffee pot' or dubbed Lawrence of Suburbia.[18] These bad puns do imply that a woman's place is in the home not politics. Arguably, they are silly rather than serious.

Graver issues about gender portrayal arise, however, from the case of the naked woman in the collar. The case also highlighted an extremely important dilemma for the news media: the line between news and entertainment. A March 1992 issue of *People* magazine had a cover picture of a naked model on all fours wearing a collar and constrained by a leash of beads. An accompanying caption read: 'Woof! More Wild Animals Inside'.[19]

The Press Council received several complaints claiming that the cover, and an inside picture, headlined 'Heel Spike' were degrading and demeaning to women and reinforced the stereotyping of women as objects of, and for, subordination. The objections covered the article itself and the magazine's street poster as well. Complaints came from several individuals, organisations and a group called Women Against Demeaning

Images, which in turn was sponsored by four women's groups. Although the council had previously adjudicated on news items published in *People*, this time it decided it could not uphold the primary complaint. According to the council, the decision was partly jurisdictional. The council said:

> First, the material complained of had already been dealt with by another body, the Office of Film and Literature Classification, which had given the issue a 'Restricted' classification.
>
> Second, the Press Council's principles were drawn up to provide guidance to the readers and editors of newspapers and other journals whose primary function is to provide information in the form of news, features and comment, although they also seek to entertain.
>
> It is not always easy or sensible to apply these principles to publications whose primary function is entertainment. What might be acceptable in a magazine like *People* might well be unacceptable in a newspaper. Publications have to be considered in the context of their readership.
>
> The Press Council . . . has neither the power nor the desire to act as a censor of publications that are legal, and that are already subject to regulation in a way that the mainstream press is not.
>
> . . .
>
> The Council has no doubt that the *People* cover and poster were offensive to many people who saw them as demeaning to women, but it notes that those who buy such magazines choose to do so knowing what to expect.[20]

The council's decision generated considerable criticism. A member of the New South Wales Legislative Council, Dr Marlene Goldsmith, objected on several counts. The council had washed its hands of the complaint, she said, because the publication was subject to regulation, unlike the mainstream press. 'While Pontius Pilate might recognise this argument, it ignores the fact that the publication was [originally] produced, displayed and sold without any restriction. It was marketed as a mainstream publication, and, by the time public complaints had led to its reclassification, had virtually sold out', she wrote.[21] The council's reference to people who choose such magazines knowing what to expect ignored the fact that it was the cover and posters, which were openly on display, that were the principal target of complaint. Goldsmith went on to catalogue several research findings that linked pornography with sexual violence. It was long past time that the council considered such issues, she said.[22] But the council chairman, Professor David Flint, had earlier gone on record — in reviewing the case — as saying: 'The proposition that a particular publication may encourage violence against women, at least in the sense that it reinforces a disparaging view of women, would either have to be self-evident to the Council or it would have to be demonstrated to its satisfaction that this were so.'[23] One of the problems here is that the council restricts its judgement to specific cases, yet the general criticism that the news media treats women insensitively is based on the proposition that the accumulation of demeaning coverage does the harm.

In an earlier ruling, the council had also failed to address itself to the possibility that, in general, lurid presentations of sexual matters were exploitative. The New South Wales Sexual Assault Committee complained of a story in *The Daily Mirror* of 26 May 1986 under the heading 'Girl's breasts slashed on terror train ride'. The story named the girl and twice told of her blouse being ripped open and her breast being slashed; it used phrases such as 'a horrifying attack', 'vicious muggers' and 'sadistically slashing'. The complainant said the paper 'could be considered exploitative of women in that not only does it use women's bodies to sell copy but also sensationalises and thereby trivialises violence against women'.[24] The page-three story was published beside a photo of a big-breasted, bikini-clad 'Miss Snow Bird'.

The council reiterated its view that a sexual assault was 'a gross invasion of privacy and dignity, involving humiliation and embarrassment as well as physical suffering. Publicity compounds the suffering and may also be a deterrent to the reporting of such offences.'[25] It saw no justification in naming the girl and upheld the complaint on that ground. But it side-stepped the general complaint about exploitation and the possible results of detailed descriptions of the attack. Indeed it seemed to place more importance on the law enforcement aspects of the case than on the prurience of the story treatment.

Naming of victims of sexual assault is generally considered unethical. But is the public interest of half the population genuinely served by dwelling on details that may incite individual copy cats and create a general climate of opinion that women are 'natural' victims? Is the value of a graphic story more important than the principle of not harming others? The Press

Council has said that a consequence of freedom is that 'journalists carry the responsibility for making a professional judgment about what will be reported'.[26] Many critics contend that the exercise of such professional judgement is often misguided and threatens the rights of others to live free from fear and abuse.

If journalists are able to select what information to include without falling foul of the law, it follows that freedom of expression cannot be jeopardised. The journalist remains free from legal compulsion to omit lurid details but may make a personal and ethical choice to place the rights of members of the community to protection ahead of other values. Or the journalist may choose to include the detail, putting commercial considerations first. In the *People* case, the council explicitly brought market considerations into its decision, as did the publisher of the magazine in a radio interview when he claimed that 'these magazines are good working class material . . . aimed at young working class men'.[27] Taken to its logical conclusion, this type of market argument suggests that ethical decisions should be dictated not by the moral rightness of the behaviour but by the social class of the audience. Freedom of the media is defined by the absence of legislative restraint; it does not mean freedom to ignore ethical considerations.

Another interesting aspect of the Press Council's decision in the *People* cover case is the indistinct demarcation between news and entertainment. The news media in a competitive economy operate as providers of information in the public interest and entertaining stories of interest to the public. Many workers in the news media call themselves journalists, whether their job is to provide information in the public interest or entertainment or a varying mix of both. As the Communications Law Centre noted about the *People* case, '[p]resumably journalists and photographers are involved in the production of these magazines, and what they produce — however trivial, offensive or kinky — constitutes "news" or "information" of a kind'.[28]

If the Press Council believes it has no power to adjudicate in entertainment areas of the press, the range of publications — and items within publications — that it can consider is narrowed immeasurably. It may be, as we argue elsewhere in this book, that the ethical resolution of some questions — such as chequebook journalism — should take into account whether the prime function of a given piece of information is public interest reporting or entertainment. But in cases where there is a clash between the principles of free speech and harm to others, that distinction is less tenable. And whether the decision can be enforced should also be remembered. Just because the council, as it often says, has no power to censor does not mean it has no power to censure material in a mixed news/entertainment publication that breaches its own ethical guidelines.

In the United States, there appears to be no distinction between news and entertainment when it comes to freedom of speech. A significant case dealt with the 1974 screening of an NBC drama depicting the harsh realities of the confinement of juvenile offenders and its effects. *Born Innocent* showed the rape of a child by four fellow inmates in a home for girls; three days later a nine-year-old Californian girl was raped in similar circumstances. It was a type of crime previously unrecorded in American juvenile casebooks. In 1978, a Supreme Court judge ruled that the drama was presumptively protected by the First Amendment, which guarantees freedom of expression, and an impending suit for personal injury damages was dropped.[29] The drama could have been defended on the grounds that, even though a fictional work, it accurately depicted a matter of public interest.

Obviously the Australian Press Council would never be asked to rule on a television drama program; but the *Born Innocent* example shows that public interest and free speech defences cannot solely be the province of the strictly news section of the media. Further, it demonstrates that broadcast self-regulators face extremely complicated moral dilemmas largely because the entertainment and information aspects of the electronic media are so entwined.

The Press Council has, on several occasions, used the public forum argument in reaching its decisions on specific complaints against sexist material. In 1990, for instance, it dismissed a complaint against *The Advertiser* in Adelaide for publishing in a column, 'At a glance with Marty Smith', a 1987 quote from a Queensland cattle-dog breeder. The quote read: 'Good dogs are like a good wife — honest, hard working, smart but dumb enough to be completely loyal and still love you despite the odd kick and frequent abuse'.[30] Although it sympathised with the complainant, the council opined it was 'better for the public to know that outrageous views exist in the community than to mislead it by omission'.[31] The rationale may have carried more weight had the quotation been contained within a contemporaneous news report; but it was three years old by the time it was recycled in *The Advertiser*.

Other sexist comments have received a varied reception from the council. A woman complained that several items in an issue of *Computing* magazine relied on sexual innuendo and suggested that women were relevant only in a sexual role. The council, however, accepted the magazine's statement that the material was intended to be satirical and dismissed the complaint, even though it agreed with the complainant that an accompanying illustration that showed a woman bound to a bed could be considered offensive.[32] Another piece that the writer argued was satire fared less well. A column written by the editor of the *Caboolture and Bribie Times* in Queensland appeared after the election of seven women to the Caboolture Council. The article speculated, among other things, that television sets would be built into councillors' benches for watching soap operas, a manicurist would be on call and premenstrual tension would be an excuse for not attending council meetings. The council found the material was insulting and upheld the complaint, saying the complainant had correctly relied on the council's existing principle 8, 'part of which says material disparaging or belittling people by reference to their sex is a breach of ethical standards'.[33] It is difficult to discern what makes the Caboolture statements a breach of ethical standards when, a year earlier, an illustration of a woman bound to a bed was not.

Reporting and commenting on gender matters requires a delicate balancing act. In determining right conduct in these areas, journalists have to recognise the changing values held by various components of their public and investigate the often-disputed facts about the effects of some types of coverage on the well-being of individuals. They must search rigorously for the boundary between free expression and the freedom to exploit others and question the universality of the concept of public interest when it is applied to reporting discrete groups of the public. They must decide the relative weighting between freedom to report and the principle of respect for others. And they must ask themselves if reporting accurately on a particular event may not sometimes contribute to untruthful reporting of the reality of a society.

Race, Ethnicity and Nationality

More than one in five Australians was born overseas; one-third of the Australian population speaks a language other than English at home. Three in every 200 Australians have a blood tie to the original people who inhabited the land thousands of years before successive waves of immigrants turned Australia into a country of racial and ethnic diversity.[34]

Despite the blossoming of ethnic radio and television and the rapid growth of Aboriginal broadcasting during the 1980s, the mainstream media remain predominantly monocultural in tone and reporting the reality of Australia's diversity throws up many practical and ethical challenges. Many critics assert that the news media do less than their best in giving fair coverage to minorities and frequently fuel tensions and divisions between ethnic groups. Like the criticism applied to reporting of gender issues, the accusations are both general and specific. The general charges are that ethnic groups are stereotyped and marginalised, that the reporting of their cultures and value systems is characterised by ignorance and prejudice and that they are portrayed as being major contributors to social ills such as crime and unemployment. Specifically, critics say that insensitive and offensive reporting legitimises racist attitudes and, at its worst, can condone injustices and incite racial hatred and violence.

The role of the media in influencing attitudes is well documented and acknowledged by the media industry as a whole. The news sector, however, asserts that its special task of recording and commenting on social issues puts it in a slightly different position from that of producers of drama or comedy and of advertisers. As we saw at the beginning of this chapter, the Australian Press Council sought to have Western Australian legislation on racial vilification changed to include, as the New South Wales law does, a defence of fair reporting of racist views put by public figures. The plea for a 'fair reporting in the public interest' clause — similar to the privilege protecting journalists against defamation when they report court proceedings — was based on the public's need to know about attitudes, even unpalatable ones, that motivate racist actions. The council chairperson wrote to the state's Minister for Ethnic Affairs that a defence of publication in the public interest 'could assist in ensuring that the press and the media are not inhibited in reporting, indeed exposing, racist events and, above all, racist campaigns'.[35]

The adoption of anti-discrimination laws in Australia has necessitated a precise definition of racial discrimination. The Victorian Equal Opportunity Act, for instance, defines racial discrimination 'as being treated less favourably than a person of another race, colour, or ethnic origin in the same or similar circumstances'.[36] Anti-discrimination laws, however, are targeted towards actions taken against individuals in their daily access to the services and opportunities provided in the community. They do not deal with words, imagery and ideas, which are the currency of the media. The move, during the late 1980s, towards enacting legislation to create offences relating to racial harassment and incitement to racial hatred focused attention on what people say, and therefore on the media's role in reporting race issues in Australia.

Australian press history is littered with gross examples of racist views. *The Bulletin* under J. F. Archibald during the late 1880s was renowned for its vicious anti-Chinese stand. *Smith's Weekly* in the 1920s railed against 'dirty dago pests'.[37] In the 1840s, it was possible for papers to write about Aboriginals thus: '. . . the sensual and animal part of their being is almost entirely in the Ascendant — and they seem only to be "at home" whilst revelling in all that is beastly and obscene'.[38] One hundred and fifty years later, awareness of the harm caused by racist invective was much improved but there were still sufficient transgressions for the self-regulatory bodies to be kept busy investigating charges of racism and for several government inquiries to restate the importance of media influence on community attitudes and actions.

The Australian Press Council was the first media organisation to determine that publishing material that disparaged people by reference to race, colour or ethnicity was unethical. The sixth complaint it adjudicated claimed that a front-page headline in a Melbourne suburban paper was offensive and that the report itself would harm the development of harmonious relations in the community. The headline — 'Greek threat of violence' — related to a story about a dispute within the local Greek community over the building of a Greek Orthodox church. The council dismissed the complaint as it did two more similar complaints that year: one from several Croatian organisations and the other alleging the Brisbane *Sunday Mail* had presented white racist propaganda in an article and letters on minority rule in Rhodesia.[39]

A little more than a decade later, the council acknowledged that racial issues were 'emerging as ever more important, reflecting on the one hand a growing ethnic press which sometimes brings to Australia group conflicts based overseas, and on the other hand an increasingly sensitive social consciousness . . .'.[40] By the early 1990s, about a score of complaints relating to racism or religious disparagement were received each year.[41]

Many complaints about racist reporting hinge on the concept of relevance of certain facts to the story, especially when the stories are negative in tone. Sometimes, the distinction between relevant reference and gratuitous reference is easy to see. Two brief items that appeared on the same page of *The Australian* in September 1993 illustrate the difference. The first paragraph of one, headlined '2 murder charges', read:

> A 67-year-old Ukrainian man was charged late yesterday with murdering two elderly people and attempting to murder another in stabbing attacks west of Newcastle in NSW. He was refused bail and will appear in Wallsend court today.

The second, under the heading 'Muslim singing prompted stabbing', read:

> The singing of Muslim songs at a Sydney restaurant led to a wild brawl in which a man was stabbed to death, a Supreme Court judge said yesterday.
>
> In sentencing 37-year-old Richard Kolalich to a minimum of three years' jail for the manslaughter of 40-year-old Bosco Davic, Justice Grove said underlying the eruptions were 'identifiable ethnic tensions'.[42]

At its inception, the Press Council incorporated into its principles the idea that no news item or headline should 'state the race, nationality or religious or political views of a person suspected of a crime, or arrested, charged or convicted, unless the fact is relevant'.[43] In the two crime stories from *The Australian*, it is clear that ethnicity is irrelevant to the reader's understanding of the first story but religious belief and ethnic tension could be an illuminating fact about the possible cause of the fight in the second.

Determining the relevance of facts in crime stories is not usually difficult, although it may sometimes cause offence to sections of the community. In 1978, for instance, several Italian organisations complained to the Press Council that a series in

The Herald in Melbourne, which investigated links between the Mafia in Calabria and some residents of the New South Wales town of Griffith, was racist and tended to damage the good name of all Calabrians; the council dismissed the complaint, noting that it would have been impossible to have written the articles 'without some danger of a reflection on the people of Calabria' but that the subject was of legitimate public interest.[44] Many Australian newspapers have in-house rules that reinforce the council principle against referring to ethnicity or race in crime or court reports unless the fact is relevant.

A more difficult problem is determining the relevance of race or other factors in stories that have a less direct negative focus than straightforward crime stories. The MEAA code of ethics requires journalists 'to report and interpret the news with scrupulous honesty . . . by not suppressing relevant available facts'. But who should determine what is relevant: the journalist or the individual or community that feels aggrieved? The twin issues of determining relevance and judging what to publish in the public interest are often tested when race matters enter the picture.

The rationale behind the prohibition on gratuitous emphasis on race, ethnicity and so on was spelled out in a council adjudication on a story about riotous behaviour of some Aboriginal tenants of a public housing estate in Perth:

> To emphasise race or religion in connection with unfavourable events to which they are irrelevant creates a misleading impression of a connection between the two and feeds the only too common human weakness to stereotype other groups in a disparaging way.
>
> On the other hand a false picture is also given if the press does not report problems that actually exist in relation to particular groups.[45]

In the Perth housing case, the council ruled that references to Aboriginality were relevant to the story. Indeed in most cases alleging 'gratuitous emphasis' that have gone to council adjudication the council has dismissed the complaint. It has, however, often cautioned newspapers to be 'sensitive to the growing community concern about matters that contribute to the development or perpetuation of group prejudices'.[46] Generally, the council appears to have ruled on the intent of the publication, rather than on its effect. In one case, for instance, it exonerated an economics commentator of any intention to stir up prejudice by the use of the term 'Mediterranean back' in a story on workers' compensation law reform but said that the term did embody a stereotype 'which unfairly [labelled] all members of a group as possessing some unfavourable characteristic'.[47] The journalist may not have intentionally set out to offend, but the offensive reference to an ethnic group could surely have been avoided without affecting the public interest.

Headlines cause particular problems when deciding whether a reference to race has been sensational. In 1986, the chairperson of the New South Wales Ethnic Affairs Commission told the Press Council that the commission had received several complaints about the headlines on two articles in the Sydney Sunday paper, *The Sun-Herald*, about conflict between gangs of Lebanese and Vietnamese youths in the city's western suburbs. The headlines read: 'Race hate grips Bankstown' and 'War in the West'. The council determined that the reports of underlying problems, manifested in the fights, were in the public interest and that, although the headlines were dramatic, they did not exceed acceptable limits.[48]

The news media, when countering criticism, often refer to people's tendency to 'shoot the messenger' who bears bad tidings. It is in the reporting of race and ethnicity in a multiracial society that the role of the messenger is under the most intense scrutiny. Unfortunately, there is little doubt that, when the media do draw public attention to certain issues, the incidence of harassment of innocent people increases. The National Inquiry into Racist Violence in Australia noted that 'evidence of victimised individuals and organisations suggests a connection between media coverage of immigration issues, foreign affairs and events involving ethnic minorities and the level of harassment experienced'.[49] The connection was made plain during discussion groups, carried out by the Office of Multicultural Affairs for the inquiry.

> Filipino women in the Northern Territory and Queensland said harassment was worse following media stories about 'Mail Order Brides' and the Aquino campaign against prostitution and crime in the Philippines.
>
> Asians in all States noticed increased harassment after reports of arrivals of Vietnamese refugees and of increased numbers of Asian students in Australia, as well as stories about Japanese purchases of real estate . . .

Arabic speakers in several States said harassment was worse after media coverage of the [Salman] Rushdie affair and any reports of terrorist action by nationals of Middle Eastern countries.[50]

The inquiry properly upheld the news media's right to report on issues of concern to the community without fear of censorship or excessive restriction and noted that most media were 'careful to provide a balanced coverage of contentious race issues and [exercised] their power to influence public opinion in a responsible manner'.[51] But it pointed to the impact of what it termed 'media shock', in which the power of headlines, photographs and dramatic introductory paragraphs have a more lasting impression on audiences than the more detailed stories with which they are associated. In such areas, the media should exercise caution, it said.[52]

If a journalist believes that respect for the rights of others is a value that must be taken into account when deciding how to approach a story, then that journalist is duty bound to place due emphasis on the possible effects of a story. But to what degree should that respect override the principle of full disclosure of relevant facts? And how much should a journalist's conduct and a story's content be modified by the possibility that some among the audience may interpret the news as condoning prejudice?

Indigenous Australians

Indigenous Australians have specific complaints about news coverage of their peoples and their concerns, some of which are similar to those of other ethnic groups. They complain that Aboriginal and Torres Strait Islander people are marginalised and stereotyped, that journalists are insensitive to Aboriginal values and belief systems, and that most reporting is negative. Such complaints take on a sharper edge because of the blighted history of Aboriginal–white relations in Australia since the intrusion of Europeans. And they pose a particular challenge for journalists because the coverage of Aboriginal issues has grown immeasurably in the past two decades. Such an expansion increases the odds that journalists will cause offence, through ignorance or unthinking prejudice or because they judge some types of story more newsworthy than others. To what degree they behave unethically is, however, another matter.

A study of the content of *The Canberra Times* in 1974 found that the main elements of the Aboriginal stereotype suggested that

Aborigines were lazy, irresponsible, dirty, thriftless and immoral, that they could not handle alcohol and were superstitious.[53] As Janelle Miles pointed out,[54] all these supposed characteristics were drawn from comments made by news sources, not journalists; yet it is the publication of such views, not their source, that lies at the heart of the Aboriginal community's objections.

Miles's own comparative study of coverage in *The Courier-Mail* and *Sunday Mail* in Brisbane in 1966 and 1981 found a general improvement in treatment of Aborigines and a change of emphasis in the type of stories run. Miles found that political stories accounted for more than one-third of all stories about Aborigines in 1981, but none in 1966. Coverage of social problems — which included discussion of education, health, housing, alcoholism and welfare — had doubled to just over 39 per cent of items; crime stories in which Aborigines were identified had dropped from 25 per cent to 3.6 per cent of items. Conversely, stories about Aboriginal culture comprised 12.5 per cent of the 1966 coverage and none of the 1981 coverage. The stories were also ranked as positive, neutral or negative. The 15-year gap showed a slight drop of 0.85 per cent in the proportion of positive stories to 17.9 per cent of the total. But the negative stories had dropped much more dramatically, from 31.25 per cent to 3.5 per cent. Neutral stories went from 50 per cent to 78.6 per cent of the total coverage.[55]

As John Hurst pointed out in a paper delivered to the Journalism Educators' Association conference in 1988, Australian journalists had 'cause for pride in having drawn public attention to some of the glaring injustices done to Aborigines in recent times'.[56] Hurst reached his conclusion from examining the first 32 years of the Walkley Awards, the national awards for excellence in journalism; he found that 18 Walkleys had gone to journalists who had focused sympathetically on Aboriginal concerns.

> They wrote about the appalling conditions under which many Aborigines lived and about their treatment as social outcasts by white society long before those issues began to gnaw at the Australian conscience. Admittedly, they saw the problem from a white cultural perspective. Nevertheless, they went out of their way to understand the reasons why Aborigines felt aliens in their own land. They looked closely at the causes of the high incidence of malnutrition, disease and infant mortality among Aborigines and at the evidence of white prejudice.[57]

It was one such report, the ABC's *Four Corners'* 'Black Death' program in 1986, that helped create the climate of opinion that led to the setting-up of the Royal Commission in Aboriginal Deaths in Custody the following year.

In 1987 another Walkley Award went to journalist Frank Robson for an article in *Time Australia* about Aboriginal deaths in custody and the general treatment of Aborigines in Queensland. Yet it was Robson who, a year earlier, had been the target of criticism for an article published in *People* in April 1986 to accompany a general article about social problems in the northern Queensland city of Cairns. Robson quoted the officer in charge of the Cairns police station, Senior Sergeant Vern Timm, who claimed that about 90 per cent of assaults and robberies in the Cairns area were perpetrated by Aborigines and alleged that welfare payments had caused an upsurge in crime; he also quoted Timm's description of Aborigines as 'coons, boongs, black bastards and dingoes'.[58] In a highly critical analysis of the coverage, journalism lecturer Michael Meadows found that 28 stories were published nationally over the next two months. In 23 of them, Meadows said, the offensive words were repeated and 15 ran the 90 per cent allegation again; not one sought to examine whether the original claim of a surge in the Cairns crime rate was, in fact, sustainable.[59] The Aboriginal and Torres Strait Islander communities of Cairns were understandably outraged by Timm's comments; they demonstrated outside the police station and called for his sacking.

The communities also took their complaint against *People* to the Press Council which found 'the magazine was justified in publishing it; indeed it did a public service in doing so'.[60] The council found Timm's language was clearly denigrating and would have inevitably caused hurt and distress. It noted, however, that the accuracy of the report was not questioned and that the item referred to the reporter being shocked by Timm's comments, thus indicating that the magazine did not endorse them. It went on:

> It was surely in the public interest that it should be revealed that the officer in charge of police operations not only held such views but was prepared to express them to a reporter. The justification for publication lay in the exposure of prejudice in a key law enforcement figure, and the article has in fact led to a police inquiry into the comments.

[Principle 8] enjoins papers from themselves promoting, or allowing themselves to be used by others to promote, racial prejudice in the community. But it does not require them to pretend that racial prejudice does not exist in the community, or to refrain from reporting the existence of such prejudice where it is in the public interest to do so. In short it is not intended to prevent papers informing the public of the real situation in the community.[61]

The case demonstrates many of the moral issues attached to reporting of race issues. A journalist intent on acting ethically rather than responding emotionally would have to ask several questions. How relevant was the fact that the person who vented such racist language and unsubstantiated claims was a police officer? Would publication have been justified if the speaker was an ordinary citizen expressing prejudice? Was the reader entitled to details of the racist slurs in order to comprehend their vehemence or would a general assertion by the reporter have sufficed? Was the principle of full disclosure more important than avoiding hurt to Aboriginal residents of Cairns? How important was it to discover the truth about the city's crime rate so the audience could judge the accuracy or otherwise of Timm's remarks? Was the general public interest in knowing that those pledged to uphold justice and the law were unfitted for the task more important that the particular right of the Aboriginal and Torres Strait Islander community to be respected?

Sometimes, however, the Press Council has come out strongly against reporting that uses racist language. In one adjudication against the *Wellington Voice*, published in western New South Wales, the council found that several articles constituted 'a litany of insulting and intemperate language, inaccurate reporting, and gross and unsubstantiated generalisations about Aboriginal people'.[62]

During the early 1990s, the mainstream media in Australia became increasingly sensitised to some of the substance of the charges levelled at them by indigenous Australians. The Special Broadcasting Service commissioned guidelines from Aboriginal broadcaster Lester Bostock for use in the production of television and film about Aborigines and Torres Strait Islanders.[63] The Royal Commission into Aboriginal Deaths in Custody had recommended in its 1991 report that 'all media organisations should be encouraged to develop codes and policies relating to the presentation of Aboriginal issues, the establishment of monitoring bodies, and the putting into place of training and employment programs for Aboriginal employees in all classifications'.[64] Two years later, in the International Year of the World's Indigenous People, the Media Entertainment and Arts Alliance, including the AJA section, adopted guidelines for reporting on Aboriginal issues.[65] The Federation of Australian Radio Broadcasters developed its guidelines for the portrayal of indigenous Australians and the federal government's Department of Transport and Communications began preparing a statement of principles.

Yet some of the difficulties of cross-cultural reporting are not necessarily solved by articulating codes of conduct. These difficulties arise from the constraints imposed by the daily operation of mainstream media. One frequent complaint from Aboriginal communities is that the mainstream media rarely presents Aborigines as authoritative figures. One Aborigine's assessment of the media coverage of a shooting at the New South Wales town of Moree in 1982 was pithy:

Who gets shot? Koories.
Who gets arrested? Koories.
Who gets interviewed? A gub! (white)[66]

White Australians are comfortable with the concept of identifiable experts and leaders with instant opinions. Such figures suit the demands of the journalist, pressured by a deadline, who is in search of an unambiguous quote. Much Aboriginal decision making, by contrast, is communal and takes time. As journalism educator Mark Pearson has pointed out, the normal news gathering methods of Australian journalists can result in inaccurate and unfair coverage of Aboriginal issues. In an overview of the sociolinguistic research into Aboriginal communicative patterns,[67] Pearson identified the absence of the reason-seeking question 'why' in some Aboriginal communities, the cultural reluctance to be singled out from the group, more leisurely timeframes adopted for the exchange of information and different linguistic structures for questioning as professional pitfalls for the reporter. However ethically reporters may wish to conduct themselves, the different values which indigenous Australians place on consensus and interpersonal relationships will continue to give rise to misunderstandings and accusations of deliberately insensitive reporting. But that reality should not prevent journalists, and media organisations, from making a concerted effort to modify those professional techniques that prove ineffective in reporting Aboriginal and Torres Strait Islander issues truthfully.

Matters of Faith

In the industry's guidelines for reporting Aboriginal issues, the news media have belatedly recognised that the beliefs once dubbed primitive superstitions are, in fact, expressions of a complex spirituality. The recognition in the guidelines is not always upheld in practice, however. One newspaper columnist, for instance, described Aboriginal beliefs as 'manifest claptrap and arrant nonsense which any self-respecting, civilised, intelligent society would treat as balderdash'.[68] Yet despite such occasional gross lapses, the mainstream media are gradually becoming more accommodating of Aboriginal religion. Other faiths fare less well, however. While complaints that journalists have disparaged religious beliefs are less common than those about gender, race or ethnicity, they still occur.

Religious references are often inextricably bound up with ethnicity and national origin. Sometimes the links are forged by ignorance; in others, they are a crucial element to understanding why community tensions arise. A further difficulty for the Australian news media stems from many Australian citizens' prior loyalties to their country of origin. In commenting on growing religious and ethnic complaints, the Press Council said the increase was in part due to an expanded ethnic press that brought 'to Australia group conflicts based overseas'.[69] Yet reporting of overseas conflict in the mainstream Australian media can be equally divisive.

More complaints about religious disparagement reaching the self-regulatory bodies relate to Judaism than to any other religion, although Islam became increasingly the target of prejudicial and ignorant reporting during the late 1980s. Several cases illustrate the Press Council's comment about imported tensions. In April 1982, the council considered a complaint from the New South Wales Jewish Board of Deputies against two articles in an Arabic paper, *An-Nahar*. The first article set out teachings that allegedly came from the Torah and the long-discredited publication, the Protocols of the Elders of Zion; the council found the tenor of the item was to bring the Jewish religion under a wholesale condemnation. It judged, however, that the second article, which attacked the Israeli state for its actions in the Lebanon, was 'acceptable propaganda in time of hostilities'.[70]

In an earlier adjudication, the council was careful to make the distinction between legitimate political comment and religious disparagement. It was one of the few occasions that the council has found against a cartoon or illustration and ruled that lack of intent to offend was not a mitigating circumstance. The Executive Council of Australian Jewry complained about a drawing, published to illustrate a highly critical article about the Israeli treatment of Palestinians living in the West Bank. The complainant described the illustration thus:

> The cartoon in question depicts a Satanic cloven-hooved Jewish figure — apparently a rabbi — slicing an infant into pieces under the background of a crescent moon dripping blood. He is apparently dropping a bomb on a mosque and, it seems, has a Nazi 'S.S.' symbol engraved on his clothing.[71]

The complainant said that the cloven-hooved image of Jews as 'agents of Satan' had often appeared in medieval anti-Semitic depictions, frequently as a prelude to a massacre or pogrom and was a symbol of hatred of the Jewish people. The artist told the council he had not intended the imagery that way. It was a reference to certain extremist rabbis referred to in the article and what had been taken as a bomb was no more than his usual logo signature. The council accepted his good faith but explained why it had upheld the complaint.

> [The illustrator] was entitled through the medium of the drawing to express his strong disapproval of the treatment of Palestinians in Israel, and to convey that he saw an ironic parallel with Nazi Germany's drive for Lebensraum. However, no doubt unintentionally, he went beyond that and used images which tapped deep well-springs of racial and religious prejudice, thereby giving deep offence to at least some Jewish people through the revival of memories of past persecution.
> . . .
> The Press Council believes that The National Times should have been more aware that the illustration, with its hard-

hitting imagery, although intended as political comment, was capable of being seen as anti-Jewish as well.[72]

Overseas political events triggered yet another complaint. The New South Wales Jewish Board of Deputies complained of three articles published in the Arabic language paper, *An Nahda*, in September 1985, claiming they were anti-Semitic, disparaging and belittling of Jews. The council censured the paper on the grounds that the articles contained 'a number of wild and unsubstantiated allegations . . . typical of the kind of propaganda that has been used to stir up anti-Jewish prejudice and justify racial persecution'.[73] Two of the three articles were reprinted from papers published in the Lebanon and the editor of *An Nahda* told the council they reflected the bitter feeling generated by the Israeli–Lebanese conflict. The council said the strong feelings were understandable but in no way justified the violent attacks on Jews as a group. Earlier the same year, the council had found a Croatian weekly, *Hrvatski Tjednik*, guilty of similarly abhorrent anti-Jewish prejudice.[74]

The Muslim community, too, has had cause for complaint about media treatment, some of which was sparked by reports of overseas events. Before and during the Gulf War of 1991, both Arabic-speaking and Muslim groups suffered the backlash of heightened nationalistic sentiment. The National Inquiry into Racist Violence found that anti-Arab and anti-Muslim feeling in Australia was largely based on stereotypes. Its report noted there was:

> . . . a generalised identification of Arabs and Muslims with violence (such as terrorism and the taking of hostages), a stereotyped identification of Arabs and Muslims with 'unAustralian values' (for example, religious fundamentalism, conservative views about women and moral issues, dietary restrictions, conservative and conspicuous clothing, prohibitions on alcohol, and a desire for a separate cultural identity . . .[75]

Media coverage had reinforced such perceptions, the report said. The inquiry made five specific recommendations about media reporting of Arabs and Muslims. It suggested, for example, that using the word 'Muslim' in phrases such as 'Muslim extremists' and 'Muslim fanatics' should be avoided unless it referred to people who were most accurately identified by their religion; when reporting on Islamic belief or practice, particularly on controversial issues such as calls for a *jihad*, or holy war, journalists should consult authoritative leaders of representative groups.[76] No journalist who values accuracy and fairness could take exception to such suggestions.

Although we have concentrated in this chapter on just a few examples of covering gender and ethnic issues, criticism of the news media's insensitivity to difference is much more wide-spread. The various self-regulatory bodies have heard complaints about coverage of homosexuality, of the aged, the physically disabled. The Press Council has adjudicated on allegations of racism in the use of words such as 'Pom' and 'Anglo-Celtic' and the disparagement of Sri Lankans, Turks, the French, Palestinians, Chinese students, Cambodian refugees and many others. As we noted earlier, difference arouses powerful emotions.

We saw in the preceding chapter on fairness and bias that people's ties to their cultural background, moral value systems and personal beliefs cannot be severed simply because they choose journalism as a career. Many recent investigations of media performance in gender and race matters have recommended greater representation of women, Aborigines and other ethnic minorities among news media workers. The recommendations are a tacit acknowledgement that journalists with different backgrounds will report differently because they understand the issues differently. Given that all journalists are to some extent prisoners of their backgrounds, how do they pick their careful way through the ethical minefields of reporting difference?

For a start, they should recognise the inherent loyalty they have to their own kind. Then when faced with a particular ethical problem in gathering and writing news about minorities, they should identify the various values that operate. The relevant values can be individual and community ones. Individual values may include fairness and respect for the rights of other individuals to live free of fear and oppression. Community values may encompass the value of social harmony and tolerance.

As professionals, journalists have then to evaluate the application of the principle of free speech in situations where groups or individuals may be subjected to harassment, distress or discrimination. While all individuals in a free society have a right to express their opinions, is it ethical for a journalist actively to seek out comment from people known to hold inflammatory views? The result may be controversial and sensational copy, but is it a fair representation of widely held views? Is the search for extremes an ethical news gathering practice or merely motivated by a desire for arresting copy? If truth-telling — or accuracy and fairness — is an important principle for journalists, the question has to be asked of whether continued reiteration of prejudice magnifies, and so distorts, the general incidence of such prejudice. The Press Council, for instance, has often argued that what public figures say, however repugnant or prejudiced, should be reported because the public has a right to know that those figures hold such views. But such a blanket defence may not be appropriate in all cases. One can also argue that it is the relevance of the views to the person's public or professional duties that should dictate whether the views are exposed. For instance, if a senior public servant in the Department of Immigration holds blatantly racist views, the fact is relevant; the bureaucrat's equally discriminatory views about women may be less so.

As we have mentioned, the loyalties of the journalist reporting difference will be sorely tested. Some loyalty to one's own race, gender or culture is inevitable. But other loyalties must also be weighed. What is the strength of the journalist's loyalty to the audience? Is a female journalist's loyalty to women more important than her loyalty to her audience as a whole? Should Aboriginal reporters working in the mainstream news media put loyalty to their fellow Aborigines before their obligations to their employer to report all relevant facts, even if those may distress or offend Aboriginal people?

None of the ethical questions that arise in minority reporting is easily answered. But journalists may well find that much of their conduct that is deemed gratuitously offensive can be rectified by putting a higher value on accuracy. The journalist who works to find out about the beliefs, customs and values of people who are different will find that respect for accuracy, fairness and truth brings greater understanding, which may in turn eliminate unnecessarily provocative coverage. At the same time, the news media should not be forced to ignore unpalatable truths, simply to avoid causing offence.

CHAPTER 4

Violence, Crime and Public Safety

Australians have voiced disquiet about the methods and motives behind media reports of crime and violence for more than 150 years. Many of the newspapers of the 1840s relied heavily on court reports of sex crimes and murders and on descriptions of floggings and the low life of Sydney. Later papers and broadsides devoted much space to gory details of murder trials and executions. *The Bulletin* cast doubt on the journalistic motives behind such content, particularly that of the *Sydney Evening News*, which began publication in 1867 and by 1884 was selling 40 000 copies a day: 'What sells certain Australian evening papers till they run into the severalth edition? Is it their leading articles — or is it the graphic account of the brutal prize-fight, the "sickening details" of the horrible murder . . .'.[1]

Contemporary critics — like their 19th century counterparts — express distaste and occasional revulsion at the detailed reportage of violence and crime, yet crime remains a mainstay of many mainstream media, especially tabloid metropolitan newspapers and television news and current affairs programs. Criminologists Peter Grabosky and Paul Wilson found that, while most

Australian newspaper editors conceded that the relative importance of crime news had declined since the 1960s, crime stories still ranked in the top two or three items for at least one Melbourne television station.[2] During an extensive national study on crime news, they discovered an almost universal acceptance among journalists that the most newsworthy crime stories were those that involved violence or death. Those in which harm befell ' "respectable" citizens, children and the elderly [received] more coverage than incidents involving more marginal members of society'.[3]

The fascination with crime is universal and enduring. One look at an airport bookstall testifies to that. Stories about crime sell because they are stories of temptation, fall and sin. They are dramatic and tell of passions and experiences beyond the personal knowledge of most ordinary citizens, characteristics that fit well the news criteria of conflict and the unusual. Criminal acts flout the age-old codes that forbid the taking of life and property; they are the quintessential anti-social behaviour, the antithesis of right conduct. Crime reporting tends, as Grabosky and Wilson point out, 'to provide a focus for the affirmation of public morality . . . [When values about which there is wide-spread public consensus] are violated, such as through the murder of a child, the news media enable members of the public to share their indignation, and provide an opportunity for the reaffirmation of those basic moral standards of society'.[4]

Crime, by definition, goes beyond debate about the ambiguities of ethics into law, or the codification of what constitutes unacceptable behaviour in a particular society. Although the boundary between ethics and law is perhaps at its most poorly defined in the coverage of crime and criminal justice, reporting crime raises several ethical issues that are not necessarily covered by law. It is here that the difficulties of balancing the demands of journalism and the needs of the community are most obvious.

The specific topics that arise in crime reporting are:

- the apparent conflict between full disclosure of relevant facts and a person's right to a fair trial;
- the glorification of criminality;
- the problem of copycat crime;
- the disproportionate reportage of crime that can distort perceptions of the actual crime rate;

- the conflict between the obligations of the media and those of enforcement authorities;
- public safety;
- the potential for the media to become involved in criminal incidents;
- detailed reports and images of distressing or offensive material; and
- intrusion into the privacy of, and harassment of, victims, witnesses and the families of offenders.

Despite the myriad ethical questions that arise when covering crime there is, surprisingly, only one direct reference to crime reporting in the existing Australian codes of practice. The little known code of ethics of the Country Press Association of New South Wales says that 'news of crime, scandal and vice should be presented in such a manner as to deter readers from imitating the criminal and the vicious'.[5] All the national codes ban intrusions into privacy except where there is a public interest component and the television and radio codes caution against the unnecessary use of violent or distressing material or items likely to cause public panic. None mentions the more vexed areas of ethical debate surrounding crime news. Matters of privacy and taste, which occur so often in crime-related reporting, are examined elsewhere in this book. This chapter looks at those ethical issues peculiar to crime reporting where journalists may find themselves at odds with the values of their fellow citizens.

A Siege Mentality

One sort of crime seems tailor-made for the news media, and it often is. It is the siege with its drawn-out tensions and looming potential for violent death of innocent hostages. It is no accident that Hollywood has made millions out of hostage movies; sieges are inherently dramatic. They are great stories and, for journalists, they are great news stories. Most crimes are reported after the event and the reporter must piece together the picture second-hand from victims, witnesses and police officers. A siege enables crime reporters to do what is rarely afforded them: to see the event unfold.

Sieges fall into two categories. There is the 'domestic' siege in which individuals — thrown off balance by alcohol, drugs, anger or anguish — lose control and lash out, using family members, friends or strangers as hostages to bargain a way out of what they see as an intolerable personal situation. Then there is the 'political' siege, in which the offenders are motivated by the desire to make a public statement about some perceived personal or political grievance. Some terrorist acts, such as hijacking and kidnappings of prominent people, are the most overtly political crimes but other sieges can manifest elements of a protest against an undefined 'system'. While both sorts pose ethical questions for the news media, the 'political' siege has an extra dimension. When publicity is the offender's main motive, the news media are forced to participate in the event. They can no longer try to operate as impartial observers for their actions have a direct impact on the outcome of the incident.

For enforcement authorities, both types of siege are essentially the same. The aim is to resolve the incident safely, and the primary goal is the lives of those involved in the siege as well as those in the vicinity, such as emergency personnel, media representatives and the general public. A siege negotiation expert from the New South Wales Police, Superintendent Norm Hazzard, told a meeting of enforcement officers and the media that peaceful resolution depended on three elements: isolation, containment and negotiation.[6] By isolating and containing the event, police seek to establish the official negotiator as the sole link to the outside world.

> The skilled work of the negotiators, advised by psychiatrists, builds up a rapport with the hostage taker, and leads, in most cases, to a peaceful resolution. However, the interference in this isolation by a third party breaks the rapport and can lead to aggressive behaviour by the offender.[7]

The third party is often the media. According to one police spokesperson, media behaviour is the one factor in a siege that the authorities cannot control. The media are the wild-card in the pack.[8] Police acknowledge that the process of negotiation 'usually takes time which inevitably causes problems for media working to deadlines under intense competitive pressure'.[9]

Domestic sieges, while not everyday events, are not uncommon in Australia; many are short-lived and are resolved peacefully. As such, they rate a few paragraphs in newspapers and rarely make the television news bulletin unless graphic footage is available or it is a slow news day. Occasionally, however, a big siege occurs and the media scramble for the story, often drawing criticism for their coverage.

One such siege occurred in the dying days of March 1993 when three men kidnapped four children near Dalby in south-eastern Queensland on Sunday 28 March, sparking a highly publicised police hunt. Two of the children were released unharmed the same day but two others, an 11-year-old boy and his 9-year-old sister, were driven south into New South Wales. On Monday, three other men who encountered the party near Armidale were killed when, according to police evidence,[10] the fugitives stole a car to swap for their own. Early on the Tuesday morning, the three holed up, with the children, in a house on the Hanging Rock station near Cangai, 80 kilometres north-east of Grafton.

By the middle of the day, two of the fugitives had given several media interviews by telephone, the first to the Sydney afternoon paper, *The Daily Telegraph Mirror*, which did not publish the scoop after being told by police that publication might endanger the lives of the two youngsters.[11] Several radio and television reporters also got through to the isolated farmhouse but it was Michael Willesee's interview for *A Current Affair* that generated the most criticism. Willesee extracted detailed confessions to murder from two of the men and interviewed both children. Soon afterwards, the children were released, and an hour later one of the men surrendered. Another surrendered shortly after 6 a.m. on the Wednesday. When emergency response police burst into the house at 11.30 a.m., they found the third man, Leonard Leabetter, dead beside a shotgun with a piece of string tied to the trigger.[12]

The day the siege ended, the police commissioners of all Australian states issued a media release, asking the media to examine their coverage of the incident and to recognise the needs for self-restraint and responsibility during such events. The commissioners listed seven specific grounds for concern. They were:

- the glorification of the offenders' actions by giving them such an extensive platform;
- the danger of inspiring 'copy cats';
- the probability of prejudicing police negotiations by extensive interviews with the offenders;
- interviewing the child victims involved;

- repeatedly divulging the location, number and equipment of police trying to resolve the incident;
- unnecessary trauma to victims' relatives;
- prejudice to subsequent court cases.[13]

The commissioners called on the media to consider adopting guidelines for reporting sieges, which had been canvassed several years earlier by the Standing Advisory Committee for Commonwealth/State Co-operation for Protection Against Violence (SAC-PAV). The guidelines suggested that media representatives should

- not take any independent or unauthorised action which could further endanger the lives of hostages;
- ensure they did not become part of the story and so add to the complexity of the situation and endanger their lives and those of hostages;
- avoid giving terrorists or hostage-takers an unedited propaganda platform by broadcasting live television or radio interviews;
- not make direct contact with hostage-takers or terrorists as the action might prejudice the work of trained negotiators; and
- ensure reports of demands should be free of rhetoric and propaganda by, ideally, paraphrasing such demands.[14]

It was not only the police commissioners who were disquieted by the media coverage at Cangai. Child psychologists, media analysts and politicians questioned several aspects of the media's behaviour, especially Willesee's interview with the children.[15] Journalists discussed the implications among themselves and Melbourne's *Herald Sun* wrote an editorial critical of Willesee's conduct.[16] The Australian Broadcasting Authority received 50 complaints;[17] but, paradoxically, the Willesee interview took *A Current Affair* to a ratings peak of 30, which made it the equal top-ranking program for the week.[18] Queensland senator Margaret Reynolds pointed out that the most contentious area, interviewing the children, lay outside existing broadcast codes of practice because 'the codes . . . would not have contemplated the use of children in those circumstances',[19] while Jock Rankin, head of news for the ABC in Victoria, noted that the journalists' code of ethics did not address itself to the problems of sieges.[20]

The Cangai incident raised most of the important areas of contention about the ethical reporting of sieges and highlighted some of the general difficulties of crime reporting where law enforcers and reporters operate in uneasy symbiosis.

Glorification of Offenders and Copy Cats

Since Ned Kelly shot it out with police at the Glenrowan pub more than 100 years ago and became an Australian folk hero in the process, people have worried about publicity's tendency to glorify criminals. The glorification theory is difficult to pin down. No journalist will admit to extolling the virtues of crime deliberately. Yet, to many observers, the extensive coverage given to crimes, especially to dramatic acts of violence and defiance, suggests that, even if crime is not a virtue, it pays in terms of increased circulation and ratings and panders to public curiosity.

It may be that devoting pages of newsprint or slabs of air time to the details of offenders' lives aggrandises the criminal in some minds, although some observers argue that the role of the media in reaffirming public morality by awakening the community's revulsion about some crimes actually works against glorification. There remains considerable doubt on the matter. The news editor of *The Age* in Melbourne was reportedly concerned about the profile of the Cangai gunmen created by the media interviews although, after deliberation, the paper carried the transcript of interviews with the two fugitives on the grounds that the information was newsworthy, but it did not run the children's interviews.[21] Whichever theory one espouses about glorification, it is undeniable that extensive media coverage does give criminals their '15 minutes of fame', if not glory.

Social scientists have voiced concern about the effects that the ego-massage of media attention may have on social misfits who dream of being the centre of attention and may be tempted to draw that attention to themselves. Grabosky and Wilson say social science research indicates 'there could be a link between the degree of media publicity attached to a homicide, suicide, or terrorist incident, and the incidence of subsequent conduct of a similar nature'.[22] The news media do acknowledge the copycat effect, in some crime categories. Many news organisations have policies not to report individual cases of suicide, except where the person is a public figure, or to detail suicide methods.[23] Most will not report bomb hoaxes, although some news managements believe the disruption caused by such hoaxes should be explained to the public.[24] The moral reasoning that sees the details of some destructive acts voluntarily withheld but allows revelations of the minutiae of rape and other violent incidents is unclear at best.

The day the Cangai siege ended, a 14-year-old boy was charged on a number of counts — including unlawful wounding and threatening a person with a firearm — relating to a siege that day at an Adelaide high school. A forensic psychologist, Tim Watson-Munro, told a *Herald Sun* reporter: 'You can't be sure without knowing all the facts of each case, but when a person who is feeling very unhappy about life picks up on the attention the others are getting through illegal behavior they inappropriately model themselves on it'.[25] But Watson-Munro said the media could not be accused of causing copycat crimes. He asserted that it was in the public interest for the community to be well informed and the benefits clearly outweighed the potential hazards.[26]

It is unlikely that anyone would argue that the news media should not have reported the Cangai siege simply because of the copycat effect. Nor could they have not reported the Hoddle Street and Queen Street mass shootings in Melbourne or the 'Father's Day' bikie gang killings, the Strathfield slayings and the 'Granny Killer' murders in Sydney during the bloody 1980s. These horrific events could not go unrecorded. For a journalist reporting big crime incidents, the potential for copycat events, even with their attendant risk of death and pain to others, is overwhelmed by the principle that the public cannot be shielded from knowledge of such disaster. Anyone who argued for total suppression would simply have a value system inappropriate to journalism.

It is the scope and type of reportage that produces more complicated ethical dilemmas, not the fact of reporting crime itself. Some of the details, such as close-ups of blood and bodies, relate to matters of taste which are discussed elsewhere. The effect of graphic detail of sexual assaults — whether in crime or court reports — on creating a climate in which violent acts against women are seen as normal behaviour was examined in the last chapter. But other issues such as allowing a platform for criminal posturing — during or after siege events — can shed light on the values of reporters and the principles they espouse. Should a self-confessed psychopath be given air time to talk about enjoying killing or detail the armoury with which he intends to 'take as many pounds of the flesh of police as [he] can'[27] because the exposure may legitimise such views?

One news organisation may decide that the public interest is not served by detailing the workings of a deranged mind; another may argue that full disclosure of all relevant matters — including an offender's state of mind — is the principle to be upheld. One journalist may place more personal value on not pandering to voyeurism; another may defend the value of allowing people to understand how others think, even if those others are criminals. One reporter may believe her prime loyalty is to her employer and her duty is to file the most newsworthy story; her competitor may feel that his prime loyalty is to an audience that will be distressed by undue emphasis on disturbing detail and his duty to society as a whole is not to promote the egos of criminals.

The glorification argument and the related problem of copy cats remain among the most problematic ethical questions for journalists covering crime. Equally ambiguous is another issue raised by the Cangai siege.

Prejudicing a Fair Trial

The concept of a fair trial for those accused is a basic principle of the Australian legal system. Most Australians would place personal value on a system that holds a person is innocent until proved guilty even if that value's relative importance is rarely tested by a brush with the law. Given that social consensus, the contempt laws forbid behaviour, including publicity, that might prejudice a fair trial. The main aim of the law is to protect the jury system by shielding potential jurors from information that might affect their attitudes to the accused when the time comes to judge the evidence brought to court.

Contempt law in Australia imposes considerable constraints on journalists and creates confusion for many law enforcers. And its effect on crime news is surely incomprehensible to ordinary citizens. One day they are exposed to a welter of detail, speculation and assertion about a crime and the person police believe may be responsible; the next day the story has virtually vanished except for a cryptic paragraph or two saying that an unnamed person has been charged with an offence. Sometimes the story is even dropped between editions.[28] The case of the disappearing story is explained if one realises that, once a person is arrested for questioning or charging, contempt laws come into force. The legally allowable information that can be published is basic. Police can divulge only the age, sex and general address of the person, the charges, court details, remand date or bail conditions and the name of the arresting officer.[29]

The arguments the Australian media put forward in favour of easing the restrictions of the contempt laws and the practical constraints that the law imposes on reporting fall outside the scope of this book, which deals with media ethics not media law.[30] But because critics cited prejudice to a fair trial as one feature of the Cangai coverage, some aspects should be mentioned here.

Under contempt rules, confessions whether given to police officers or other parties cannot be published, except as evidence in open court. The principle here is that people should have the right not to incriminate themselves. Further, confessions are not an infallible guide to the truth. The interviews with the children and accounts of other witnesses — which may later have been brought forward in evidence — were widely published during the Cangai siege. Because the men had not been charged at the time, the media were not acting unlawfully. The question remains whether they were acting unethically.

By publishing the confessions were the news media putting their desire for a graphic story before the value of accuracy? By broadcasting available material that assumed the guilt of the three men did the media deny the two survivors the right to a trial at which the jury could weigh up all the facts? In a case like this, is full disclosure of available facts in the public interest more important that the public interest inherent in the value of a system in which a person is regarded as innocent until proved guilty?

A siege, conducted in the glare of publicity, may seem to be a cut-and-dried case in which guilt can be reasonably assumed. But examination of the same underlying principles and values is as necessary during a siege as in other criminal events when the available facts paint a less clear picture. However, the intense competitive pressure of reporting a siege — when news editors are insisting on the best possible story — places the journalist in a difficult position. There is little time to consider the long-term implications and no time to seek legal counsel. Yet many people, who believe that the fair trial principle overrides the journalists' professional principle of disclosure or their duties to their news organisation, would argue that lack of time is an explanation for unethical behaviour, not a justification.

Intervention in Police Operations

Many who censured the media's behaviour at the Cangai siege did so on the grounds that the journalists impeded the police's ability to end the siege peacefully and quickly. The critics had three specific grievances: journalists tied up the only phone line into the farmhouse, thus impeding the official negotiators' contact with the offenders; the media took it upon themselves to act as *de facto* negotiators; and a television helicopter flew into restricted airspace which may have caused the fugitives to take fright and respond violently.[31] The belief underlying the three explicit accusations was that the media acted unethically in putting their quest for the best story before the palpable threat to the hostages' lives.

The relationship between the media and police is very fragile. Reporters, particularly those who do not specialise as crime reporters, are profoundly dependent on police for information. Without information from the police, journalists simply cannot do their job. To get stories, reporters often cooperate with police in angling stories or withholding information if police request it.[32] On the face of it, such behaviour does not match up to the professional principle of disclosure. Yet few reporters feel ethically compromised by their actions. As one reporter told Grabosky and Wilson, 'We're all on the side of law and order'.[33]

Immediately after the kidnapping that ended in the Cangai siege, authorities enlisted media help to publicise the description of the fugitives and their car. Later one of the fugitives was to tell Willesee: 'We needed a car and you media fellows kept on giving the rego plate number out . . . it was all over the radio that we were heading south in our car, which we were, so we needed a car'.[34]

Once the siege began, however, the situation changed and police priorities shifted to ensuring isolation, containment and negotiation, which meant isolating the fugitives from the outside world, containing the information available to them and negotiating the release of the hostages. Part of their activities was aimed at managing the news; but modern technology makes that hard. The siege location would seem to suggest that isolating the incident would be much easier than in a city; however, the ubiquitous presence of the radio in a country in which there are nearly two radio sets for every person[35] makes isolation from incoming information extremely difficult. Television signals, too, can penetrate a police cordon.

Police and psychologists almost universally condemned the journalists' telephone contact with the offenders. There was criticism that the media tied up the single phone line with their constant calls and did not allow the police through. There was one report that Leabetter asked a persistent ABC reporter to get off the line so he could speak to police about arrangements for releasing the children.[36] One forensic psychologist, however, moderated his criticism. He said the interviews may have alleviated tensions within the farmhouse by giving the offenders the chance to ventilate their feelings. But media coverage of high-profile crimes was a two-edged sword, he maintained.

> Insensitive, 'scoop-orientated' handling of a delicate crime could aggravate the problems . . .
> One of the dangers of the media becoming too involved during delicate negotiations is that the wrong questions may be asked at the wrong time.
> With the offenders probably hyped up on adrenalin and potentially trigger-happy, . . . lives could be lost.[37]

Common sense would suggest that the law enforcement team at sieges — with its trained negotiators, its psychologists and its access to the offender's history and possible mental state — is better equipped to conduct calm negotiations than a reporter with a deadline looming. Certainly none of the reporters who phoned the farmhouse at Cangai had specific negotiation skills, although all could claim formidable professional interview skills. Several months after the siege, Willesee discounted the objections to him acting as negotiator: 'The police called me back and said "Look, you're getting more out of these guys than our negotiators are. Could you call them back and see if you can get an admission on the [other] murder".'[38]

The news media's use of another piece of modern technology, in the eyes of some critics, compounded their improper conduct. A Channel Nine helicopter twice crossed into the zone cordoned off by police. The journalist on board, Mike Munro, was later reported as saying he was unaware of entering restricted airspace although 'the media had a responsibility to get as close to the scene as possible'.[39] Police, however, argue that low-flying helicopters can disturb evidence at a crime scene through the turbulence caused by their rotors, and during sieges can trigger potentially dangerous action by offenders.[40] Television journalists point to the problem that news crews face when covering events in isolated places of how to get heavy equipment close to the scene; they cannot do their job without the chopper.[41]

Possible media interference in police operations is not always made as visible to the audience as it was at Cangai. Police files are full of instances where media action may have affected the resolution of a case. In all of them, the public right to know is a central issue.

One case is the 1984 Geelong water extortion case in which an extortionist threatened to poison the city's water supply with polychlorinated biphenyls, or PCBs, unless $150 000 was paid into a Geelong bank account. If the police were called in, the lives of the mayor and his family were at risk. The *Geelong Advertiser* was tipped off anonymously but sat on the story when the police asked. On the third day of the crisis, all media agreed to a voluntary national ban on reporting the threat.[42] Although many journalists agreed with the *Geelong Advertiser* editor, Graeme Vincent, that 'everything about [the ban] really went against the grain',[43] the shaky agreement held. A radio journalist, Bill D'Arcy, vehemently disapproved of the ban and left his fill-in job with 3AW when management told him he would be cut off, through the seven-second delay mechanism, if he did as he had threatened: to blow the whistle on the sixth day.[44]

On Friday 14 September — exactly a week after the threat was issued — the ban was lifted. Nobody had been arrested; testing of the water supply had still to be completed. Immediately after the ban was lifted, police received more than 100 calls from the public, some of which contained 'valuable' information.[45] On the Sunday, a 20-year-old man was arrested.

The justification for the ban was principally the immediate threat to the mayor and his family if the offender knew — through publication — that police were involved. Public panic was another consideration. The Geelong case raises several questions. Did the citizens of Geelong have a right to know that their water supply was at risk and take whatever action they felt necessary to protect themselves? Did the possibility of public panic outweigh their right to information of grave importance to them? Who, and what, determined that the threat to the mayor and his family, serious though it was, was greater than the threat to the 180 000 residents of Victoria's second largest city?

A former editor of *The Sydney Morning Herald*, David Bowman, was the only person to join Bill D'Arcy in publicly questioning the news media's actions. He recalled a similar incident in which Sydney editors — himself included — had applied a voluntary ban to publishing the information that the seats in Sydney's suburban trains were highly flammable until the seats could be replaced. Derryn Hinch, then editor of *The Sun* in Sydney, objected because the public had a right to know the danger but he lost the argument.[46] In retrospect, Bowman doubted whether his acquiescence about the seat ban was correct, just as he worried that the Victorian news media had accepted too readily the police reasons for the Geelong blackout. By that ready acceptance, the news media may have, Bowman speculated, put police operational considerations ahead of the basic professional principle of the public's right to know.

It was perhaps Derryn Hinch's experience with the train seats that led him to break the embargo on information about an extortion threat against Ansett airlines in mid-1989. On 15 June, Ansett executives received three letters threatening a media campaign to scare away customers unless a ransom of $1.5 million was paid. Police in New South Wales and Victoria mounted an operation to catch the extortionist but the Sydney media got wind of the story two days before contact was to be made with the extortionist. They agreed to hold the story to allow the contact attempt to be made. The following day, Victorian news media attended a briefing at which they, too, were asked to hold the story because premature publicity could mean that the extortionist may not be caught and Ansett's business would be disrupted. It was, police said, a purely commercial extortion threat, aimed at affecting Ansett's revenue. They assured the news media there was no threat to the safety of airline staff or passengers.[47] That night, Hinch went on air to tell his audience the public had 'a right to know about the threat, especially if you are about to fly Ansett'. Hinch denied he had broken any undertaking with senior Victoria Police, although his Melbourne producer had attended the Victorian briefing; his story had been gathered from 'independent sources' in Sydney.[48]

Both the Geelong water and the Ansett extortion cases raise interesting ethical issues about coverage of police operations. Can journalists make valid ethical choices when their only source of information about the real risk to public safety are the police? If reporters attempt to verify the information independently, as they are required to do by their obligation to be accurate and to make judgements based on all available facts, may they not jeopardise police operations and/or public safety? How binding are promises of confidentiality made to the authorities when challenged by the public right to know, particularly when public safety is at issue? Is it ethical for journalists to waive the right to know in deference to the police's duty to catch offenders?

Conflicts between the police duty to enforce the law and the journalists' duty to report are inevitable. Yet both claim their duty is in the public interest. It may well be that in dealing with some types of crime, the two groups can agree to disagree about the primacy of their public interest claims. In cases where individual lives are at stake or public safety is jeopardised, however, one public interest claim could be stronger than the other. Media analyst Trevor Barr summed up the non-journalist's view when commenting on the Cangai siege.

> Instead of talking about public interest, surely the higher public interest is the potential danger to human life.
>
> Of course we want a free society where a lot gets reported, where there is a great deal of scrutiny of people . . . But if you have a circumstance where there is a possibility that even more people are going to be killed, then I think there is a higher public ideal of a protection of life.[49]

It must be pointed out that a journalist who agrees to place the potential for loss of life before other specifically professional principles does not have to jettison entirely the notion of reporting in the public interest. He or she may simply postpone the exercise of the journalistic duty to inform the public. The details can be published after the threat to life has receded. However, the decision is still not simple because the journalist must also assess meticulously the evidence that the potential risk to life is indeed genuine.

Live to Air Reporting

When the American CNN correspondent Peter Arnett breathlessly faced the television lens in his room at the al-Rashid Hotel in Baghdad on 17 January 1991 and told the world about the opening shots of Operation Desert Storm, his image ushered in the era of the real-time television war. Although vision was lost a few minutes later when a laser bomb hit Baghdad's main telephone exchange and satellite dishes,[50] the CNN reports and those from the American Broadcasting Corporation's Gary Shepard were an awesome display of communications technology which, because of its global significance to the conduct of war, focused public attention on just what the news media were capable of doing. But journalists had been using live crosses to different battle scenes for a number of years. The first Australian television live-cross to an unplanned news event, rather than the planned outside broadcast of managed events, came with the introduction of electronic news gathering technology in the late 1970s.[51] Live reporting of the war against crime raises new ethical dilemmas, some of which have been canvassed in the preceding section because they include the effect of reporting on successful police negotiation to resolve the incident without loss of life. But several aspects need closer examination.

Some of the most telling examples of the difficulties of live-to-air crime reporting come from the United States. On 27 September 1990, a gunman invaded a college bar in Berkeley, California, and held 33 people for nearly seven hours. When the siege ended, the gunman was dead — shot by a police SWAT squad — one student had been killed and nine other people were seriously injured. Local television and radio stations aired live cut-ins throughout the evening and extended their coverage in the early morning hours. Inside the bar, the television set was tuned to KPIX-TV.[52] Later 25 of the hostages signed a letter, written as part of a post-trauma counselling session, and sent it to the station's general manager. The hostages accused the station's coverage of endangering their lives.

> Watching your channel with the gunman from inside the bar, we sat and stood in disbelief, watching the broadcast of negative and derogatory remarks. Not only was the terrorist aroused by these comments, but frustrated and angered, believing that his demands, because he was publicly acknowledged as deranged, were not being taken seriously. Your station put the lives of 33 individuals in serious jeopardy. Fresh threats of violence and death ensued . . .
>
> Knowing that a SWAT team was on the way, [the gunman] became apparently more eager to demonstrate his seriousness, calling for volunteers to die.[53]

While recognising the victims' anger, KPIX challenged the accuracy of their claims. The station had not called the gunman deranged but had repeated police statements that his demands were 'irrational and strange';[54] it had referred to the SWAT team presence hours after the siege began. The station's news director said 'as crazy as he was . . . I don't think we told him anything he didn't already know'.[55] Irrespective of the intepretation of the literal details, the incident highlights the problems in going live to air.

Live television coverage was not a big issue during the Cangai siege, although some radio stations did broadcast interviews live. Willesee's controversial conversations with both the offenders and the children went to air several hours after the children were released. What was at issue was the delicate balance of negotiation, which may have been disturbed by the phone interviews (and to which we have already referred), and the distinct possibility that the offenders were hearing or seeing news reports that either enraged them further by provocative speculation and derogatory descriptions or revealed details of police activity. For instance, the police appeal to the editor of the *The Daily Telegraph Mirror* not to run the paper's scoop interview was based not on any fear that the gunmen would see the paper itself but that the electronic news organisations would pick up the story and broadcast it.

In any hostage situation, the negotiator tries to get the offenders' confidence and talk them out; if that proves impossible, the police try to manoeuvre the hostage-taker into a position where they can move in. It is this latter process that involves tactical positioning of special operations officers. If live radio or television reports reveal police positions or police strength, the vital element of surprise is removed. Not only may hostages' lives be endangered but so may those of officers and observers. An inspector in the Victoria Police Special Operations Group told a group of media and police personnel of his experience during a domestic siege in an outer Melbourne suburb.[56] The inspector was crouched down behind cover in the garden. He raised his head to find a shotgun at his throat. The offender, having monitored the live television coverage of the police activity, had pinpointed the inspector's whereabouts.

After the Berkeley incident, one television news director said that next time he would assume the hostage-taker was watching the coverage. He issued a memo the day after the siege forbidding his reporters to 'cover live, or insert live by tape, anything which shows the tactical movements of the police department in an ongoing situation'.[57] After Cangai, all state police commissioners called on the media to adopt the self-regulatory practice incorporated into the Radio Television News Directors' Association of Canada's code of ethics in 1986. The clause reads, in part:

> Reporting of criminal activities, such as hostage-takings, will be done in a fashion that does not knowingly endanger lives, hamper attempts by authorities to conclude the event, offer comfort and support or provide vital information to the perpetrator(s) . . .[58]

In March 1994, television and radio broadcasters agreed to restrict their siege coverage in return for greater police cooperation.

These days it is almost impossible for police to control the information flow fully, however much reporters accuse them of manipulating information. Radios, telephones and television sets are everywhere, and are becoming less dependent on wiring and power supplies, which can be relatively easily cut by authorities. Also the reporters themselves may not be on the scene — as some were not at Cangai — and therefore less knowledgeable about the situation on the ground than either their field colleagues or the authorities. If, in making an ethical decision in a given event, it is important for journalists to take account of all available facts, those not at the scene are surely obliged to be cautious.

Information that may assist an offender is not always as direct as filming police in position or broadcasting aerial shots of the scene, showing the focus of police activity; common sense should tell a journalist that such visuals could be of use to the offender.

It can be as indirect as broadcasting live on radio a telephone interview with a shopkeeper in the vicinity of an incident. When asked what is going on, the interviewee might inadvertently describe the type of vehicles and estimate the number of officers on the scene. Even a reporter aware of the dangers of revealing tactical details has no control over information broadcast live in such a situation.

Live coverage is fraught with other dangers for journalists. The rush to be first with the latest may seriously compromise the accuracy of a report. When a crime is in progress, nobody — including the police — knows exactly what is going on. Journalists have a professional duty to verify information, a demand not easily met when chaos reigns. The incidence of inaccurate reporting in the heat of the moment was well demonstrated during the coverage of the Queen Street killings in Melbourne in 1987, when a man ran amok in a city building shooting dead eight people and injuring another five. Broadcaster Neil Mitchell was conducting the drive-time show for 3AW, whose studios were just a few blocks from the scene of the carnage. Mitchell devoted his program to a running report of events. Initial reports suggested an armed hold-up in the Telecom Credit Union office in the Telecom building had gone 'horribly wrong'. In fact, there never was a hold-up and it was the Australia Post building. Mitchell broadcast the erroneous information with increasing confidence during most of the two hours of his program, converting suggestion into fact. Despite having reporters with mobile phones on the scene and a newsroom team checking all the obvious sources of information, the station did not correct the basic errors of fact until its six o'clock bulletin, two hours after the shooting started.[59] It may appear to be a small detail but it had the capacity to make people panic needlessly and illustrates how difficult it is to achieve accuracy in adrenalin-charged situations.

Reporters often monitor police radios on scanners to get information about what is happening. But such information, particularly during the initial stages of a crime incident or a disaster, is not reliable because it is often based on garbled first versions of events. The use of live eyewitness accounts is also problematic. Experienced journalists know that eyewitnesses, because of a desire to please the reporter, the excitement of the moment or plain ignorance, may provide inaccurate — but graphic — information in good faith. The principle of truth dictates such accounts should be verified or placed in context by other information, a process not easily carried out on the run.

When a siege or similar criminal event is happening, the duties and values of the police are clear. Their duty is to minimise harm to victims, emergency personnel, the general public and the offenders, to end the incident as quickly as possible and to catch the perpetrators. The values that drive them are the importance of human life and the law. The duties and values of the news media can be more muddled. As ordinary people, journalists may put human life above all else. As citizens, they may value the rule of law and believe criminals should not be assisted to evade capture. As journalists, they are torn by the principles of truthful reporting and the public's right to know and by their obligations to their employers to produce the most competitive and compelling work with its attendant impact on ratings.

There is no question that refusing to broadcast live from a dramatic crime scene — or to confine live coverage to uncontentious material — would be failing to uphold one's employee duty. But the public's right to know would still be maintained, if somewhat delayed. The problem is, as most journalists and news media managers concede, that delaying or modifying coverage can only work if everyone does it; otherwise the prudent news organisation loses its audience to its competitors.

The Australian media have not drawn as much criticism about live coverage as their American colleagues, perhaps because there have been fewer big crime-in-progress stories. But in the absence of definite evidence that the news industry overall modify its practice on live coverage, many critics remain concerned about the potential dangers of irresponsible instant coverage.

Psychological Effects on Children

One measure of a society's moral worth is the way it treats its children. The principle that children should be protected from harm imposed by adults motivated those who campaigned against sending small boys up chimneys in 19th century Britain and drives those who fight today against the economic and sexual exploitation of the children in many countries, including Australia. Most people agree that child protection demonstrates the ethical values of fairness and trust. Children are smaller, weaker and less knowledgeable than adults. Until they grow in stature, strength and understanding equal to that of adults, it is unfair to take advantage of their relative powerlessness. And exercising unequal power destroys the trust children have in adults to care for them.

The community duty towards children is reflected in countless pieces of Australian legislation and in several sections of the self-regulatory television program codes which, although they allow violent material in news bulletins, caution against unnecessary violence when children may be watching and forbid violent content in news flashes broadcast during the officially designated children's viewing times.

Despite the mention of children in the television codes, the Cangai siege showed, as Senator Margaret Reynolds observed, that small people could fall between the self-regulatory cracks. Although a Sydney psychiatrist voiced concern that the coverage in general would have disturbed many primary school children who saw it,[60] it was Willesee's interview with the two child hostages — in which he asked if the children had seen anyone killed and if they had seen 'bad things'[61] — that aroused the most passionate condemnation. The interviews were 'totally irresponsible and unnecessary'[62] and had put the children's lives at risk. Willesee's questioning, according to a *Herald Sun* editorial, 'suggested, however unintentionally, less concern with the children's welfare than with getting answers that made good television'.[63] A few months later, the Herald and Weekly Times Limited became the first major media outlet in Australia to set specific rules aimed at avoiding exploitation of children while gathering news. At the time, most criticism was based implicitly on the concept that children should not be exploited in a commercial setting. Willesee defended his actions on air the evening after the interviews were broadcast, saying his only concern had been to discover whether the children were unharmed.[64] The children's father, who reportedly learned from a radio bulletin that Willesee had interviewed the children and they were alive, said: 'I reckon Willesee did right'.[65]

The children appeared on *A Current Affair* six days after the siege, talking to Willesee in the Channel Nine Sydney studio and on the beach. He did not ask them about their experiences. The program reportedly paid $1000 for the story, flew the children and six family members to Sydney and picked up the hotel tab for the weekend.[66] *New Idea*, which paid $2000 to take the children's photographs, did not question them either but asked them to draw pictures based on what had happened.[67] Finding out whether the children were alive was a matter of public interest. It is highly debatable whether the interviews themselves — in which the children simply answered 'no' to a series of leading questions — were of overriding public interest.

Reporter John O'Neill visited the family for *The Independent Monthly* a month after the Cangai seige to discover the effects of the media coverage on the children. He found them displaying aggressive, demanding and clinging behaviour.[68] Whether this was the result of the traumatic experience itself or its magnification by the subsequent media attention, we will never know. But what is clear is that the news media have an ambivalent attitude towards the treatment of children. Australian journalists have done excellent work — exposing, for instance, child pornography rackets, child abuse and the inadequacies of child protection services and the juvenile justice system — on behalf of children and in the general public interest. When individual children get caught up in crime as victims, however, it seems they are just another part of the story. There are numerous cases of children being subjected to journalists' questioning to extract stories about a parent's alleged misdoings.[69] Such behaviour can rarely be justified on public interest grounds; most of the time, it appears that the children are being used to produce attention-grabbing copy at the expense of their well-being.

Rigorous ethical decision making requires the journalist, at the very least, to add another factor for consideration in the complex process: the principle that children have a special right to care and protection.

Recorders or Actors?

One of the fiercest debates about the process of news gathering is whether journalists are primarily objective observers who record what has happened or whether objectivity is an outmoded, false and impossible ideal. The implications for the debate on the practice of ethical journalism are examined in the chapter on fairness and bias. In this section, however, we will look at those occasions where journalists are openly, deliberately and inevitably cast as leading actors in a news event. The political siege, the terrorist act and, to a lesser extent, the public demonstration are just such occasions. The participation of the media is essential to these activities because publicity is the end goal.

In the Cangai siege, the journalists who interviewed the gunmen took it upon themselves to enter the action, even if unaware that their behaviour could have a very real impact on the outcome. By becoming participants, they forfeited a defence that they were simply telling it as it was. But other cases demonstrate more directly the tug of principles and values that occurs when journalists are forced centre stage.

Media exposure was the motivation that led to a 45-hour siege of the Bendigo Prison in central Victoria in August 1987. John Dixon-Jenkins, who styled himself the Anti-Nuclear Warrior, was sentenced in the Melbourne County Court in late 1984 to a six-year jail term on 29 counts. The charges arose out of a series of threatening letters to community leaders and bomb hoaxes in schools and shops earlier that year. The hoaxes had sparked a three-state police search and headlines such as 'Mad "Bomber" Hunt', 'Mad bomber plotted against US President' and the more moderate 'Big hunt for bomb hoaxer'.[70] At his trial Dixon-Jenkins, after dismissing his defence counsel, had told the jury he planned the campaign because it seemed the only way to attract media attention to the nuclear threat.[71]

Three years later — just before midday on 20 August — Dixon-Jenkins took six Education Department officers and three fellow prisoners hostage in the Bendigo medium security prison educational unit. He claimed he was armed with a homemade firearm and had an incendiary device strapped to his body.[72]

Dixon-Jenkins was intent on publicity — of the right kind. His list of demands, which he had left in his cell for police to find, began with instructions about news coverage. His 'statement to the people' and his demands were to be printed on the front pages of all metropolitan daily papers and presented on all major television stations; police were to provide copies of the papers, a television set, videorecorder and tapes to the jail so coverage could be monitored. He wanted an open and unrestricted press conference and a federal government assurance that his ideas on a unified theory of existence would be fully and publicly evaluated. And he sought to defuse sub-editors' colourful and pithy language: 'The term "mad bomber" is no longer to be used in headlines regarding me or my actions. That misleading term should be replaced with the more appropriate name, "The Anti-Nuclear Warrior" '.[73] The demands were leaked to *The Age* by a prison reform group and the paper ran them, not on page one, but on page 17. Police had not released them.

The situation was tightly controlled. Special Operations Group police negotiators talked to Dixon-Jenkins by phone. The only other contact with the outside world was a radio in the education unit. By the second day, four hostages had been released. Dixon-Jenkins charged one of them, education unit principal Glen Carey, with the task of getting publicity; 'He made it quite clear the lives of my staff depended on me getting a radio news broadcast'.[74] Carey said police were reluctant to allow a broadcast but, after the assistant commissioner for operations agreed, Carey spoke to the local radio station 3BO. Little other information was available.

Outside the prison's main gates, the reporters milled about, eating refreshments provided by the Salvation Army. One of them, Michael Gawenda of *The Age*, summed up the media's frustration and bewilderment in a colour piece headlined 'Waiting for man with a mission'. There was not much else to write.

> In some ways, this hostage drama is fundamentally a media event. Inside the jail, John Dixon-Jenkins still holds five hostages, and we are told he wants our cooperation so he can publicise his ideas, which he believes are of great importance to mankind.
>
> In the circumstances we would, of course, be perfectly willing to oblige Dixon-Jenkins — if we could find out what these ideas are. But to do that we would have to talk to him and, for what are probably the best of reasons, the police have told him this is not possible.
>
> The police, it must be said, tell us very little, and we must assume that this, too, is based on sound and rational reasons. In other words, we do not know why they tell us next to nothing. So we stand there on the lawn, waiting and wondering what it is that Dixon-Jenkins has to offer the world.
>
> . . .
>
> But the questions are: what are we actually doing here? Are we reporting the news? Are we helping the police? Are we a group of key players in what is happening?
>
> Yesterday morning, for example, Dixon-Jenkins let a hostage go free because, after perusing the morning papers, he

declared himself satisfied with the coverage. Thank God for that. How, though, are we to know what will satisfy him today?

Later yesterday morning, he released another hostage, Mr Glen Carey . . .

Mr Carey seemed anxious to talk to us about what had been a horrendous experience, but he couldn't because the police had told him that to do so would be dangerous. Why? We were not told.

So we know nothing about conditions inside that room inside the jail where the people have been held for almost two days. Are there lavatories? We don't know. Is there food? We don't know.

And yet the media are leading players in what is going on in the Bendigo jail. It is apparently happening for our benefit, so that the man holding the hostages can get space in the newspapers, on television and on radio.

It is space granted under duress, really, and we can only pass on information that the police think is safe to pass on. Bendigo is calm, but for the scores of media people on the lawn, this is a real drama. What part we are playing, however, is not at all clear.[75]

The Bendigo siege ended peacefully at 9.15 on the Saturday morning. Dixon-Jenkins's firearm and incendiary device were, according to police, 'not operational'.[76] Police and prison staff were praised for the way they had handled the situation; a prominent anti-nuclear campaigner congratulated Dixon-Jenkins for a 'wonderful experience' for the movement.[77] But the news media were none the wiser about their role or the ethical implications.

Had the media found information about Dixon-Jenkins's views independently would it have been in the public interest to publish? Was it necessary for the police operation to withhold available and relevant details about conditions under which the hostages were held? What principle, if any, underpinned the police reluctance to allow the media to interview released host-ages? If the media had interviewed the hostages without police permission, would they have been behaving ethically? And, perhaps most important of all, what are the ethics of publishing information under duress? Is it in the long-term public interest for the law enforcement authorities and the media never to accede to terrorist demands? Or do specific circumstances call for a flexible interpretation of seemingly inflexible rules? For instance, did Dixon-Jenkins's avowed pacifist principles make the situation less dangerous than it outwardly appeared and so enable greater coverage than in fact occurred? Such questions were barely tested at Bendigo but remain crucial to the consideration of the journalist as an actor in a crime drama.

Another important question arises when journalists are forced to become actors: is it possible, and ethical, to take off one's journalistic hat and behave as a non-journalist? Two very different cases illustrate the point: one was another siege involving children, the other the storming of the Iranian embassy in Canberra.

At about 10 a.m. on 9 May 1989, an armed man burst into the Manresa kindergarten in the Melbourne suburb of Hawthorn. The kindergarten director, her assistant and a mother managed to usher 15 children out of the building but the man snatched four four-year-olds, doused them with petrol and locked himself and the children in a toilet cubicle. A seven-hour siege followed. Later the kindergarten director told the court: 'He said he didn't want to frighten anybody, but he wanted me to ring Channel Nine. He said, "They won't listen to me, but after this they will".'[78] The man had a grievance against doctors who he alleged had caused his wife's infertility after a caesarean operation 10 years earlier. His claims had been ignored and he and his wife had staged two vigil protests on the steps of Parliament House, one in 1985 and once in March of the siege year.[79] During the second vigil, Channel Nine reporter Sally Gluyas had interviewed the man.

Gluyas was on a day off when she heard radio reports about the siege. Parents of children at the kindergarten had also heard the reports before police had managed to contact them officially.[80] Gluyas had a feeling the hostage-taker was the man she had interviewed; her fears were confirmed when the Nine newsroom rang, telling her the man was demanding she be brought to the kindergarten. There was no question she would go there as a reporter because she knew she could not report objectively; she made her position clear to her chief-of-staff who agreed.[81] A Nine news crew was already at the scene.

When Gluyas arrived at the kindergarten she was ushered past the scene-of-crime tape, to the annoyance of a crew from another channel. In an open row with the police media director, the reporter complained that it was unfair that Channel Nine got 'all the breaks'.[82] The reporter was mollified when he found that Gluyas was not getting a scoop, but his tantrum shows just how strong the competitive urge to get good footage is. Gluyas knew nothing of the altercation; she was with the police, scared of getting shot — although the man's gun proved to be an imitation — and deeply affected by the sound of the children whimpering in the building. Some of her colleagues later told her, had they been her, they would have taken advantage of her special position. But that option did not cross her mind. She had been cast, unwittingly, in a different role. She acknowledges a distinct difference between the professional journalist and an ordinary person. Journalists must learn to distance themselves from the emotional impact: 'Without the distance, like police and doctors, we could not do our jobs'.[83] At the kindergarten, there was no distance — so she felt she could not report ethically.

Coincidentally a second journalist was involved in the Manresa siege as a private citizen. He was Alan Kohler, then a journalist on *The Australian Financial Review* and later editor of *The Age*. Kohler was the president of the kindergarten's parents' association and was called to the scene to help comfort the parents whose children were held hostage. For him, too, there was no difficulty in setting his professional persona aside. He acted that day as a concerned parent and does not believe that, even though the siege was not the sort of story his paper would have run, he would have wanted to file a story even had he been a general reporter.[84]

Later Kohler's professional understanding of the media was enlisted when he acted as spokesperson for the parents to shield them from the attentions of reporters eager to follow up the story by finding out more about the children's experiences. The four hostages suffered chemical burns and from fume inhalation; many of the children later exhibited many behavioural symptoms of trauma, such as nightmares, bedwetting and fear of separation.[85] In adopting the role of intermediary, Kohler did not believe he was behaving unethically towards his fellow professionals.

What is interesting about the attitudes of Gluyas and Kohler is that they easily assumed the different values of participants. This suggests that the frequent assertion — often used to justify seemingly callous or insensitive behaviour — that a journalist is on duty 24 hours a day and always holds fast to professional values above all other things is not universally applicable.

An SBS news crew drew public wrath after it responded to an anonymous tip about an impending demonstration at the Iranian embassy in Canberra on 6 April 1992. Within seven minutes of the crew arriving, the demonstration was over and the protestors had fled. Cameraman Mick O'Brien had captured graphic images of more than a dozen demonstrators smashing windows and furniture, painting slogans on the walls, lighting fires and attacking embassy staff.[86] One official was attacked with a screwdriver and a spanner; blood flowed. O'Brien, a few metres from the heat of the action, kept filming — and received an avalanche of blame and praise for doing so.

Two specific criticisms emerged. Should SBS have told police about the demonstration before the event and should O'Brien have ceased filming and tried to stop the attack on the embassy officials? The equally important question of the degree to which the very presence of news cameras alters events was raised only in passing. Opinion was divided about whether police should have been alerted. One metropolitan newspaper editor said media organisations had an obligation to inform police even at the risk of losing the story.[87] The SBS head of news and current affairs, Andrew Potter, disagreed. The crew had not notified police in advance but had handed over film afterwards, which assisted police in identifying the offenders.[88] Most journalists would maintain that telling the police was ethically permissible, but not obligatory. If they had stopped to think about it, the SBS crew members would probably have assumed that a police presence was already at the embassy, given that the first wire service reports of similar attacks on Iranian missions around the world reached Australia just before three o'clock that morning.[89]

The intervention aspect generated more heat. Talkback radio programs testified to public upset that O'Brien did not stop filming. One distressed woman, in a letter to *The Age*, wrote: 'Do they not become accessories to such crimes when they refuse to provide aid to the victims? What if the man had been killed? Would they have filmed that too?'.[90] Those who defended the newsmen's actions did so by appealing to the principle that they had a first responsibility to record the event. Alan Sunderland, the reporter involved, told *The Australian* he doubted whether he and O'Brien could have done much about the incident anyway but that they had acted 'on gut instinct' during six and a half minutes of 'rapid and chaotic action'.[91]

Everyone connected with the media who commented on the matter drew the distinction between media behaviour at the

Iranian embassy and at a more extreme hypothetical situation. If the threat to life had been worse, different action should have been taken: 'The television camera, the photographer's lens or the reporter's notebook should not in all cases come between his or her duty to come to the aid of a person in extreme circumstances'.[92] O'Brien himself said he would have stepped in had the situation been different. 'My experience as a cameraman allowed me to assess the situation, and I knew that that wasn't [life-threatening] . . . even though it was horrific and I didn't enjoy it one little bit'.[93]

O'Brien had something to say about a more intractable problem. 'I think, in all honesty, that that is the case [that camera presence alters events] but only [to] a marginal extent. When someone makes a protest, some of the things they do may be spurred on [by the camera]. On the other hand the camera is also a bit of a protection against too much happening.'[94] One of the crew's staunchest defenders was the ABC's Tim Bowden, biographer of the Australian foreign correspondent and cameraman, Neil Davis. Bowden said the SBS team had been filming combat. It had behaved impeccably in continuing to film. 'They scored what will probably prove to be the scoop of their lives, at grave risk to their safety. I look forward to hearing about their Walkley award for the best news film story of the year.'[95] Bowden accurately assessed the profession's judgement of the ethics of the SBS filming. The team got its Walkley.

Reporting crime and violence is an ethical labyrinth. It is in this area that journalists are most powerfully confronted with the conflicts of their profession. It is here they must weigh the value of life, of public safety, of a 'good' story. They must recognise the occasional clash between the principle of the public right to know and the principle of the rule of law. They must differentiate between the public interest and public curiosity. They must identify the strength of their loyalty to their employer, their audience, their sources and their fellow citizens. Above all, they must ensure that they have done their best to gather all the available facts about a situation before they decide to act. And, last, they must accept that very often they will be accused of making the wrong judgement.

CHAPTER 5

Private Lives and Public Life

The news media are never welcome at the scene of tragedy. The mere sight of journalists, photographers and television camera crews is sometimes enough to provoke hostility among people grieving over the loss of relatives and friends. From their point of view the media are intruders — 'vultures' or 'heartless ghouls'. Yet in perhaps eight cases out of ten the media have a right to be there. Tragedy is news, and it is the media's job to report it. The difficulty is to report it adequately without treading on the sensitivities of people in shock or grief.

Every day journalists have to make hard decisions about how far they should go in the pursuit of news. It is not always clear when a person's right to be left alone is transcended by public interest criteria. Does a public figure have a lesser claim to privacy than other people? If so, where does a public figure's public life end and private life begin? Are the media entitled to report and photograph anything that happens in a public place, or should some scenes go unrecorded because they may cause pain or embarrassment to the people directly involved, or offend against canons of decency or taste? When are close-ups of the dead, the dying, the injured and their distraught relatives justified? And how close is too close? Who should decide? There are no pat answers to these questions because the journalist must weigh in each case the principle of respect for the rights of the individual against that of the need of the community to be informed.

The steady flow of complaints to the Australian Press Council and the Australian Broadcasting Tribunal demonstrates growing public concern about media intrusion into privacy and grief.[1] The problem is not yet as acute as in Britain, where invasions of privacy by the mass circulation tabloid newspapers have led to threats of further government control of the press.[2] Nor are Australian media as obsessively interested as their American or British counterparts in unveiling the sexual peccadilloes of people in public life. Nevertheless, more than 120 complaints of invasion of privacy have been received by the Press Council since it was established as a watchdog of the media in 1976, and the statistics tell only half the tale. Many people are still unaware of the council's existence and others see little point in complaining because the council has no power to impose any penalty or to enforce its decisions. Even fewer know about the alternative grievance procedures operated by the Media, Entertainment and Arts Alliance (MEAA) because its judiciary committees hear complaints in private and their decisions are never published in the mainstream media, or in any journal likely to come to general public notice. There would probably be a lot more complaints but for public ignorance of the means of redress.

It may still be true, as the Australian Law Reform Commission said in 1979, that the number of privacy-invading publications is small and that most journalists are sensitive to privacy issues,[3] but there is evidence that lapses now occur more frequently. And as the Australian Law Reform Commission also noted, from the victim's point of view, it is the effect of invasion, not the frequency, that matters.[4] Bereaved people speak bitterly of the loss of dignity and sense of personal violation they feel when the media intrude upon their grief. Graham Glisson complained angrily to Peter Couchman of the ABC how he had been woken between 4 a.m. and 5 a.m. one morning by 'two Rambos, one with a tape recorder and one with a camera', who wanted to interview him about the death of his daughter, which had occurred at 4 p.m. the previous day. He was still in a state of shock and his brother sent them away. 'But an hour later they woke us out of our beds again to get a story.'[5]

Marija Bandish would also have preferred to be left alone on the day that her son was drowned in a lagoon in a national park near Sydney. Nevertheless, she agreed to be interviewed by a Channel Nine news team about dangers of the lagoon when they offered to airlift her and her husband to the scene in the network's helicopter. She believed, perhaps naively, that they would film only the stand-up interview. However, that night Channel Nine showed film of them wading into the lagoon to see how deep the water was near the spot where their son had drowned. Mrs Bandish felt that she had been manipulated, that Channel Nine had filmed them in the lagoon without their permission, and when they were obviously in distress. She recalled: 'I was totally shocked — at no time aware that I was being filmed while I was in the lagoon. I wasn't aware of my surroundings. That wasn't all. They let the *Mirror* use one of their clips and I had no knowledge of it until a friend showed me the newspaper. That was my first experience of the media and I thought, how can they use my pain for sensationalism like that.'[6]

'Death-knocks'

No journalist or photographer likes doing a 'death-knock', the somewhat macabre term for the task of interviewing and filming people still in shock and grief. It is probably the least popular assignment in journalism, next to covering funerals. In both situations emotions run high, nerves are on edge and the anger mourners feel as a natural response to death may turn to aggression against the presence of unwanted strangers. The media are an obvious target with their video cameras and microphones. Highly strung relatives or their friends may react instantly to any sign of insensitivity by gung-ho reporters. Tempers flare, abuse follows and sometimes punches are thrown.

The brawl between mourners and the media at the funeral of Robert Trimbole is a case in point. The bereaved family's belief in their right to privacy clashed with the media's belief in their right to be present because of the 'public right to know'. Trimbole was a notorious public figure. He had been named in three Royal Commissions and shortly before his death from cancer he had been hunted in Europe by federal police, who suspected him of being involved in drug trafficking. His family believed they had the same right as other mourners to the dignity of a private funeral, without media onlookers, no matter what Trimbole's reputation might have been. Journalists disagreed. Max Uechtritz, the ABC television reporter who went to the aid of a cameraman who was punched while filming the funeral, commented: 'This man had by his own actions in fleeing the country made himself a figure of mystery and intrigue. We were right to be there.'[7]

Journalists and media commentators tend to agree that intrusive reporting tactics are a predictable consequence of the intense competition in the news business and the fear of being scooped by the opposition the next day.[8] Even when most reporters at a disaster scene approach grieving relatives of the victims with sympathy and discretion their job can be made more difficult by the clumsiness of a few.

These were among the reasons for the breakdown in relations between the media and the local community when 12 men were entombed by a coal mine explosion in the small Queensland town of Moura, Queensland, in July 1986. One reporter at the scene said that a lot of journalists were paranoid about being beaten to the story by competitors partly because the police and mining company officials gave such scant information to the media in the immediate aftermath of the disaster.[9] Desperate for a story, some journalists did a middle of the night death-knock, calling at houses with the lights still on to get interviews with families waiting anxiously for word from rescuers.[10]

The Anglican chaplain at the Moura mine, Father Dennis Vanderwolf, blew the whistle on the media the following day when he announced that the pregnant widow of one of the trapped miners had been approached by a journalist at 1.30 a.m. and offered money for her story. From that point the townspeople turned on the media and press conferences with the authorities became tense and sometimes angry affairs. Police instructed journalists not to attempt to contact relatives of the entombed men and journalists were abused on the streets and warned they could expect no protection if the mourning turned to violence. Reporters covering a mass meeting of 300 miners two days after the explosion had 'the comforting assurance that if miners decided to kick a few heads they would do so with police blessing'.[11] Defending his colleagues, David Bentley of *The Sunday Sun* in Brisbane conceded that the media group contained 'its usual quota of hot-heads and show-offs' but said that most reporters carried out the distasteful but necessary business of interviewing relatives with sensitivity.[12]

Despite the general condemnation of the media by the mining company, the unions, the police, the Church and the townspeople, John Harrison, the communications coordinator for the Uniting Church, argued that the conflict was inevitable immediately the mine blew up because 'anger is an integral and normal part of the grief process'. The media came to grief, he says, because they were 'the scapegoat of a town's wrath'. They were not primarily responsible for that wrath. However, the journalists there were probably professionally ill-prepared to do a death-knock story in a town where everyone knew at least one of the men killed.

They and their city-based editors probably assumed they were dealing with 12 grieving families rather than 3000 grieving people. Moreover, the competitive nature of the media made it difficult for them as a group to take any substantive steps to restore the confidence of the townspeople in journalists once the conflict exploded. If there is any lesson to be learned from Moura's explosion of anger against journalists, it is that the profession needs to take more seriously the task of training journalists in dealing with death and grief.[13]

The Australian Broadcasting Corporation and the Herald and Weekly Times acknowledged the importance of such training in 1993 when they adopted detailed policies on intrusion into grief.

Some areas are regarded by the media generally as out of bounds. The law forbids identification of rape victims and most newspapers follow a policy of not disclosing the names of victims of other kinds of sexual assault; the few reported breaches of that standard have been condemned by the Press Council, which stated in its comments on one complaint:

A sexual assault is a gross invasion of privacy and dignity involving humiliation and embarrassment as well as physical suffering . . . In these circumstances the publication of any identifying particulars of the victims of a sexual assault can only be justified by some compelling reason of public interest or fairness. This will rarely occur.[14]

Arguments for Intrusion

The media argue that in some situations the identification of victims can serve socially useful purposes, and they are not alone in that. For example, pictures and background information can help police trace missing persons or lead to the apprehension of offenders, a point made by a senior reporter for the Melbourne *Herald Sun*, John Sylvester:

> Detectives who want to keep a story alive know that relatives can make good copy. They know that the longer a story is active the more chance of someone coming forward with information. More than once a seemingly hopeless investigation has turned for the better as a result of a public response to a newspaper story.[15]

In other situations the media justify intrusions into privacy and grief on the presumption of the public need to know. For example, it is often argued that news and pictures which convey the horror and pathos of major disasters help to mobilise emotional and financial support for the victims, and focus public attention on problems such as road, rail and air hazards, deficiencies in safety regulations or public health facilities, inadequate policing, or the need for stricter gun laws.

Another common rationalisation is that families of victims find it therapeutic to talk about their grief to the media. Grief counsellors, however, argue that following sudden news of the death of loved ones the bereaved are in no state to make rational judgements about whether they want to be interviewed, and may be manipulated by the media. Some journalists share the same qualms. A former police rounds reporter for *The Age* said she found the whole idea of intrusions distasteful and added: 'I think people are often taken advantage of when they're at their most vulnerable and probably just looking for a shoulder to cry on. The journalists ends up being the shoulder. I'm sure a lot of victims and their relatives end up regretting it later.'[16] Some other journalist agree, arguing that in the immediate aftermath of tragedy the most helpful reaction is usually silent sympathy.[17]

Criminologists Peter Grabosky and Paul Wilson found that some journalists they talked to were prepared to be 'super-assertive, and sometimes manipulative' in obtaining information from distraught relatives. Others talked of the tricks of the trade used to con photographs out of a bereaved family and one reporter accused his opposition of stealing photographs off mantelpieces.[18] Their research led them to the conclusion that 'for many journalists the pressure to deliver a story tends to eclipse ethical considerations'.[19]

Some of the most difficult ethical problems for the news media are caused by the use of dramatic photographs and television film showing horror and grief. It has been said that one graphic picture has a greater impact on the audience than a thousand words could do. The portrayal of human agony may well be good for newspaper sales or television ratings. Nevertheless, it is not always clear why the public needs to see close-ups of anguished relatives who have just lost their kin in an air crash or a bushfire.

Media executives usually say they weigh the news significance of the pictures against the pain and embarrassment that may be caused to individuals by showing them. Choices have to be made not only about what pictures should be used but about what prominence they should be given or, in the case of television, how long the cameras should be allowed to linger on a gruesome or harrowing scene. Sometimes the decisions are made for them by the authorities at the scene of the disaster. For example, when 83 people were killed and many others injured in the Granville rail disaster in Sydney in 1977 police kept television cameras away from the most seriously damaged carriages. As a result, film of the accident consisted mainly of long shots which conveyed the horror without identifying the victims, and the photographic close-ups were mainly of 'walking wounded' who consented to be interviewed.[20]

Usually, police interfere only when there is a possibility that the media will impede rescue operations, and the hard decisions about how far journalists and camera crews should go and what material should be used are left to news editors.

Most news organisations say that they try to avoid stories which merely capitalise on people's grief although they acknowledge that competitive pressures sometimes make it difficult for them to ban material which other channels are showing. At the same time they are against 'sanitising' the news to the point that it no longer bears any resemblance to actual events. Channel Seven's Melbourne news editor, John Gibson, keeps a film record of gruesome or gut-wrenching scenes that have been cut from the news because of fears that they might be offensive to the audience. 'Gibbo's ghoul tape', as it is known in the Seven newsroom, is the channel's response to viewers who might accuse them of insensitivity.

The station also has a policy of not showing bodies, except when it serves the purpose of illustrating the horror of an overseas disaster or war.[21] That policy was put to the test on 30 May 1992 when a freelance photographer offered Channel Seven a series of pictures of a man who had set himself alight after dousing himself with petrol in Geelong's Market Square. The incident had occurred in full view of shoppers and retailers, some of whom had tried to put out the flames. The pictures reached Channel Seven too close to the evening news deadline for them to get a clear story of what had happened. Without that information Gibson and other Seven executives decided that showing the pictures would be merely a gratuitous display of the man's agony. However, they made one of the pictures available to the *Herald Sun* at that newspaper's request.

The following day the *Herald Sun* used the picture across six columns with a story quoting rescuers who had used their clothes and pieces of blanket to smother the flames.[22] The newspaper story changed Channel Seven's view. They ran film of the incident that evening. 'What we did, in effect, was a follow-up', said Gibson, 'because we now had a story of people who had risked injury trying to help the man. It was a story of bravery so we had a reason for using it.'[23]

It is sometimes said that media intrusion begins where consent ends. However, sick and injured people are often not in a condition to indicate whether they give their consent, and many dramatic pictures have been taken without permission, including several which have won journalism's national Walkley Award. For instance, Ray Saunders won the 1958 prize for his picture of a would-be suicide clinging to Brisbane's Victoria Bridge and Stephen Cooper earned the 1986 award for his photograph of a police sergeant carrying the body of a 12-year-old girl who had been drowned in a Sydney flood.[24] In neither case could the victims give their consent yet Saunders and Cooper could argue that a strong public interest in both events overrode the individual right to privacy.

Another case in point was the picture taken of two men who received terrible burns when they were showered by molten metal following an explosion of a metal factory in Footscray, Melbourne, on 30 September 1986.[25] The picture was taken by an industrial photographer, Carmine Cozzolino, an eyewitness of the accident, who gave a copy to *The Age* in Melbourne. It showed one of the victims with his back to the camera but the other was completely naked, his clothes having been stripped off in the blast. One member of *The Age* staff argued that the picture should be used as it was, but a more senior executive suggested that the man's genitalia should be painted out as a matter of decency, and his view prevailed. The picture was altered, though the man could still be identified, and displayed across eight columns of *The Age's* front page. On the same day the picture was also published in *The Canberra Times*, then in the same newspaper group, John Fairfax, as *The Age*. *The Canberra Times* gave it less space than *The Age*, spreading it across three columns, but left in the genitalia.

Readers of *The Age* reacted in outrage at the photograph, protesting that the injured men deserved compassion, not the degradation of being shown naked in their pain. However, the decision to publish was defended by Professor J. Masterton, Associate Professor of Surgery at Monash Medical School. In a letter to the paper he pointed out that the photographer had not gained financially (he had donated the money paid for the picture to a fund for the accident victims) and had been devastated by the criticism levelled at him. Professor Masterton added:

> This is not an attempt to expose people cruelly at their most vulnerable moment. It gives us a lesson and hopefully a telling lesson of the horror of what, after all, was a limited explosion. The onlookers and the victims are standing in shock. The victims are terribly burned. This is no different than what we see coming almost daily from South Africa and the Lebanon. It also shows in miniature what would happen to thousands of people in the event of a nuclear attack or even another Chernobyl. The message should be noted by all.[26]

Photographers at the scene of tragedy rarely have time to ponder the ethical implications of what they are doing. They must shoot instinctively or the opportunity for the best pictures will have passed them by. While they try not to be obtrusive or insensitive, some take the view that the safest policy is to 'shoot first and edit later'. They may still be criticised by the public simply for being there, 'like vultures'. However, they cannot be blamed later for being beaten by their competitors. The pictures of pathos are in the bag and the decision about whether they should be used can be discussed calmly with superiors, who are paid to bear the responsibility if anything goes wrong.

Unfortunately, the luxury of postponing tough decisions often does not exist in the case of television.[27] Modern technology that enables television to report live from the scene causes several ethical dilemmas, which we noted in the previous chapter. In matters of privacy, however, live-to-air coverage poses another difficulty. Distressing footage that may once have been cut in the studio editing process now goes straight to air as the cameras roll. Either a spur-of-the-moment decision to stop intrusive filming must be made at the scene or the news channel must live with the consequences when the complaints flood in.

Legal Remedies

One of the difficulties of dealing with complaints of intrusion is that there are no legal precedents to go by. Unlike the United States, Canada and some European countries, Australia has no general law protecting personal privacy although the legal system does punish trespass and in some states it imposes restraints on disclosure of information that is defamatory. For example, the courts have held that television 'walk-ins' to private property or business premises with cameras rolling and sound equipment running are a form of trespass despite attempts to justify them in the public interest[28] and may subject journalists to punitive damages.[29] However, trespass laws cannot prevent media taking photographs or film from neighbouring land or premises, or stop the use of secret surveillance devices to penetrate a person's house, workplace or other area he or she occupies.[30] Defamation laws also afford only limited protection. In New South Wales, Queensland, Tasmania and the Australian Capital Territory there is no legal remedy for publication of non-defamatory private facts and in other states and territories even defamatory private facts may be published provided that it can be shown that they are true.[31]

The lack of effective legal remedies has meant that the only avenues for redress are the journalists' union and the Australian Press Council. The journalists' state judiciary committees have power to rebuke, fine, suspend or expel any member who breaches the journalists' ethics code. In fact the only case of intrusion severely punished by the AJA involved a photographer who posed as a doctor to gain unauthorised entry to a hospital where he took pictures of an actress suffering from a drug overdose. The photographer was expelled but later readmitted to the union.[32]

Most other complaints about privacy now go to the Australian Press Council. However, the council is financed by and under the domination of newspaper publishers and editors. It can hear complaints only against the press, not the electronic media, and is widely regarded as a paper tiger because it has no power to enforce publication of its only sanction, a rebuke.

It was largely because the council lacked power to impose penalties that several Australian states attempted to enact privacy legislation in the 1970s and why the Australian Law Reform Commission put forward a draft Bill to protect people against exposure of information about their health, private behaviour, home life or personal and family relationships. In fact, in recommending legislation the commission stated that a mere reprimand of an offender by a conciliation body such as a privacy committee or a press council appeared to be 'an inadequate redress for a wronged person' and had not been shown to be an effective deterrent to privacy-invading publishers.[33]

None of the proposals for legislation succeeded. They foundered largely because of disagreement about what areas of privacy should be protected, what invasions could be considered unreasonable and what circumstances would excuse the publication of otherwise private information. The first chairman of the Australian Press Council, former High Court judge Sir Frank Kitto, argued that

> the concept of privacy is so elusive, so insusceptible of satisfactory definition, that legislation to create a legal right to damages for it is as undesirable as uncalled for, and is likely to do more harm than good by placing unpredictable restraints upon the freedom of the press.[34]

As an alternative to legislation Kitto urged the Press Council's claim to be the arbiter of complaints about privacy. He argued that the Law Reform Commission had 'not given sufficient weight to the advantages of allowing the council to handle privacy matters'. He described the commission's draft Bill as

> a misconceived, unsuccessful and dangerous attempt to introduce the certainty required for statutory regulation into a subject which is so intangible that in the public interest it ought to be left in the realm of ethics and dealt with by the non-technical persuasive processes of such bodies as the Press Council.[35]

Despite the council's lack of punitive powers it has developed a set of ethical principles on privacy which attempt to strike a balance between individual rights and the public right to be informed. Those principles state that the moral right to privacy should not be infringed 'except where over-riding considerations of public interest are served by the publication of information about the private life or concerns of the individual'. Reporters and photographers are required to act with sympathy and discretion and to do nothing that will cause pain, humiliation or embarrassment to bereaved or distressed people 'unless it is clear that publication of the information or picture will serve a public interest and cannot reasonably be obtained otherwise'.[36]

In cases where the affront to privacy has clearly exceeded the value of the photograph or information to the public the council has usually admonished the offending newspaper. It has been especially concerned to protect children from unnecessary publicity. For instance, the council reprimanded *The Sun* in Sydney for publishing a picture of a 12-year-old boy whose head had been shaved and dyed red by his father as a punishment for truancy. The fact that the boy's parents had given authority for the picture made no difference. The council said the newspaper had 'added to the boy's humiliation'.[37] In a similar case it rebuked *The Daily Telegraph* for publishing the names of and photographs of two children whose mother had become hysterical and threatened violence following an eviction notice. The council acknowledged that the incident was a matter of public interest but said the newspaper's identification of the children had attached to them 'the stigma of their mother's irrational behaviour'.[38]

Critics of the council have noted the lack of logic and consistency in some of its privacy rulings. For instance, the council acted against the advice of the New South Wales Privacy Committee when it refused to censure *The Sun News-Pictorial* for publishing a photograph of two grief-stricken women who had just heard that their husbands' bodies had been found in a blizzard at Mount Hotham, Victoria. The picture was taken without the women's consent by a photographer using a long-distance lens. Their complaint was rejected by the council because the photographs were taken in a public place where other members of the public could see what the photographer saw.[39] However, in a similar case the council admonished *The Sun* in Sydney for publishing a picture of a woman and her two sons as they were leaving a hospital where her husband was being treated for shotgun wounds. The council acknowledged that the photograph was taken in a public place and without discourtesy or 'undue intrusion'. However, on this occasion it argued that the photograph 'merely pandered to morbid curiosity'.[40]

The council seemed reluctant to apply its own principles in another case which was brought to its attention by two federal parliamentarians, Senator Ruth Coleman and Mr Ross McLean. They complained that a front-page picture in *The West Australian* of a naked woman being rescued by firemen from a Sydney fire was a breach of her privacy and also sexist. However, the council declared that in the absence of any evidence that the woman herself felt that her privacy had been invaded it was unable to uphold the complaint.[41] This argument seemed objectionable on several grounds. Firstly, the woman was in no condition to say whether she opposed publication of the photograph. Secondly, the mere fact that she may not have seen it in print was not a sufficient reason for using it, even by the council's own erratic standards of judgement. Other dramatic pictures of the fire were available without showing the woman naked. Thirdly, the council had upheld a number of other complaints of intrusion which had been initiated by people other than those directly involved. It was therefore disingenuous for members of the council to argue that they could take no action because the woman herself had not protested.

At times the Press Council has also seemed ambivalent in its approach to the question of how far newspapers should go in their scrutiny of people in public life. Its promulgation on privacy states:

> The fact that a person is a public figure, by accepting a position of significance to the public whether official or not, does not of itself give the public the right to know facts about his private life or concerns where those facts have no relation to his public position or activities.[42]

However, the council seemed to go against its own principles when it ruled on a complaint about intrusion involving a university lecturer and a woman who was widely known as a television journalist. The woman had separated from her husband and the mass circulation Melbourne paper, *Truth*, investigated her personal life to find out whether there was 'another man'. This involved camera surveillance of the woman, interviews with the man in which he was questioned about his relationship with her, extended camera surveillance of his home and the photographing of about 40 guests entering a party attended by the couple. The man declined to comment, insisting that the matter was private. *Truth* twice ran stories on the relationship.[43]

The complaint had been referred to the Press Council by the New South Wales Privacy Committee, which believed it would be upheld. To its surprise, however, the council dismissed the complaint simply on the ground that the woman was a public figure. The committee made the acid comment: 'The council did not indicate how the woman's television capacity was affected by her alleged love life, nor advert to the fact that the man, the complainant, whose privacy was equally invaded, was certainly not a public figure'.[44]

The council's current thinking seems to be that because public figures, especially politicians, regularly seek publicity for what they say and do they must expect closer scrutiny of their private lives than the media give to other people. The council's general philosophy was explained by its chairman, David Flint, in an address to the National Press Club in Canberra:

> There is now a consensus, I think, here and elsewhere, that to the extent that an aspect of a public figure's private life directly affects or relates to the holding of and carrying out of public office, it is a matter of public interest. Prima facie, the sexual life of a public figure is a private matter; however, there can be occasions when the sexual life of a public figure is of legitimate public interest.[45]

Flint drew attention to the tendency of public figures to open up their private lives to media inspection in the hope that it would help to get them elected, only to scream 'you're invading my privacy' when those same private moments damaged their chances of success. 'There I think you have it,' he said. 'If a public figure introduces his or her private life — by promoting familial themes — one can hardly claim that the media must stay with the promotional story.'[46]

In its adjudication of complaints the council has sometimes been severe with newspapers that have invaded the privacy of public figures without good cause. For example, it upheld a complaint by the parents of Australian actress, Nicole Kidman, about an article in *Woman's Day* referring to her relationship with American actor Tom Cruise on the grounds that it failed to respect her privacy and sensibilities. The article purported to reveal behind-the-scenes secrets of Kidman's new film *Billy*

Bathgate. However, the council said the magazine had an obligation to ensure that statements in the article were true or, if they were rumour or unconfirmed reports, to identify them as such.[47]

Private Conversations

In a more contentious case the council censured *The Age* and the *Sunday Observer* in Melbourne for publishing transcripts of alleged tape-recorded conversations between Prince Charles and his then wife-to-be, Lady Diana Spencer.[48] The recordings were allegedly made by a Telecom employee when Prince Charles visited Australia in April of 1981, and the transcripts were first published in the German magazine, *Die Aktuelle*, only 24 hours after a Nuremberg court had ruled that they were an invasion of the couple's privacy.

Prince Charles and Lady Diana denounced the tapes as fakes through their London solicitors, Farrer and Co, who after studying the transcripts, declared that the conversations had never taken place. An investigation by the federal police and Telecom Australia seemed to confirm this. It showed that the telephone line through which the calls were supposed to have been routed did not exist and the methods by which the calls were allegedly intercepted were impractical and would not have been considered by a person with technical experience. Moreover, the supposed source of the information, a Telecom engineer with republican leanings, proved to be a fictitious person with a bogus address.[49]

On 3 May the Press Council learned that a version of what *Die Aktuelle* had published had been made available to most Australian newspapers by the Australian Associated Press wire service. The council's chairman, Sir Frank Kitto, immediately issued a warning that the council would view with strong disfavour any publication of the material by any Australian paper. Most Australian papers refrained from using the Australian Associated Press story but on 9 May *The Age* published extracts from the transcripts in defiance of the council's warning.[50] *The Age* admitted that its own inquiry into the authenticity of the so-called Charles tapes had concluded that they were 'probably fraudulent'. However, proof was lacking and in any case *The Age* claimed to have other sound reasons for publishing the material, which it outlined in an editorial on 11 May.

The Age said that it would not have bought the tapes (even assuming that their authenticity had been established) and would not have been the first to publish them. However, it argued that because the material had been widely published in Germany and had been made freely available to Australian newspapers on open telex lines the privacy of the original conversations (assuming they had occurred) had already been massively invaded. The issue of respecting the privacy of the speakers therefore no longer arose.

Rejecting this argument, the Press Council said that a conversation did not cease to be private merely because someone other than the participants had illegitimately gained knowledge of what was said and had spread this knowledge around. It said *The Age* had done a 'disservice to the maintenance of high journalistic standards'. The position adopted by *The Age* might well have the effect of weakening resistance in the journalistic profession to the 'exploitation of private information obtained by morally or professionally dubious methods'. Although the council recognised that considerations of public interest (as opposed to public curiosity) might in special circumstances override the right to privacy, it said that this was not such a case.[51]

Another argument of *The Age* was that if the Australian press had maintained a mysterious silence following publication of the material overseas the public might have concluded that the tapes contained scandalous or sensational content which it was better to conceal. Was it therefore not better to publish the stuff, show how innocuous and how lacking in political dynamite it was? (In fact the transcripts contained little of substance apart from an alleged disparaging remark by Prince Charles about Malcolm Fraser's sense of humour, and alleged chit-chat about whether Charles might be offered the job as Australia's next Governor-General.) Nevertheless, the Press Council said *The Age's* decision to publish had gone against the wishes of the two people who had been 'victimised by this inexcusable journalistic malpractice' after they had insisted that the tapes were fraudulent.

The Sunday Observer had gone a stage further than *The Age* by publishing the full transcript of the tapes and with a banner headline on the front page.[52] The Press Council declared that by publishing in 'a deliberately sensationalist manner' the *Sunday Observer* had treated the wishes of the royal couple in a 'very high-handed way'. It also dismissed that newspaper's excuse that it had a duty to clear the air of mischievous guesswork about the contents of the tapes by publishing the actual text. The acceptance of that justification, the council said, would provide 'an extremely wide area of exemption from the duty to honour the privacy of private or public persons'.[53]

Although the hullabaloo over the so-called 'Charles tapes' soon died down, the case seemed to have established the principle that private conversations were sacrosanct. As the council put it, they did not cease to be private merely because someone illegitimately gained knowledge of what was said and then spread it around. However, the council overturned that principle six years later when it upheld the right of newspapers to publish the contents of a secretly taped car telephone conversation between the Victorian Opposition Leader, Jeff Kennett, and the federal Liberal foreign affairs spokesman, Andrew Peacock.

During their late night conversation the two men had made some very frank and unflattering comments about the federal Liberal leader, John Howard. Kennett was heard on the tape saying that he had told Howard after the by-election for the Victorian seat of Central Highlands that he did not have his support and never would have it. He said that after he had abused Howard 'the poor little fella didn't know whether he was Arthur or Martha'.[54]

The tape of the conversation was supplied to *The Sun News-Pictorial* by a man who had accidentally picked it up on a $299 scanning device. The paper's editor, Colin Duck, was at first worried about the legality of using secretly taped material, but after getting advice from the paper's solicitor he decided to publish it on the ground that the public had a right to know what a potential Liberal Premier of Victoria and a potential Liberal Prime Minister had to say about the Liberal Party leadership.

The front-page story caused immediate political repercussions. On the day it appeared Howard demoted Peacock from foreign affairs spokesman to backbencher. Although he was accused by some Liberal MPs of over-reacting, Howard said that Peacock's explanation of the conversation was unsatisfactory and implied disloyalty to him.[55] The first story contained only the substance of the conversation, not the actual dialogue, which was heavy with expletives. *The Sun* explained that it felt the details would 'embarrass both parties because of the strong language and the personal nature of some of the comments'. However, in interviews with other media Kennett bitterly attacked the *Sun*, saying that it had established 'a new low in journalism ethics and professionalism' by publishing a private conversation which it knew had been obtained by surreptitious means.[56]

The next day *The Sun News-Pictorial* published the full transcript of the conversation, with only the expletives deleted, saying that it had a right to defend itself against Kennett's challenge to its integrity and motives. However, as Colin Duck acknowledged, another reason was that verbatim parts of the conversation had been used on radio and television and he had learned that other newspapers around Australia intended to publish extracts. He felt that as the *Sun* had originated the story it now had a duty to its readers to publish the full contents.[57]

In the view of electronics specialists and private investigators, Kennett and Peacock should have known how easy it was to monitor car telephone conversations, even with unsophisticated equipment, and were unwise to discuss sensitive political or private business in that way. And as if to rub salt in the wound, the former state politics reporter for *The Age*, David Broadbent, indicated that several years earlier he had warned Kennett about the dangers of eavesdropping after a radio station had monitored their conversation on Kennett's car phone.[58]

Nevertheless, Kennett maintained that the only possible justification for publishing a private conversation would be if it brought to light treasonable or criminal activities, and then only if the disclosure was sanctioned by the courts.

Colin Duck argued that the private rights of public figures did not go that far.

> I suppose everybody is entitled to believe that any conversation they have is private. Unfortunately, because of human nature that doesn't always occur and there are plenty of cases where letters, which I guess are as private as a telephone conversation, have been leaked to the media.[59]

Duck pointed out that politicians spent a lot of time either leaking information to the media or complaining about leaks, and their attitude usually depended on whether the stories that came out were favourable to them.

> Take the example of a caucus meeting in Canberra. Within minutes of the meeting breaking up all those loyal members of whatever party it happens to be are telling members of the media what actually went on, and I'm very happy with that system because it means we can give the public the news. You

will get verbatim quotes appearing in the newspapers and on television from meetings that were supposedly personal and private and where they are making decisions on what course the government is going to take so I don't think that if something is said on a telephone it makes it anything special.[60]

Duck admitted that he would not be happy if someone secretly taped one of his private conversations but said that if it was published because of its news value he would just have to put up with it. So where did he draw the line between the public figure's right to privacy and the public right to know?

That's extremely difficult. My line would normally be that I wouldn't publish any material between two politicians talking privately about their wives or romantic attachments or children. But you couldn't completely exclude even those matters because there could be a good reason for publishing them. It could be very much in the public interest.[61]

Arguments like this carried no weight with Kennett, who complained to the federal police and the Director of Public Prosecutions, Ian Temby, QC. However, Temby decided against prosecution because he was not convinced that the case would lead to a conviction before a jury.

Under the Telecommunication (Interception) Act of 1979 it was illegal for anyone to intercept telephone material without government or judicial approval, but it was not illegal to publish it. The legislation seemed to give no clear protection against disclosure of the contents of private phone conversations. To close this loophole the Attorney-General, Lionel Bowen, introduced amendments to the legislation in federal parliament in May 1987. Bowen acknowledged that the whole question of telecommunications interception required a balancing of conflicting interests:

Broadly those interests are the need to provide Australian law enforcement authorities with the important additional tool of interception powers for use in the investigation and prosecution of serious offences and the need to ensure that the privacy of individuals is protected from unwarranted intrusion.[62]

The legislation would make it illegal for the media to publish political revelations from private phone conversations, as in the Kennett–Peacock affair. Kennett welcomed it, Colin Duck thought it a backward step, and the Press Council made it clear whose side it was on when it rejected a complaint against *The Courier-Mail* in Brisbane for publishing excerpts from the conversation. It stated:

> The fact that a conversation, or indeed document, is intended to be private does not mean that media are to be forever restrained absolutely from publication. This would impose restrictions on the media which would be against the public interest. Rather, each case has to be examined on its merits. Public figures, like other citizens, are entitled to privacy, but that privacy must give way whenever and wherever the people are entitled to be informed. This conversation was one such matter . . .[63]

Private Documents

In another more recent landmark case the Press Council was confronted with the thorny problem of what newspapers should do when they received private documents which had 'fallen off the back of a truck'. This time the council's decision was attacked because it went in favour of the complainant, and because it was regarded by some journalists as creating a precedent for further restrictions on the freedom of the press. Nevertheless, the case was important for another reason. The council laid down new principles which could be applied in future cases to determine whether a particular 'leak' should be used by a newspaper. As the council indicated, the test to be applied would be whether the leak was in the public interest.

The case concerned the use made by the *Geelong Advertiser* of documents which had been posted to Joan Creati, a member of the Victorian Local Government commission, but which had been inexplicably found in a car park and delivered by the finder to the newspaper. The documents included confidential legal opinions and a letter from the Victorian local government minister, Caroline Hogg, to the director of the Local Government Commission, Russell Badham, relating to controversial proposals for the amalgamation of local councils in the Geelong area.[64] The report published in the *Geelong Advertiser* described the documents and included direct quotations from the minister's letter. The contents of the legal opinions were reported briefly and in general terms, and the newspaper also described how the documents had come into their possession, along with a letter from Creati protesting at their action.

Creati complained to the Press Council that the newspaper was wrong to read her mail and to print a story based upon it. She maintained that the source was not 'a whistle-blower' who might have had legitimate access to the material but, at best, 'an un-involved busy-body who had access to stolen goods'. She said her reputation had been damaged because the confidentiality of the documents was breached when it was thought they were in her charge, and that her privacy was invaded, not only by the reading of her mail but also by the unnecessary publication of the street and suburb in which she lived.

In reply, the newspaper's editor-in-chief, Daryl McLure, said the material extracted from the documents was obviously on a matter of considerable public interest. He said it was not unusual for newspapers to publish reports based on material that had been leaked, found by chance or allegedly stolen. He cited recent examples in other newspapers. 'This was simply another leaked document', he said. 'How the information was obtained — as long as it was not stolen by my staff or on the orders of my staff — is irrelevant.'

In its adjudication of the case the council said the *Advertiser* was justified in reporting that confidential and sensitive material on an issue of considerable local interest — and allegedly stolen — had been found in a car park. It was also right to publish Creati's criticisms of its actions and had shown restraint and prudence in deciding not to report the more sensitive infor-mation in the documents.

However, the main issue, as the council saw it, was whether the newspaper should have revealed information extracted from the documents. The council rejected the newspaper's contention that the manner in which the documents were obtained was irrelevant. It stated:

> The source of information, particularly if it involves an alleged criminal offence, is clearly a matter a newspaper must take into account in deciding whether to print it. The basic question is whether the printed report added so significantly to public knowledge on what was certainly an issue of public

interest that such ethical and privacy considerations were outweighed. On balance, the Council believes it did not.[65]

In admonishing the paper, the council said it recognised that documents and other information which reached newspapers through unauthorised or even illegal channels could be a valuable and legitimate source of news. It was often only as a result of such material that newspapers were able to reveal facts that had unjustifiably been kept secret and to expose wrongdoing and incompetence. However, the council said that by its nature such material confronted editors and reporters with serious ethical issues. It added:

> Often the information reaches them only because someone has stolen it or breached a confidence. This does not mean that newspapers must never use such material; it does mean that they need to be very sure that the public benefit to be achieved through publication outweighs the harm of taking advantage of somebody's misdemeanour or crime, even where the motives of the person responsible for the 'leak' are honourable. That responsibility becomes even more onerous when publication would involve the invasion of an individual's privacy.[66]

The decision infuriated senior executives of the *Geelong Advertiser*, including McLure, who sent a letter to the council protesting at the implication that the matter was not of sufficient public importance to warrant publication. McLure was struck by the irony that the council had commended the newspaper for its restraint in leaving out sensitive material and had then rebuked it for publishing a watered down version of it. He commented: 'The *Geelong Advertiser* appears to have done everything right except to publish the story'.[67]

Journalists were also puzzled by the council's conclusion that it was wrong to publish information which it had admitted to be of 'considerable local interest'. In countless other cases material which had fallen off the back of a truck had been published by newspapers without so much as a murmur from the Press Council. Of how much public interest did material have to be before it could be published? The council's ruling had not clarified that issue. In McLure's view, it had clouded it.[68]

Although the council has received more brickbats than bouquets its procedures for dealing with complaints are at least as effective as those of the journalists' union. While the MEAA has greater punitive powers than the council, its code of ethics offers no clear guidelines about when and in what circumstances it is an offence to invade privacy.

Clause 9 of the code states that members 'shall respect private grief and personal privacy and shall have the right to resist compulsion to intrude on them'. On its own that seems clear enough. However, the clause appears to be contradicted by the preamble to the code, which states that 'respect for truth and the public's right to information are overriding principles for all journalists'. In other words, the union also believes that intrusions are sometimes justified, though the code does not indicate when public rights should override private rights, or vice versa. In fact, the AJA Ethics Review Committee appears to have left the issue deliberately vague when it formulated the new code in 1984. It then stated: 'The question of when overriding considerations of the public's right to know may justify such intrusions is subjective and variable. AJA members should be secure in the knowledge that the Code respects individual professional evaluations.'[69]

Lack of faith in Press Council and union grievance procedures has led some people to adopt more direct forms of protest. For example, an article in the Melbourne newspaper, the *Sunday Herald Sun*, revealing that the distinguished Australian ballet dancer, Kelvin Coe, was suffering from AIDS provoked a bitter reaction from Coe's partner, Stuart Robertson, a lecturer at the Victorian College of the Arts. The article, written by the newspaper's arts editor, Bob Crimeen, was published on 25 August 1991 despite Coe's request that his illness be kept private. Two days later Robertson confronted Crimeen in the courtyard of Melbourne's Regent hotel and threw red paint over him. He wanted to humiliate Crimeen publicly, and chose red to symbolise that Crimeen had blood on his hands.

Kelvin Coe died on 9 July 1992, and on 27 July Robertson pleaded guilty in the Camberwell Magistrates Court to criminal damage and assault. He was put on a two-year good behaviour bond with the conditions that he pay $1000 to the court fund and $1500 compensation to Crimeen for damage to his clothes. According to Robertson, the story had exacerbated Coe's illness, and had caused both of them incredible stress and strain. He rejected the argument that he could have used the usual channels of complaint. He said he had thrown the paint because he was not convinced that the findings of the Press Council or the AJA judiciary committee would have had the same impact on Crimeen's life as the article had had on the remainder of Coe's life.[70]

Public figures know that by complaining to the Press Council or the Australian Broadcasting Tribunal they may risk having their private lives raked over a second time. Sometimes the cure seems worse than the disease, especially if the decision goes against them. Nevertheless, the high-profile women's magazine publisher, Ita Buttrose, was so incensed when the Sydney television station Channel Nine sifted through the contents of her rubbish bin to get a story that she lodged a complaint with the New South Wales Privacy Committee.

Bits of Buttrose's rubbish were used on Terry Willesee's *Eye on Australia* program in an attempt to show what it revealed about her habits and lifestyle. It seemed a cheap, sordid little stunt and although it aroused some amusement among the audience the Privacy Committee thought it a poor excuse for entertainment. In a report to the New South Wales parliament the committee said that disclosing information obtained by searching a person's rubbish bin was an invasion of privacy, and it added: 'A person does not forfeit his (her) expectations of privacy simply because rubbish must be left in the street for collection and proper disposal'.[71]

Channel Nine officials refused to apologise. So far as they were concerned, the contents of Buttrose's bin were matters of public interest. And despite the Privacy Committee's judgement the case left a few questions unanswered. Would the media be justified in rummaging through the bins of other public figures in the search for evidence of dishonesty, corruption or other malpractice? In other words, would the ends ever justify the means? And at what point did rubbish cease to be private property — when it had been placed on the nature strip, or in the garbage truck or at the tip? Once it had left the house was anyone — the media included — entitled to search it? And if a person's rubbish was not sacrosanct what was left of one's private life? As one commentator noted, no wonder shredders were becoming so popular.[72]

While Ita Buttrose was accused by some observers of making much ado about nothing the case illustrates the difficulty of obtaining redress through normal channels when privacy has been invaded. Buttrose could not have complained to the Press

Council because it deals only with complaints against news-papers, or to the AJA, which can discipline only its members and has no power to take punitive action against television station management, or any other employer for that matter. Neither the AJA nor Broadcasting Tribunal have been very active in dealing with complaints of ethical transgressions and the New South Wales Privacy Committee could offer little satisfaction because, like the Press Council, it lacked the power to punish offenders. Channel Nine was obviously unaffected by the committee's mild rebuke. The station could claim that its action in going through Buttrose's garbage was merely a harmless bit of fun. However, for her the issue was why the fun had to be at her expense, and how much her privacy was worth if it could be invaded with impunity by a banal peep and freak show.

In a few cases news organisations have disciplined staff for breaching in-house rules relating to intrusion into grief and privacy. For instance, a Channel Seven reporter and producer in Perth were sacked in May 1990 after taking responsibility for a piece of graphic news footage of a family tragedy. The story was about a boy who had been buried alive while playing with friends in a sand trench. The section of news film which Seven executives and some viewers found offensive showed close-ups of the victim's mother having the news broken to her, and soundtrack of her agonised screams as the words sank in.

Some commentators thought the penalty unnecessarily severe, among them Melbourne television personality Derryn Hinch, who was no stranger himself to controversy over lapses in journalistic ethics. Hinch said he would have run the report but, bearing the Broadcasting Tribunal and the viewers in mind, he would have deleted the audio of the mother's cry. However, in his weekly column in *The Sun News-Pictorial* Hinch also argued that the case illustrated some of the hypocrisy in Australian attitudes to invasion of privacy and grief, both among television network executives and in the minds of viewers. He asserted:

If that young boy had suffocated in India or Bangladesh — and a TV crew had captured that moment of the mother's grief — it would have been shown in this country without compunction. Whether you agree with it or not the TV bulletins almost daily show carnage. In the Middle East — bodies in Beirut, grieving mothers in Iran or Iraq during that war. From Belfast TV footage showing victims of that public conflict — including chilling pictures of two young British soldiers being battered to death. So when it comes to news-worthiness do we really subscribe to the cynical newspaper equation that goes something like this: One Australian equals 10 Brits, equals 20 Americans, equals 100 Canadians, equals 100,000 Indians, equals Columbians, equals Africans.[73]

Hinch argued that viewers were responsible for the large number of disaster scenes in television news because they wanted slick stories with plenty of dramatic pictures. They wanted to see it all. If they did not want that they would watch 'learned and worthy news reports from all parts of the globe on SBS or the ABC'. However, the last thing they wanted was for television to see into their own private worlds. 'Intrude anywhere you like but not in my street or suburb.'[74]

Law Reform Proposals

The lack of what the Law Reform Commission called 'an effective deterrent to privacy-invading publishers' and the increase in complaints about media intrusions in the early 1990s led to renewed discussion by governments of the arguments for and against privacy legislation. In 1991 the Attorneys-General of New South Wales, Victoria and Queensland proposed the creation of a new uniform defamation law which would include provision for protection of individuals from revelations about their private affairs.

Predictably, the Press Council was lukewarm about the proposal. It could see that its authority as a conciliation and disputes-settling body would be eroded if privacy issues became the province of the courts. It also reiterated the difficulty of drafting a generally acceptable definition of 'privacy matters'.

Broadly, the legislation envisaged by the three governments was designed to protect people from publication of sensitive facts about their health, family or private behaviour unless it could be shown that the information was 'relevant to a topic of public interest'. It made no distinction between the private rights of public figures and those of ordinary citizens. In fact, the Attorneys-General strongly opposed the Press Council's suggestion that the legislation should include a 'public figure' category of the kind that had been adopted by the American courts.

The public figure doctrine had been developed by the United States Supreme Court in a series of controversial defamation cases between 1964 and 1974. The court established that plaintiffs in public life were entitled to less protection in defamation and privacy cases than ordinary citizens. It held that a public figure should be prohibited from recovering damages for defamatory falsehood unless he or she could prove that the media defendant knew that the statement was false or had shown a reckless disregard for the truth. The justification for the harsher rule for public figures was that they usually enjoyed greater access to channels of effective communication and therefore had a better opportunity to counteract false statements than private persons, and secondly that those in public office had to accept greater public scrutiny of their actions.[75]

Although the American courts have asserted that public figures have fewer rights to privacy than other people the definition of 'public figure' has tended to vary from case to case. At one point the Supreme Court defined public figures as government officers or 'those who, by reason of the notoriety of their achievements or the vigour and success with which they seek public attention' should be classified as such.[76] As if this was not vague enough to keep an army of lawyers busy for years, the American courts have now created different categories of public figures such as 'all purpose' public figures, 'limited' public figures and even 'accidental' public figures who have been thrust into the spotlight by chance.[77]

The Australian Press Council argued that appropriately worded legislation could overcome difficulties of the kind experienced in the United States. However, the three state governments remained unconvinced. As they saw it, there was no satisfactory way of determining which persons should fall within, or without, the public figure category.

The Attorneys-General believed that the American system gave too much latitude to the media and too little protection to public figures whose privacy had been invaded. Rather than go down the American path they preferred that the onus should be on the media to provide proof that intrusions were justified in the public interest. By late 1992, however, the tripartite government discussions were close to breaking down and it appeared there would be no privacy legislation. For the time being complaints about invasion of privacy would have to be resolved within the realm of ethics rather than the realm of law.

To people with grounds for complaint the Press Council's limited powers of censure and moral suasion might seem a weak alternative to a legal remedy. Yet experience in the United States has shown the legal remedy also to be unsatisfactory. Contradictory decisions by the American courts have created uncertainty in the minds of lawyers and their clients. The prospect of compensation has to be weighed against the potentially huge costs if the case fails. In any case the courts cannot restore what has been lost. As one commentator has noted:

> A huge monetary award can make a plaintiff rich, but it cannot return that sense of control the initial invasion takes away. For this reason alone the law provides an unsatisfactory solution. Ethical thinking prior to broadcast or publication is preferable to a court battle.[78]

CHAPTER 6

A Question of Taste

In matters of taste we are as fickle as the weather. What we liked last season grows stale and tiresome by the following season. Nowhere is this more evident than in the news media, whose day by day reports reflect the wild vicissitudes in public taste. As a pluralistic institution the media must also cater for many different tastes; the interests, passions and tolerance levels of one group of readers, listeners or viewers are often dramatically different from those of another group. Even one newspaper or broadcasting station will find it impossible to please all of its audience all of the time, so wide will be the variety of its inclinations, expectations and general tastes. That being so, it is extremely difficult for organisations responsible for setting standards in journalism, such as the Australian Press Council, the Australian Broadcasting Authority and the Media, Entertainment and Arts Alliance, to set down permanent rules or make lasting judgements about what is in good or poor taste.

The difficulty is acknowledged by the Press Council in its adjudications on public complaints and in its general pronouncements on matters of taste. For example, in replying to criticisms that the media sometimes displays a lack of sensitivity and taste in the reporting of crime, natural disasters, terrorism and other forms of violence the council stated that there was no single set of community standards available to editors as the basis for making judgements. It added: 'What is offensive to one section of the community may be equally acceptable to another'.[1]

The council is slow to reprimand offenders because of its reluctance to be seen to be acting like a censor in matters of taste. Nevertheless, it is at times extraordinarily reluctant even to arbitrate on specific complaints. For instance, in defending the right of columnists and cartoonists to express views which some people might regard as offensive, the council said it did not set itself up as a general arbiter of taste and therefore intervened 'only in extreme cases'.[2]

Because the range of tastes is, in the council's own words, 'as wide as the range of finger prints',[3] it has argued that the promulgation of a code setting out specific rules is neither desirable nor feasible. On the whole it prefers to leave questions of taste to the 'professional integrity, judgement and commonsense' of the people working in the news media.[4] The council's Statement of Principles is also more permissive than restrictive. Principle 7 states: 'A newspaper has a wide discretion in matters of taste but this does not justify lapses of taste so gross as to bring the freedom of the press into disrepute.'[5]

Some newspapers and broadcasting stations have in-house guidelines to assist editors and chiefs-of-staff in making decisions about the appropriateness of reporting or filming stories in ways which may arouse revulsion or distaste among readers or viewers. Some of these guidelines were created as a response to public criticism of media intrusions and reporting of violence. However, breaches of the guidelines are rarely punished and are sometimes justified on the basis that they were the only means of obtaining information that the public has a right to know. The primary duty of the news media, it is argued, is to inform the public of important events, not to act as moral guardians. The Press Council has said as much itself, though it is sometimes timid in its response when it can be demonstrated that the media have overstepped the boundaries of good taste.

As we have tried to show in other chapters, some kinds of media behaviour offend against more than one principle of right conduct. For instance, intrusions into people's privacy may also lead to reporting and filming that sensationalise lurid details, in defiance of generally accepted canons of decency and good taste. Likewise, overtly demeaning portrayals of women of the kind mentioned in Chapter 3 are clearly also in extremely poor taste from either gender's point of view. Nor can there be much doubt about the tastelessness of a promotion campaign by the magazine *Picture* in its edition of 6 February 1990 when it invited readers to win a prize by picking the date, time and the VIP passengers killed in the next airline crash: 'Play JUMBO BLOTTO and win $20,000'. In his defence the publisher said that death or gallows humour, known in contemporary life as black humour, was as old as Shakespeare. He cited, for instance, the droll comments of the gravedigger in Hamlet, and added: 'So the lineage of this kind of humour is impeccable'. The Press Council was partly won over by this brand of chop logic. It acknowledged that many readers would find the *Picture* promotion offensive but said it did not believe it to be a lapse of taste so gross as to bring the press into disrepute. Dismissing the complaint, the council said the publisher's reference to black humour was a reminder of the wide spectrum of views and tastes which was 'an inherent feature of a free society'. It saw no advantage and considerable danger in trying to prohibit such material.[6]

Of course, as the council implies, the mere fact that an article or photograph could cause offence is not of itself a reason for not publishing it or, subsequently, for censuring it. Objections on grounds of poor taste need to be weighed against the usefulness or importance of the information that is published. In short, did the story do more good than the harm it caused, and could the harm have been avoided by gathering the information and telling the story in a different way? There is no easy answer. The problem of withholding information to avoid giving offence is to know where to draw the line. One kind of censorship easily leads to another. The newspaper or periodical that is always being praised for common sense and good taste is also likely to be mocked at times for its stodginess and lack of originality. But the more permissive approach is potentially as dangerous. Material that gives serious offence can result in widespread public disapproval, reflected in a decline in circulation and revenue. Again, it is a matter of knowing where the line should be drawn.

The controversy over the reporting and filming of major disasters and acts of violence further illustrates the point. Generally the media would argue with sound justification that it is in the public interest to show things as they are, not as some people would like them to be, or as governments and others in authority would like them to seem. 'Tell it as it is — as you see it and hear it' is an almost hackneyed injunction by editors to reporters and photographers. However, in some circumstances there may be equally compelling reasons for arguing that some of the realities should be concealed because they are so grossly offensive to prevailing standards of morality and good taste. On the one hand there is a danger of distorting the truth and misleading the public by sanitising the realities of war and disaster. One of the most recent examples of that is the reduction of the Gulf War, in media terms, to little more than a high technology video show which, as the authoritative defence writer Peter Young has noted, never showed the bloody end result or the failures.[7] On the other hand there is the risk that showing everthing in close up and in explicit detail may cultivate a taste for horror and yet more horror until there is no line to be drawn. Blown-up photographs or extended television clips of the maimed or the dead cause not only anguish among relatives and friends of the victims but also more general public outrage. However, the Press Council rarely seems to utter more than a mild 'tut, tut!' over the complaints in this category that come its way. For instance, it offered only muted criticism of *The Daily Sun* in Brisbane when that newspaper gave two-thirds of its front page to a blown up picture of the body of a murder victim slumped in the front yard of his home. Replying to criticisms in parliament and by its readers, the paper said the photograph served the public interest by bringing home more forcefully than words the brutality and finality of murder. The council seems to have recognised that the story might have been overblown. It acknowledged that the picture and the detailed medical description given in the story about the state of the dead man would have caused distress to his family and recommended the exercise of restraint in the reporting of violence. However, it said that the incident did not amount to a gross lapse of taste and dismissed the complaint.[8]

The council meted out a little more severity in its judgement of an article by the *Herald Sun* in Melbourne about the discovery of a body thought to be that of a six-year-old girl who had been abducted three months earlier. The council agreed that the reference in the story to the possible mauling of the body by animals was 'unnecessary'. The public interest could have been equally well served, in the council's view, by 'less explicit reporting'.[9]

Some of the worst cases do not reach the council because no one is sufficiently concerned to make a formal complaint about them or perhaps because of a belief that the council lacks the power or the will to change anything. Many other complaints are beyond the jurisdiction of the council because they are about stories which appeared on television. One such complaint was against the ABC for showing the decapitated head of a murder victim being removed from a grave.[10] Another was described by one of the journalists interviewed by criminologists Peter Grabosky and Paul Wilson during their research on the reporting of violence and crime. The journalist recalled a case in which the body of a murder victim was retrieved from a river by police divers:

> No sooner had the remains reached dry land than a television camera crew arrived on the scene. Acutely frustrated with their unfortunate timing, the TV crew saved their day (and their story) by prevailing upon the police to return the body to the water, and to retrieve it once again for the cameras.[11]

As we have said elsewhere, there is an obviously legitimate public interest in the reporting of disasters and crimes of violence. The objections are usually about the scope and type of reporting rather than the reporting of violence itself. What causes particular concern is the sometimes heavy focus on the blood and gore of serious accidents or explicit details of cruel and sadistic homicide or sexual assault cases. A common complaint is that television comes far too close without any respect for human dignity or anguish. A typical media response is that the depiction of horror serves as a reminder to others of the stupidity of war or the dangers of easy access to drugs, drunk driving and lax gun laws. Sure, close-up filming can be disturbing but reportage of crime and disasters is meant to be disturbing and anyway, how close is too close, and who is to judge: the police in charge of the scene, the traumatised survivors or the media?

Changing Tastes

Rapidly changing public views about acceptable behaviour make it extraordinarily difficult for editors and for regulatory bodies like the Press Council and Australian Broadcasting

Authority to make definitive judgements about what is currently in good or bad taste. Sometimes they can only guess at it, and the fierceness of public reaction may be the first they hear of it. Some of the issues that were taboo a decade or two ago nowadays hardly raise an eyebrow. Nowhere is this more obvious than in the airing given by the mass media to matters of sex. As Richard Glover noted in a commentary on the new permissiveness in society, when close-up shots of vaginas and ultrasound pictures of intercourse are appearing on television and mass circulation teenage and women's magazines are offering free condoms and explicit sex guides there seems little left to give, yet the stakes continue to be raised.[12] In this almost-anything-goes society it is hardly surprising that the Press Council looks rather nonchalantly at some of the complaints that come before it alleging poor taste in matters of sex. For instance, the council had little difficulty in dismissing complaints about a review in *The Age* of a television program titled 'Everything you always wanted to know about sex and were afraid to ask'. The objectors complained on the ground that intimate sexual details were made the subject of jocular comment and a source of hilarious entertainment — 'a lapse of decency indefensible in a paper circulating in families of varied age groups'. The council conceded that the film might be offensive to some sections of the community but said that did not mean the newspaper had no right to review it, and it had done so in a 'restrained and responsible' manner.[13] Another story published in *Fishing News* drew the complaint that it referred to explicit sexual behaviour, belittled handicapped people and contained offensive language. The council acknowledged that many people would find the article coarse and vulgar and totally inappropriate for a sporting magazine. Nevertheless, it conceded that some people might consider the story humorous and although it lacked taste the council doubted whether it would bring the press into disrepute. It dismissed the complaint.

The council's toleration of swear words and other potentially offensive language also reflects the changes in community attitudes of the past 15 to 20 years. For instance, in dismissing a complaint about four-letter expletives published in an interview with actor, Bryan Brown, in *The Weekend Australian*, the council accepted the newspaper's view that such profanities were no longer confined to the factory floor or dockside and that the use of the word 'fuck' in full was justified in that particular context.[14]

Of much greater concern to the council is the use of language which reinforces and perpetuates prejudice and crude stereo-typing. It condemned without equivocation the publication by the *Northern Territory News* of a letter to the editor, written under a pseudonym and headed 'Ban poofters', which disparaged homosexuals and suggested that they be banned from Darwin's free beach.[15] It also upheld a complaint against the *Kilmore Free Press* for using the words 'boong' and 'poofter' in a regular personal opinion column.[16] The council pointed out that although the use of these derogatory terms was still widespread in Australian society they were deeply offensive to the groups concerned and were generally avoided by newspapers, even by the writers of idiosyncratic columns. However, as another of the council's rulings indicates, the context in which some expressions are used determines whether they are to be regarded as being in questionable taste. It dismissed a complaint against *The Ovens and Murray Advertiser* for using the term 'mick school' to describe a Catholic school at Beechworth. The council was persuaded by the editor that the terms 'micks' and 'proddies' were used interchangeably and in a light-hearted vein by the resident columnist and were not intended to give offence.[17]

The council has frequently defended the right of columnists to express views which many people might regard as offensive, or in dubious taste. Thus, the council upheld the right of feminist Germaine Greer to write an article for *The Age* describing the Pope as 'an abominable, publicity-seeking, sanctimonious s . . . !'[18] and another accusing Mother Teresa of using charitable actions to foist Catholicism on vulnerable people. Dismissing the complaint in the second case the council stated that while the feelings of those who viewed Mother Teresa as a saint were understood the censorship of opposing views was 'unthinkable'.[19]

Similarly, the council has shown little sympathy for attempts to restrict or censor the work of cartoonists on grounds of poor taste. It has strongly defended the centuries-old press tradition that cartoonists should have freedom of choice about the subject of their cartoons, remarking on one occasion:

> In a democratic society it is appropriate that opinion, in-cluding extreme and even unpopular opinion, should not be proscribed from publication . . . A cartoon is one form of opinion and it is traditional that the cartoonist be given wide

licence because exaggeration and caricature are inherent in his or her art.[20]

The council's policy is reflected in its arbitration of a complaint about a cartoon by Paul Zanetti of *The Daily Telegraph* in Sydney that marked the sudden death of the New South Wales Attorney-General, Paul Landa. The cartoon, published four days after the death, showed a cemetery in which a number of well-dressed men, obviously contenders for the Cabinet vacancy, were fighting furiously on top of a grave marked 'R.I.P. Paul Landa'. The Premier was seen standing to one side looking distressed while from the grave a voice was saying 'Will you blokes knock off that noise — it's enough to wake the dead.'[21]

The cartoon drew a strong protest from the Orange Trades and Labor Council. However, it was vigorously defended by the newspaper, which said that the cartoon was not meant to amuse but was a caustic and perfectly legitimate comment on the political situation that followed Landa's death. The Press Council said it could sympathise with relatives of Mr Landa who were distressed on seeing the cartoon. However, it saw some substance in the paper's argument that what was distasteful was not the cartoon itself but the situation it depicted of politicians squabbling over a dead man's position. It dismissed the complaint.

Two years later an even more controversial cartoon on the subject of AIDS earned *The Bulletin* a deserved rebuke.[22] What is remarkable is the excuse that the council made for it. The cartoon appeared with *The Bulletin's* cover story on the disease and showed one flower in a garden asking the question 'How do you know if your garden has AIDS?', to which another flower replies: 'All your pansies die'.

In its complaint the Public Interest Advocacy Centre argued strongly that the punch line made light of the immense suffering to which people with AIDS, their families and friends were subject and perpetuated the myth that AIDS was solely a homosexual disease.

In reply *The Bulletin's* editor stressed that the magazine had at no time sought to trivialise what it regarded as one of the country's major problems and it would not have donated so much space to the issue and to a question and answer section designed to provide information to the public if it had not believed this. While he would not have printed the cartoon had the matter been left to him, because it was not in keeping with the serious tenor of the story, he did not believe it constituted irresponsible journalism. However, because he accepted that some people would find the cartoon offensive *The Bulletin* had published a strong letter of protest from the complainant in a subsequent issue.

The council said that the cartoon would undoubtedly have been considered hurtful by AIDS sufferers and by many others. However, the fact that it was published in *The Bulletin* did not mean that the interpretation placed upon it by the complainant had the imprimatur of that journal. The council had attempted to weigh, on the one hand, the necessary freedom that a publication must give to its cartoonists, and to other commentators, and on the other, the principles of responsible journalism. Although the cartoon was harsh and in questionable taste the council felt that on balance it was not deserving of censure but rather of the publication of a letter of protest from the complainant. As this had already been done the council saw no reason in pursuing the matter further. Once again it had washed its hands of a sticky problem.

CHAPTER 7

Protection or Prison? Confidentiality of Sources

Journalists have demonstrated that they are prepared to go to gaol rather than breach their code of ethics by revealing the sources of information given to them in confidence.

Three cases illustrate the point. The first involved Tony Barrass, a senior journalist for the *Sunday Times*, Perth, who on 12 December 1989 refused to reveal in court the source of confidential tax documents relating to former merchant banker Laurie Connell and Connell's wife, Elizabeth. Barrass was found guilty of contempt of court by Perth magistrate Peter Thorbaven, and subsequently sentenced to seven days' jail.[1]

Barrass had to endure the indignity of being strip searched by warders three times while in detention at Wooroloo prison farm near Perth. He was released after serving five days of his sentence, having been granted two days off for good behaviour. But ten months later — in September 1990 — he again refused to reveal the source of information leaked to him from the Tax Department and, as a result, was fined $10 000.[2]

The two stories based on that information, entitled 'Tax secrets for sale' and 'Police probe tax leak', were clearly in the public interest. Barrass and his newspaper acted responsibly by not disclosing details of the Connells' tax affairs. Their purpose was to highlight breaches of security in the Taxation Office. Had Barrass not agreed to protect his source the public would not have been told of the ease with which their apparently secret tax documents could be made available to anyone willing to pay the right price.

Barrass's defence counsel, Martin Bennetts, argued that his client had chosen to remain true to his honour rather than to his oath to tell the whole truth in court. However, Judge Toni Kennedy said Barrass's honour had no foundation in law. His crime struck at the heart of the administration of justice, she said. The rule of law would break down if witnesses refused to answer questions put to them in court.

Here was a classic demonstration of the conflict over what represents the public interest. Both the news media and the judiciary claimed to represent the true interests of the wider community. Who was right? To argue that the judiciary are right implies that the news media should never break the law, however bad the law, and should answer all questions put to them in court, even if that results in dire consequences for their informants and denies the public information that they have a right to know. To argue that the media were right would be to suggest that they should enjoy a special privilege over other citizens when called upon to give evidence, and should have a right to withhold information even if it is considered necessary in the interests of justice.

For obeying his conscience Barrass could have been jailed for five years or fined $50 000, but Judge Kennedy accepted testimonials to his 'high integrity and professionalism as a journalist' and said she did not think prison was the appropriate answer.

The $10 000 fine, which was paid by the *Sunday Times*, is the highest ever imposed on an Australian journalist for refusing to disclose a source. Barrass was also the first Australian journalist to be imprisoned for protecting the identity of his informant.

However, history repeated itself on 20 March 1992 when former journalist on *The Courier-Mail* Joe Budd was found in contempt of the Supreme Court in Brisbane after repeatedly refusing to disclose the source of his story about alleged police misconduct at a Toowoomba football carnival in 1989. The story was the subject of a libel writ against the newspaper.

Mr Justice Dowsett said he could not understand how a responsible member of the community could seek to put himself above the law. He sentenced Budd to 14 days' jail.[3]

Predictably, the sentence provoked outrage among journalists and civil libertarians. *The Courier-Mail's* editor, Des Houghton, told a public rally in Budd's support: 'The day journalists get into the witness box and spill the beans is the day that people will stop giving us vital material about wrong-doing in public office.' Investigative journalist Bob Bottom added that the ability of reporters to expose crime and corruption depended on confidential sources trusting them with sensitive or incriminating information.[4]

In the third case, a former ABC radio journalist, Chris Nicholls, was sentenced on 19 April 1993 to four months' jail by Judge David Taylor of the Adelaide District Court for refusing to reveal the source of bank documents which he said had been given to him in confidence. Nicholls had been asked to name the source the previous week, during a trial in which he was acquitted of charges of false impersonation and false pretences.

During the trial the prosecution alleged that Nicholls had impersonated Mr Jim Stitt, the partner of a South Australian government minister, Barbara Wiese, to obtain the bank documents. Nicholls had been conducting an investigation into whether Wiese was involved in a conflict of interest over the introduction of poker machines.

Despite the not guilty verdict the prosecution argued that Nicholls had interfered in the legal process by refusing to identify someone who might have committed a criminal offence, and in passing sentence Judge Taylor said: 'This court will not accept an undertaking not to disclose criminal behaviour'. He said Nicholls would be released from jail if he revealed his source.[5]

In each of these cases the journalist was placed in a no-win situation. Barrass, Budd and Nicholls were all bound by the Australian journalists' code of ethics to respect all confidences given to them in the course of their work.[6] However, the law does not recognise the right of journalists to remain silent. Priests, doctors and lawyers are not compelled to reveal what they have been told by their clients but that privilege is not extended to journalists. If ordered by a court to do so a journalist must reveal his or her source or face the consequences. The three journalists who were jailed had the choice of betraying the confidence of a source, thus breaking their code of ethics and facing disciplinary action by their peers, or, on the other hand, breaking the law and facing fines or prison. As they saw it they had a duty to honour their obligation to their sources, and no alternative except to go to jail.

Pros and Cons

Journalists have good reasons for refusing to compromise over this principle. In the first place it would be largely self-defeating to do so. The journalist who betrays a confidence loses credibility. Word gets around that he is not to be trusted. His news contacts desert him, and his usefulness as a news gatherer is extremely limited.

There is an equally cogent argument that the public will be deprived of important information if journalists are forced to say where it came from. Stories about corruption, incompetence, injustice and other social wrongs come from people who, for their own protection, insist that they must not be identified as the source. Exposure would lay the whistle-blowers wide open to official or unofficial reprisals — intimidation, dismissal and, in the worst cases, violence or death threats. Journalists must therefore be able to guarantee that their sources will remain anonymous. If they cannot do so their 'inside' sources will dry up and the public will be denied information it needs to know.

The other side of the argument is that the courts would in some cases be unable to arrive at the truth if journalists refused to disclose the sources of their information. If witnesses answered questions only as they saw fit the administration of justice would become impossible. This point was emphasised by the Western Australian Law Reform Commission in 1980 when it recommended against giving journalists a statutory right to withhold sources of information given to them in confidence. The commission said the refusal of a journalist to disclose a source in a defamation case could deny the court evidence of the truth or falsity of the alleged libel or the degree of malice involved. The consequences of withholding the information in criminal cases could be much worse, since it could result in the denial of evidence essential for the conviction of a person on a serious charge, or more importantly, for his acquittal.[7]

Similar difficulties could arise if journalists refused to divulge sources of their information in evidence to Royal Commissions, parliamentary committees and other tribunals set up to investigate allegations of political or social abuse or other areas of public concern. 'If the investigating body had no coercive power to get at the truth material facts would remain uncovered, public anxiety would be unallayed and any abuses would remain unremedied.'[8]

The commission said that the public's entitlement to accurate information had to be balanced against other claims such as national security and the right of individuals to protection of their reputation and privacy. It commented:

> The public interest is not synonymous with whatever the public finds interesting, nor is the question of what is proper to publish a matter for the exclusive judgement of the media itself. The enactment of a journalists' privilege could encourage informants to leak information which should not be published, as well as informaion which should. It might be difficult for the media, or at least some sections of it, to resist the temptation to publish such information.[9]

The commission was not convinced that the public's knowledge of events was advanced by the publication of material obtained from unidentified sources. It stated: 'It is difficult, if not impossible, to assess properly the accuracy of purported information unless the identity of the person is disclosed so that his reliability and knowledge of the subject can be evaluated.'[10]

Journalists admit that the convention of confidentiality is open to abuse. Under the cloak of anonymity an unscrupulous informant could spread lies and half truths. Likewise, an unethical journalist could fabricate comments by an unnamed and non-existent source to enliven a story or give seeming substance to a speculative 'think-piece'. However, the scope for that kind of blatant dishonesty is rare. Journalists learn from experience which contacts can be trusted to give them accurate information and editors and sub-editors have a nose for the suspiciously fanciful and unverifiable stories that occasionally come their way. Moreover, in most news reports the sources are identified by name and title and often by background. Journalists are taught during training that this is essential if readers or listeners are to judge what weight should be given to the information provided by the source.

One of the reasons why confrontations between journalists and the courts rarely occur is that there are not many cases in which the journalist's source is relevant to the outcome of the case. A second possibility, mentioned by the Western Australian Law Reform Commission, is that even when penalties for contempt for non-disclosure are imposed they do not work. Knowing that a journalist will adhere to the code of ethics and go to jail rather than reveal a source, the parties to proceedings may feel it is pointless to press the matter.[11]

Third, governments may be reluctant to force the issue in Royal Commissions and other inquiries because they prefer not to appear to be attacking the press. Knowing the power of the media to retaliate, they would see little value in making a martyr out of an uncooperative journalist.

There is some sympathy in legal circles for the view that journalists should have a statutory right to protect their sources of information. Nevertheless, courts and other tribunals have fined and jailed journalists whenever, in their view, the refusal to reveal a source has obstructed their inquiries. For example, in 1939 the then editor of the *Truth* newspaper in Melbourne, Frank McGuinness, refused to disclose to a Royal Commission the source of information for his articles alleging that unspecified members of parliament were being bribed to stop the passage of two bills through the parliament.[12] McGuinness was convicted of an offence under the Evidence Act and fined £15. His appeal to the High Court was rejected and subsequently, in its report to the Victorian parliament, the commission accused him of hampering their investigations. It must have seemed a poor reward to a man whose stated objective was to bring to public notice evidence of political corruption.

However, in dismissing McGuinness's appeal the court made clear that neither a journalist's conscience, code of ethics nor good intentions would absolve him from the obligation to give evidence considered necesary for the purpose of arriving at the truth. One of the judges, Judge Dixon, said:

No one doubts that editors and journalists are at times made the repositories of special confidences which, from motives of interest as well as of honour, they would preserve from public disclosure, if it were possible. But the law was faced at a comparatively early stage of the growth of the rules of evidence with the question how to resolve the inevitable conflict between the necessity of discovering the truth in the interests of justice on the one hand and on the other the obligation of secrecy or confidence which an individual called upon to testify may in good faith have undertaken to a party or other person. Except in a few relations where paramount considerations of general policy appeared to require that there should be a special privilege, such as husband and wife, attorney and client, communications between jurors, and by statute, physician and patient and priest and penitent, an inflexible rule was established that no obligation of honour, no duties of non-disclosure arising from the nature of a pursuit or calling, could stand in the way of the imperative necessity of revealing the truth in the witness box.[13]

It is in libel cases that journalists are usually subjected to the strongest pressure to divulge their sources of information. A number of Australian journalists have been fined for refusing to do so. Their non-cooperation has also increased the risk of heavy libel damages being awarded against their news organisations.

Plaintiffs and their counsel can argue — and judges have sometimes agreed — that the truth or falsity of defamatory statements can only be tested if the source is revealed and is subject to cross-examination. Moreover, a judge may direct that unless the source is identified the jury is entitled to believe that it is either unreliable or does not exist. If no credence is given to the source it follows that the defendant newspaper will be unable to rely on the defence of fair comment or to demonstrate the truth and public benefit of the matters reported. Heavy damages and costs could ensue because of the difficulty of establishing a sound defence.

Journalists have usually received little sympathy from the judiciary when refusing to give evidence on ethical grounds. For instance, when the Sydney *Sun's* state political reporter, Joe Buchanan, refused to identify his informant in a defamation case in 1964 he was directed to appear before the Full Supreme Court, which found him guilty of contempt and fined him $300.

It was urged on Buchanan's behalf that he had to choose between breaking the law and breaking his code of ethics; between his duty to the litigants and his duty to his informant. But the court stated that litigants could not be constrained by the private codes of strangers, and added:

> If the law of the land is to rule it follows, of necessity, that the courts which administer the law must not be impeded in the performance of that function by any who give their allegiance, however sincerely, to the private codes of minorities, however admirable those codes may for other purposes be.[14]

Buchanan was fortunate. The AJA paid for the costs of his defence and the newspaper paid his fine. And as the judges told him, they considered the penalty lenient. In ordinary circumstances, they said, they would have sent him to jail until he purged his contempt by answering the questions that had been directed at him. They added that any similar offence in future would not be dealt with as 'tenderly'.[15]

Twelve years later, on 17 November 1976, the Supreme Court of the Australian Capital Territory punished another defiant journalist for withholding information in a defamation case brought by the chairman of Qantas, Sir Lennox Hewitt, against *The West Australian* newspaper.

The journalist, Tony Warton, was asked during cross-examination for the names of people who had supplied the allegedly defamatory information for his article, but he persistently refused, saying that he was bound by his code of honour not to do so.

Mr Justice Franki said he appeciated the difficulty in which the journalist found himself and he had tried to find a solution which would not impede the rights of either party in the case. However, no solution had emerged and the journalist was in contempt of court. Nevertheless, Judge Franki said no useful purpose could be served by imprisonment since the question the journalist had refused to answer had not been pressed by the plaintiff's counsel. He imposed a fine of $500.[16]

'The Newspaper Rule'

The law has gone part of the way towards recognising the desirability of protecting journalists' sources of information by applying what has become known as 'the newspaper rule'. This principle originated in the practice of the English common law courts of refusing to compel the defendant newspaper in defamation proceedings to reveal the source of its story before the trial took place. As barrister and *Australian Law Journal* editor, J. G. Starke, points out, the commonly accepted rationale for the rule was the need to discourage plaintiffs from making a fishing expedition for other possible targets for a defamation action.[17]

However, in practice the newspaper rule gives journalists only limited protection from the obligation to give evidence about their sources. Judges generally regard the rights of litigants as more important than the rights of journalists to maintain the confidentiality of their informants. They will usually direct journalists to name their sources in either pre-trial or trial proceedings if, in their view, it is 'in the interests of justice'.

The Australian Press Council takes the view that the judiciary have been over-zealous in protecting the rights of plaintiffs, to the detriment of the public's right to information.[18] By way of example it cites the case of foreign affairs commentator Peter Hastings, who was ordered by three courts to reveal the sources of his information for a series of articles alleging corruption by Eduardo Cojuangco and other close associates of ex-President Marcos of the Philippines.

The article, published in *The Sydney Morning Herald* in February 1985, stated that Marcos and his associates, including the millionaire Cojuangco, had squandered $9 billion of the Philippines foreign debt.

Hastings attributed the information to 'a senior American bank official and prominent local businessman'. Several months later Cojuangco, who owned land in New South Wales, asked the New South Wales Supreme Court to order Hastings to identify the banker, the bank and the businessman to allow him to sue them for defamation. Judge Hunt directed him to reveal his source and his decision was subsequently upheld by the New South Wales Court of Appeal and again, in October 1988, by five judges of the High Court. The High Court held that the order was necessary to provide Cojuangco with 'an effective remedy in respect of the actionable wrong of which he complains'. It said his reputation could be gravely compromised by imputations attributed to the source mentioned in the publication.

Hastings' refusal to identify his sources exposed him to the threat of a jail sentence, and the Press Council, the AJA and prominent journalists around the world expressed outrage at the court's decision. The main objections were highlighted by the *Australian Law Journal* editor, J. G. Starke, QC. They were:

1. The decision would mean the compulsory disclosure of sources of information even before the commencement of a trial and this would be intimidating and unjust to newspapers faced with defamation proceedings;
2. The High Court's approach would disastrously undermine the free flow of information. For instance, whistleblowers in the public service would be deterred from drawing attention to incompetence and corruption on the part of superiors. Other people would be discouraged from supplying vital information

to the media if their privacy or anonymity could not be guaranteed.[19]

Why did Cojuangco, a Philippines citizen, press his case in Australia rather than in the Philippines courts? One reason suggested by media commentator David Bowman was that Cojuangco's reputation had not counted for much in the Philippines since his friend, the erstwhile President Marcos, had been driven from power. On 1 August 1988 *The Age* reported that the Philippines Government had brought a civil action against 44 people, alleging that they had helped Cojuangco, 'an ally of the deposed president', to enrich himself through his political connections. In this and two other civil actions the government sought a total of 101 billion pesos ($A7 billion) damages. Other reports indicated that Cojuangco was under investigation by a government anti-corruption body in the Philippines. All this, Bowman noted, seemed to have passed over the heads of the Australian High Court; in commenting on the damage that might be done to Cojuangco's reputation, they had virtually overlooked the realities of the Philippines revolution.[20]

An even more disturbing feature of the case was that the courts were, in effect, asking Hastings to 'rat' on his informants and expose them to the risk of reprisals. When the New South Wales Supreme Court first ruled in Cojuangco's favour Marcos was still in power. As Bowman noted, Hastings was being ordered to identify the critics of 'a notoriously corrupt president and his clique, who would use any methods to say in power'.[21] Naming them could have exposed them to physical danger even if they did not become the target of a libel action.

The final episode in the Cojuangco case was played out when the publishers of *The Sydney Morning Herald*, John Fairfax and Sons, gave an undertaking that they would not call Hastings as a defence witness in any subsequent defamation proceedings. This meant that the newspaper could no longer rely on the defence that what Hastings had written was in the public interest (the defence of qualified privilege). By withdrawing Hastings from the firing line the newspaper weakened its defence but relieved him of the obligation to name his informants and break his code.

The case produced what Melbourne libel lawyers Grant Hattam and Stephen Maloney called 'a bizarre situation'. If a plaintiff in a libel case sought preliminary disclosure of a journalist's source he would not obtain a court order if he had an effective remedy against the newspaper and/or the journalist. However, where it appeared that the newspaper had a strong defence then the court could order disclosure of the journalist's source of information 'in the interests of justice'. It was therefore in the plaintiff's interest to demonstrate to a court when making application for disclosure that he did not have an effective right of action against the newspaper. It was also in the newspaper's interest to show that the plaintiff already had an effective remedy against it. Hattam and Maloney noted: 'It's a weird situation when the parties to an action try to demonstrate the weaknesses of their case'.[22]

While the High Court was considering the Cojuangco case three journalists working for *The Herald* in Melbourne — William Hitchings, Anne-Marie McCarthy and Penelope Debelle — were ordered by Justice Gobbo of the Victorian Supreme Court to reveal their sources of information for an article about a state government investigation into the affairs of the Guide Dog Owners' and Friends Association, which had been published on 8 December 1987. The association strongly denied the allegations in the article and its associate director, Phyllis Gration, said she believed *The Herald* had been tipped off by a source in the Attorney-General's Department or the Corporate Affairs Office. The association wanted to know the sources so that it could sue them as well as *The Herald* for defamation.[23]

Justice Gobbo agreed that disclosure was necessary in the interests of justice. However, his decision was later overturned by the Full Supreme Court. The judges ruled that once *The Herald* had dropped its defences and thus cleared the path for being sued there was no longer any need for the association to sue anyone else. Therefore, there was no need for the journalists to name their source.[24]

Royal Commissions

Royal Commissions, parliamentary committees and other tribunals will sometimes excuse journalists from the obligation to identify sources if it can be shown that the information is not essential or can be obtained from other sources. This was the approach adopted by the Vassall tribunal in England in 1963. The tribunal had been set up by parliament to investigate the circumstances in which offences under the Official Secrets Act had been committed by an Admiralty clerk, William Vassall, who had been convicted of spying for the Russians.

Among the matters considered by the tribunal were newspaper reports that Vassall was a known homosexual and that because this allegedly made him susceptible to blackmail he should never have been employed on secret work. A number of journalists called before the tribunal refused to name the sources of the information for stories they had written. Three of them were sentenced by the High Court for contempt — Desmond Clough and Reginald Foster of the *News Chronicle* for six months and Brendan Mulholland of the *Daily Mail* for three months, although Clough was spared jail when his source in the Admiralty identified himself as the supplier of the information.

Other journalists who declined to name their sources were not pressed to do so. The tribunal explained that this was because most of the published statements were either beyond the fringe of what was relevant to the inquiry or could be obtained from official and other easily accessible sources.[25]

Royal Commissions in Australia have seldom attempted to compel journalists to reveal their sources for the simple reason that it does not usually work. Fining or jailing journalists will not make them talk. Nevertheless, every now and again an uncooperative journalist is punished as a warning to others.

For instance, in 1981 author and journalist Richard Hall was fined $1000 for refusing to name the source of his information to Mr Justice Stewart's Royal Commission into corruption. Hall had learned from one of his police contacts that two important witnesses, both women, were being flown out from London to give evidence to the commission about the activities of the 'Mr Asia' drugs syndicate. One was a former drugs courier and the other had been the lover of one of the alleged leaders of the syndicate. When they arrived in Sydney Hall tipped off *The Sydney Morning Herald's* chief-of-staff, Ian Frickberg, who assigned a reporter to cover the story.

The witnesses were brought out under police escort because of fears that they would be 'got at' or silenced. The commission also planned to take evidence from them in private, for their own protection. Mr Justice Stewart was furious when the story got out, and worried that it might endanger the security of the commission. He directed Hall to appear before him and examined him closely about the identity of his source. But Hall refused to capitulate and at one point caused nervous laughter among lawyers at the

bar table when he said he would not respond to 'salami questioning' technique. This sounded dangerously like 'slimy
questioning' and raised the judicial eyebrow until Hall's lawyers
explained what it meant. Salami questioning was a way of
obtaining information through the process of elimination: you
cut off a slice here and another there until eventually there was
only one slice left to give — only one possible answer.[26]

Hall's $1000 fine and the legal costs of his defence were paid
from the proceeds of functions organised by his supporters and
the AJA. However, in retrospect it is difficult to see what purpose
was served by punishing him. Knowing the identity of Hall's
informant could not have advanced the commission's investigation
into drug running and corruption. Nor could the commission
show that the story based on Hall's information had in any way
frustrated or impeded its inquiries. In fact, as the AJA's federal
president, John Lawrence, pointed out, the matter was considered
so unimportant by Mr Justice Stewart that it did not rate a mention
in any of his voluminous reports.[27]

The use of federal and state police to search for evidence of
journalists' sources has added salt to the wounds caused by court-
imposed penalties. Police have searched newspaper offices and
journalists' homes and confiscated notebooks and other work
materials in attempts to discover the identity of informants. Such
raids have usually stiffened the resistance of journalists rather than
coercing them into capitulating. Nevertheless, as the following
cases show, there is growing concern over police actions, directed
from above, to force disclosure.

On 20 May 1988 the West Australian police raided the offices
of *The Daily News* in Perth in an attempt to discover the source of
a document relating to the management of the Burswood Casino.
The document related to the investments of many small shareholders in the casino and the journalist involved, M. B. Saxon,
refused to say how he had obtained it. He was supported by
senior executives of the newspaper, who took the view that
the raid was 'an intimidatory tactic' and protested to the Press
Council.[28]

On 5 July 1990 federal police raided the Sydney offices of *The
Australian Financial Review* as part of an investigation into alleged
breaches of the Crimes Act by a Commonwealth public servant.
Armed with a search warrant, two detectives spent two hours
going through the desk of journalist Ian Rogers for documents
and other material relating to reports on the privatisation of the

Housing Loans Insurance Corporation. They also seized Rogers' notebooks. The warrant referred to 'reasonable grounds' for believing that a Commonwealth officer had disclosed information, an offence under section 70 of the Crimes Act, which carried a maximum penalty of two years' jail.[29]

However, the circumstances did not seem to warrant that kind of a witch-hunt. As the Australian Press Council pointed out in a letter of protest to the then Prime Minister, Bob Hawke, the person whom the police were trying to identify had leaked a document which was not confidential and involved neither national security considerations nor the commission of a crime involving serious life or injury.[30] The council described the police raid as 'an unwarranted misuse of State power' and *The Australian Financial Review's* editor-in-chief, Peter Robinson, said it had 'all the hallmarks of overkill — an extremely heavy-handed pursuit of a bureaucratic problem'.[31]

On 12 December 1992 federal police raided the offices of *The Canberra Times* in search of information that might identify a 'whistle-blower' who had leaked details of the Australian Capital Territory government's health budget. In an editorial the next day the newspaper accused the ACT government of 'an adolescent exercise in futility' and 'an authoritarian approach to public administration'. It said the government had sought to intimidate its own public servants to reduce the flow of information.

In reply, Greg Ellis, a senior press adviser to the ACT government, said the police were merely investigating a breach of the law relating to disclosure by public servants of confidential government information. He said no one seriously questioned the right of journalists to protect their sources but the notion that this right was 'inviolable' and not to be tested by law could never be in the best interests of a democratic community.[32]

On 27 January 1993 a posse of about 12 federal police raided the offices of *The Age* and *The Weekly Times* in Melbourne and seized material which they hoped would lead them to a report by the Australian Bureau of Crime Intelligence. The report had been the basis for a series of articles alleging that organised crime groups had used the meat industry as a cover for various criminal activities, including money laundering, drug trafficking, fraud, corruption, arms dealing, standover of Asian restaurants and possible meat substitution rackets.

The police searched the offices of the head of *The Age* Insight

team, David Wilson, and his colleague, Jo Chandler, and the editor
of *The Weekly Times*, Stephen Cooper. Later they searched the
homes of Wilson and Cooper. They seized copies of the leaked
report, computer disks, audio tapes and other material.

Search warrants were also served on *The Age* editor, Alan
Kohler, the secretary of the Australasian Meat Industry Employees'
Union, Wally Curran, a Kew private detective, Greg Hooper, and
the federal National Party MP for Gippsland, Peter McGauran,
who had raised the issue of meat industry corruption in the federal
parliament in October 1991.

According to the officers who led the raids, they were seeking
evidence against a National Crimes Authority officer who had
leaked information to the media.[33]

The Age obtained a temporary injunction stopping the police
from using the material. Later, however, the Federal Court ratified
an agreement between the paper and the police which allowed
the police to have access to the material but only in the presence
of the newspaper's legal advisers.

It is difficult to see what the police achieved in any of these
four situations. The raids gave the impression that the police were
barging in like stormtroopers but did not achieve their stated
purpose. They forced journalists to yield up documents but not
the names of their informants. As fishing expeditions they were
a waste of time.

Shield Laws

The recurrence of such raids and the draconian penalties handed
out by the courts have led to renewed pressure by the Media,
Entertainment and Arts Alliance and the Australian Press Council
for legislation to exempt journalists from the requirement to disclose their sources. Following the jailing of Tony Barrass and Joe
Budd, the Press Council chairman, Professor David Flint, called
for shield laws similar to those in Sweden, Austria and 26 states
of the USA. This would mean that journalists would no longer
be liable to fines or jail if they refused, on ethical grounds, to
identify their informants. Nevertheless, the media could still be
held responsible, both at civil and criminal law, for what was
published, and the courts would not be obliged to accept the truth
of statements attributed to confidential sources.

Flint argued against following the example of British reforms, which had been progressively watered down by judicial interpretation. He suggested that before a journalist could be compelled to reveal a source the court should first establish that:

- there was reasonable cause to believe that the journalist had information that was clearly relevant to a specific and serious violation of the criminal law;
- the information sought could not be obtained by alternative means that were less destructive of freedom of the press;
- there was a compelling and overriding need for the information sought.[34]

Earlier proposals that journalists should have an absolute privilege to withhold their sources from any court, Royal Commission or official inquiry met with strong resistance from federal and state Attorneys-General and from sections of the judiciary and legal profession. There is still little sympathy for the idea. The courts continually reaffirm the principle that the interests of justice must take priority over the ethical rules by which journalists consider themselves bound. Judges stress the elementary rule of justice that people facing trial or seeking redress in a civil action are entitled to know the names of their accusers or traducers. As Doogue notes, experience in America has shown that a defendant's right to a fair trial can be seriously eroded by a gag that would prevent his accuser from being cross-examined by counsel before a judge and jury.[35]

David Flint's proposal was designed to deal with the problem. As he saw it, journalists should be required to disclose their sources only if, in the courts' view, the circumstances were 'compelling' and 'overriding' and the information could not be obtained in any other way. This would seem to go a long way towards satisfying the individual citizen and the general public that the needs of justice were being served, and were not being frustrated by overly rigid adherence to journalists' ethical principles. However, whether Flint's criteria for disclosure and non-disclosure could work in practice would again depend on how they were interpreted by the courts. Would the media always accept the judicial view of what were 'compelling circumstances', and what would be the attitude of informants if they knew that their anonymity could not be guaranteed by journalists when 'the interests of justice' required disclosure?

Another objection to granting an absolute privilege is that it would enable unscrupulous journalists to publish a false or exaggerated account of events, secure in the knowledge that no judicial inquiry could compel them to disclose their sources. Moreover, unscrupulous informants could spread lies and mis-information for their own advantage in the knowledge that the journalist's oath of confidentiality would shield them from exposure.

The Press Council has argued that any danger of fabrication by journalists is minimal because codes of ethics and peer assess-ment are adequate controls on unethical behaviour.[36] However, as a number of commentators have noted, the concealment of sources does provide opportunities for deception. The refusal to disclose a source may simply hide the reality that no bona fide source actually exists and that the story was derived from un-verified rumours or a vivid imagination.

The council has acknowledged the difficulty of establishing the authenticity of material obtained from anonymous sources. It has also criticised the publication of unsubstantiated allegations and innuendoes under the cloak of confidentiality. For instance, in July 1985 the council rebuked *The Sydney Morning Herald* for publishing an allegation by an unidentified informant about the former New South Wales stipendiary magistrate, Murray Farquhar.

Farquhar had been jailed for four years after being found guilty of attempting to pervert the course of justice. Nevertheless, the court upheld a complaint by a former newspaper editor, Mr R. S. Harvey, that part of *The Sydney Morning Herald* story was an un-warranted slur on Farquhar's wartime service record and would be seen by many readers as 'a case of kicking a man when he is down'. The council commented:

> The fact that a man is in gaol with part of his reputation in tatters, and in no position to defend himself, does not diminish a paper's duty of fairness. If anything it would increase it. The story itself suggests that, whatever he may have done after-wards, Mr Farquhar's war record was something in which he could continue to take pride. To besmirch it with no better authority than the 'suspicion' of a 'cynical' acquaintance whose identity the paper was 'not at liberty to disclose' was harsh indeed.[37]

The council said that the newspaper's right to use material from confidential sources did not justify the publication of every rumour that someone was prepared to spread but not stand by.

It added: 'In the present case it is difficult to see what public interest was served by according a cynical acquaintance of Mr Farquhar the privilege of ventilating his hurtful suspicion under the cloak of anonymity.'[38]

In a subsequent case the council cast a jaundiced eye over a report in *The Daily Telegraph*, Sydney, which attributed an allegation against members of the federal parliament to an unnamed steward in the Members' Bar at Parliament House. The report, under the byline Col Mackay, was headed 'Is the national capital a city of rorts? Canberra's good life and who foots the bill!'. The final paragraph read:

> A steward in the Members' Bar at Parliament House had a far better grip of the situation when he told me over an off-duty drink: 'The local coppers might have a bad record for solving crimes, but most of the crimes being planned by pollies in the members' bar could never be solved'.[39]

That one paragraph caused the stewards to place a temporary ban on refreshment services to journalists in the parliamentary press gallery, and as a result Wilma Spence, the Deputy Industrial Registrar in Canberra, was called in to mediate in the dispute. Spence told the council that the stewards were extremely conscious of the confidentiality required in their position and resented what they considered as a slur on their integrity and fidelity to parliament.

In support of the complaint the seven permanent stewards employed in the Members' Bar each made an affidavit denying knowledge of or friendship with Mackay or being the person referred to in the article.

A journalist with the National Media Liaison Service, Geoff Sorby, gave evidence at a mediation conference that Mackay had told him that he had gathered the information two months earlier from a friend in Sydney who had been talking to a bar steward from Parliament House. Mackay said Sorby must have misunderstood him. He stood firm on what he had written and refused to reveal his source.

Without the power to compel the giving of evidence or to test it by cross-examination, the council could not resolve the conflict in the case. It was unable to establish the identity or reliability of Mackay's source. However, the council said it could see no justification in publishing the statement attributed to a steward. Censuring *The Daily Telegraph* it said:

The quoted statement is so vague that it provides no useful information and, if it is to be given any meaning, serves only to smear politicians generally with an allegation of criminality and to taint the stewards generally with responsibility for the smear. This is unfair to both groups.[40]

As some of the foregoing cases illustrate, the journalistic ethic of confidentiality may sometimes work for and sometimes against the interests of the general community. Clearly, the community could be deprived of useful and sometimes crucial information if journalists were unable to protect the anonymity of 'inside' sources. But equally, the community has as much to lose if the convention of confidentiality is deliberately used by the source or the journalist to spread lies, disinformation or vindictive rumours. Moreover, it can be argued that in some circumstances the full truth may be made known, and justice done, only if the courts are able to identify and test the veracity of journalists' sources.

For journalists the risks are as great as the benefits. If they reveal a confidential source they can be censured, fined or even expelled by their union for having breached their professional ethics code. For refusing to do so they can be jailed for contempt of court. They are damned if they do and damned if they don't, so to speak.

One of the rewards is the additional information to be gained by protecting the anonymity of sources. Exclusive stories come from contacts who prefer not to be named. However, the countervailing risk is that some people may use the cloak of anonymity offered by journalists to peddle lies or half truths. Moreover, it is the journalist who usually carries the blame for misleading information planted by the covert source, who is safe from censure because he or she cannot be identified. As media commentator Rodney Tiffen points out:

If sources publicly say something foolish or problematic then any resulting odium normally attaches to them. But when the source remains private the news organisation and reporter are held centrally responsible for the content. If details or nuances are slightly wrong it is easier for those offended by the story to discredit it, especially if it cannot be confirmed by the covert source.[41]

From the point of view of the covert source — the whistle-blower — the main risk is that his or her cover will be blown, possibly leading to dismissal, or an even nastier form of retribution may follow. The politician who is identified as the source of a leak may lose the trust and goodwill of colleagues or be demoted from Cabinet. He is also likely to be laughed at for being found out.

As Tiffen points out, misunderstandings sometimes arise over whether informants want their comments to be used but not attributed, or intend only to provide reporters with background information.[42] Former Prime Minister Malcolm Fraser was sorely embarrassed when casual criticisms which he made to journalists on his VIP plane about President Carter's handling of the United States economy subsequently appeared in print as 'the Prime Minister believes . . .'.[43]

Misunderstandings are inevitable but what the anonymous informant expects is that the journalist will not deliberately break the convention of confidentiality, even under pressure by courts or Royal Commissions. Some journalists believe there are exceptions, for instance if they learn that the source has deliberately misled them for personal gain.[44]

Editors have also sometimes insisted on knowing journalists' confidential sources before they will authorise publication of stories.[45] Their rationale is that they need to be absolutely sure of the reliability of the source, and may have to disclose the source if the law requires it in a libel case, or if it is necessary to set the record straight.[46] However, most journalists remain extremely reluctant to surrender to editors, or to any other news executive, their right to make independent contractual arrangements with sources. One obvious reason is that editors are not required to be union members and are therefore not bound by the journalists' code of ethics. Moreover, the informant who trusts an individual journalist because a good relationship has been built up between them will not necessarily trust an editor with the same kind of information. Why should the informant if the editor pays lip service to the principle of confidentiality yet reserves the right to divulge the source?

The anonymous source knows that the more people who are aware of his or her identity the greater the risk that it will be revealed. He or she needs to be sure that the terms of the agreement are not only clear but will be consistently observed by the reporter, chief-of-staff, editor or whoever else happens to be a party to it. If that undertaking cannot be given the agreement is worthless.

Bearing in mind that journalists attach so much importance to the principle of confidentiality it is hardly surprising that they lose credibility on the rare occasions that they depart from it. One such case occurred on 7 December 1990 when political journalists in Canberra reported a speech by the then Treasurer, Paul Keating, to the annual Press Gallery dinner.

By tradition the dinner was supposed to be an off-the-record affair. Television cameras were not allowed and it was understood that the guest could speak frankly without fear of being reported and that journalists could also relax with the pollies over the port and cigars and not worry about rushing to meet story deadlines. However, on this occasion the choicest parts of Keating's speech, in which he described himself as 'the Placido Domingo of Australian politics' and implied that only he had the capacities to lead the Australian Labor Party to victory in the next election, were reported by several Sunday newspaper journalists who had not been at the dinner but had learned about the comments from other sources.

Keating had made no secret of his impatience to be prime minister and his comments were interpreted as a thinly veiled criticism of the incumbent, Bob Hawke, and as part of a renewed challenge for the leadership. They were more widely reported by the print and and electronic media the next day. As the convention of confidentiality had already been breached by the Sunday newspapers other Canberra journalists had the perfect excuse for saying it no longer applied.

Keating was reportedly furious that the media had broken the rules, and as the president of the Canberra Press Gallery, Don Woolford, later admitted, the tradition of confidentiality could not count for much if the gallery could not keep it.

Some of Woolford's colleagues were convinced that Keating expected his remarks to be reported, though perhaps not as fully, or in the form in which they appeared. They argued that because Keating was manipulating the gallery the media were entitled to tell the public what he was doing. Woolford was not persuaded by this rationalisation, and said the breach of the tradition was wrong on ethical grounds. Nevertheless, he acknowledged that it was uncharacteristically naive of Keating if he really believed that the kind of remarks he had made to a room packed with journalists would remain totally within the four walls of the building.[47]

According to Keating's press secretary, Greg Turnbull, Keating was upset because his comments were taken out of context and 'beaten up' — not because they were reported. 'To pretend that a room full of 200 journalists is going to regard everything as off the record is a bit unrealistic,' he said.

> The off-the-record arrangement has usually been honoured in the years when the speakers have not said anything particularly newsworthy. When the speaker says something newsworthy it's reported. A lot of journalists who attend the dinner do comply with the rule, but some never attend and always report what's said. They pick up the information elsewhere and absolve themselves from any ethical dilemma by reporting second hand what they have heard. If clever ploys can be used to get around the rule what's it worth, anyway. Frankly, I think the notion that the dinner is not reportable is fanciful and ought to be ignored.[48]

Since the reporting of Keating's remarks at the 1990 dinner no one has really believed that the off-the-record convention can be made to stick. As one reporter explained: 'There's no point in having the rule if we adhere to it only when there is no story. In one-to-one deals the reporter will honour the obligation but there are practical difficulties in making everyone stick to a promise when a hundred or more people are involved.'

Any residual loyalty to the tradition seemed pointless when in 1992 the guest speaker at the dinner, Keating's close friend, Senator Graham Richardson, voluntarily went on the record. Ostentatiously, Richardson put a switched-on tape recorder in front of him as he began talking and explained that it was there because he wanted to make sure that the journalists present quoted him correctly. This was naturally taken as an invitation to report him, which he fully expected, and most journalists did so. Press gallery president Don Woolford was from that point on entitled to think that the convention had become obsolete since both sides had departed from it.

Yet the central ethical issue is whether journalists are going consistently to observe the principle of confidentiality or only when it suits their own purposes. Clearly, there will continue to be situations in which they will be tempted to disclose sources of information, either because they realise that they have been misled, or because they are under pressure from an editor or a court or a Royal Commission. Most journalists, however, have resisted the pressure. Experience has shown it to be the risky way, but it is also the ethical way.

CHAPTER 8

Misleading Appearances, Deceit and Subterfuge

Journalists divide into two camps on the question of whether clandestine methods of news gathering are justified. One group asserts that using concealed cameras and hidden tape recorders to obtain information is morally wrong and ought to be punished and condemned. The other group argues that undercover methods are sometimes necessary to root out evidence of corruption and inefficiency by government officials and other people in public life. Deception may be deplorable, they admit, but sometimes the ends justify the means.

The more pragmatic approach was put to the test in the New South Wales Supreme Court in the first week of April 1988 when television journalist Michael Willesee and members of his Trans Media Production Company faced 12 charges of illegally making secret tape recordings.

Four of the charges were proven. They related to tape recordings of a conversation on 15 January 1986 between David Miller, proprietor of the Talent Scouts model agency, and one of Willesee's researchers, Jaqui Donaldson, who had posed as a young aspirant for a modelling career.

The court was told that Willesee's television program had received a number of complaints about Miller's operations. However, in passing judgement on the case Mr Justice Finlay rejected the idea that secret tape recording could be justified on the ground that it was the only way of obtaining information of public interest. He commented:

> If the means are illegal, then they are not justifiable by the ends that a corporation or person may have in mind. The invasion of privacy. . .is not excused because it was done in the cause of investigative journalism. I agree with the observation . . . that electronic surveillance is the greatest leveller of human privacy ever known.[1]

Donaldson was convicted under the Listening Devices Act for having secretly taped a private conversation in which she had taken part, and she was fined $500. The Trans Media production company, of which Willesee was a director, was found guilty of causing the illegal tape to be made and of possessing it and broadcasting it, and was fined $25 000. The charges against Willesee, one of the program's reporters, Michael Munro, and a freelance sound recordist were found not proven.

Willesee left the court still smarting over the rather unflattering description of his role by his own lawyer, Peter Hely, QC. Hely had put it to the court that Willesee on air merely parroted what someone else had written. This had inspired an artist to paint a picture of a galah bearing the Channel Nine logo on the footpath outside the Supreme Court. A group of people believed to be from a rival television channel also paraded outside the court wearing Big Aussie Galah T-shirts.

Not amused, Willesee told the press he would have preferred a conviction to being labelled a parrot. Moreover, despite the heavy fine against his company he said if he found someone 'ripping people off' and there were no legal means of dealing with the situation he would break the law in the same way.[2]

Many journalists would agree with Willesee that deception is justified if the story is big enough and the information cannot be obtained in any other way. However, there is still room for disagreement about the kind of clandestine methods that should be used and the circumstances in which they should be used. For instance, some journalists would agree to the secret taping of conversations to detect corruption but would stop short at stealing documents to obtain equivalent information. Others would perhaps agree to the planting of suction microphones and other bugging devices but would feel hesitant about posing as a police officer or some other public official to gain access to places from which they would otherwise be excluded. Members of the general public, on the other hand, would probably object to any forms of deception by the media, especially as they are rarely given a sound rationale for covert behaviour.

The attitudes of Australian journalists to the use of hidden recording devices were measured in 1983 by a visiting American academic, Dr Tom Rood, head of the Journalism Department at the Central Michigan University. A total of 153 Australian editors and sub-editors working for 38 daily newspapers responded to Rood's survey. Of these, 41.5 per cent agreed that it would be ethical to use a hidden tape recorder to gather information on suspected underworld characters and 45.4 per cent disagreed. However, 76.9 per cent disapproved of hidden recorders being used to gather business material (10.5 per cent approved) and 72.4 per cent were against their use to gather political information. Moreover, 77.6 per cent thought it would be wrong to hide a tape recorder on a reporter posing as another person (only 16.5 per cent approved).[3]

Results of the survey suggest that Australian editors are more likely to agree to clandestine methods if the objective is to uncover evidence of crime and corruption, as indicated by the high positive response to the question about 'underworld characters'. Nevertheless, the survey also showed consistently high disapproval of the use of hidden devices, whatever the circumstances. Clearly, a lot of those questioned had qualms about the excuse that the ends sometimes justify deception.

Means and Ends

The argument that dishonesty of any kind is justified for the achievement of some greater good is difficult to sustain. In the first place not everyone accepts that the media as a whole or journalists as individuals are necessarily the best arbiters of what is or is not good for the public. Secondly, the critics argue that two wrongs do not make a right, and that journalists who use deception merely add to the general sum of immorality. As a former distinguished editor of *The Washington Post*, Ben Bradlee, put it: 'How can a newspaper fight for honesty and integrity when they themselves are less than honest in getting a story.'[4]

The reverse side of the coin is that some stories of vital importance to the public would not have been made known had the reporters been scrupulously honest in their news gathering methods. If all people were open in their dealings with the media there would be no problem and journalists would not have to answer dishonesty charges in court or face disciplinary action for breaches of their professional ethics code. However, the reality is that people in public life often go to extraordinary lengths to conceal information which could prove embarrassing or damaging to them but which the public has a right to know. In such circumstances journalists are tempted to use various forms of subterfuge to get at the truth. If they are caught doing it they could be fined, of if the boss disapproves, they could be sacked. If they try the honest approach they could be beaten to the story by their competitors, who may not be as ethically pure. Whatever they do could lead them into a no-win situation. As David Anderson and Peter Benjaminson say in their book, *Investigative Reporting*:

> The reporter is often left in the classical ethical dilemma: he's damned if he does and damned if he doesn't. By lying to the double dealing official the reporter will shock many people's sensibilities. But if the story doesn't appear, the corrupt official will continue to enrich himself at public expense.[5]

Even if they escape the rigours of the law, Australian journalists who engage in subterfuge risk being reprimanded, fined or, in the worst cases, expelled by the judiciary committee of their own union. Yet neither the journalists' section of the Media, Entertainment and Arts Alliance nor the Australian Press Council have laid down firm rules about undercover methods of news gathering.

At first glance the AJA's code of ethics seems to prohibit deception. Clause 7 of the code states that journalists 'shall use fair and honest means to obtain news, pictures, films, tapes and documents' and clause 8 that they 'shall identify themselves and their employers before obtaining any interview for publication or broadcast'.[6] However, the preamble to the code changes the emphasis from prohibited behaviour to permissible behaviour and clearly provides for circumstances when subterfuge and deceit may be used. This was acknowledged by the AJA Ethics Review Committee when it introduced the revised code in 1984. The committee commented:

> The new preamble, by stating that one of the overriding principles for journalists is the public's right to information, provides for the very rare occasions when the public interest may require activity which would normally be regarded as unethical. The main approach is that subterfuge and deceit are not justified in gaining a story.
>
> However, there can be — as instanced by both British and Australian Press Council decisions — occasions when subterfuge is justified as the only means by which information can be exposed in the public interest. Rather than try to qualify statements of principle which serve for 99.9 per cent of cases, it is suggested that a statement that journalists are committed to truth and the public's right to information is more appropriate.[7]

In similar vein, the Australian Press Council's statement of principles states that news obtained by dishonest or unfair means should not be published 'unless there is an over-riding public interest'.[8] To some observers this also seems indefinite and vague. However, the council's principles are flexible enough for the most blatant cases of dishonesty to be condemned and for subterfuge and deception to be defended if important news and pictures cannot be obtained in any other way.

Both the AJA and the Press Council have rejected public complaints about dishonesty by the news media when it seemed to them that the means were justified by the ends. One notable case, arbitrated by the Press Council in March 1983, involved a complaint by the Rajhneesh Organisation, also known as 'the Orange People', against a cadet reporter of the *Weekend News* in Perth. The reporter had posed as an unemployed person to find out whether a youth worker, Mrs J. Cornish, a member of the Rajhneesh group, was directing young people 'to a sect that preaches free love and destruction of the family unit'.[9] After interviewing Cornish the cadet passed on information to a senior reporter for an article published in the paper under the headline 'Young jobless led towards sect'. As a result of the article Cornish was suspended, though she was later reinstated.

The Press Council drew attention to an earlier adjudication by its counterpart, the British Press Council. The British tribunal said it generally deplored the use of subterfuge but added:

It recognises, however, that in the investigation of criminal and other misconduct little information would be obtained from the individuals concerned by police, journalists or others if they disclosed their true identity and purpose. Investigative journalism is a legitimate activity which has more than once served a useful public purpose. It may necessarily involve a degree of subterfuge on the part of those conducting it.[10]

The Australian council said it accepted those general principles but stressed that subterfuge should be a last resort and should be avoided 'in any personal interview for the purpose of using it for publication'. It said it could understand the motives of the *Weekend News* in the course it had followed but it was not possible for the council to determine whether there were reasonable alternatives to the subterfuge practised. However, no comments by Cornish during the interview had been published, only allegations about the topic of the conversation. On that ground the complaint was dismissed.[11]

Former associate professor in journalism at Deakin University, John Avieson, described another case in which a reporter was sent by his chief-of-staff to cover a meeting of a group of people who did not want their activities reported by the media. The reporter and his newspaper knew that the meeting was not open to the media. Nevertheless, the reporter sat in the body of the hall without revealing to anyone that he was gathering information for a story. When his report was published in a capital city newspaper the next day the group complained to the AJA that he had broken the AJA code of ethics by failing to identify himself while getting information for publication. However, when defending his actions the reporter was able to show the AJA's judiciary committee that the meeting was held for an illegal purpose and he argued — successfully, as it turned out — that lawbreakers should not seek the protection of the law to conceal their activities.[12]

Because of the difficulties which journalists often have to overcome to obtain information the AJA and Press Council probably err on the side of leniency when considering the methods used. It may be said that they are quicker to condone than to condemn. However, both stress that subterfuge of any kind should be the exception rather than the rule and they have come down heavily on offenders who were unable to demonstrate that the ends were important enough to justify the means.

Impersonation

The expulsion from the AJA of a photographer who posed as a doctor to get pictures of a hospital patient, mentioned in Chapter 5, is a case in point. It involved such a gross violation of the code of ethics that, in the view of the AJA judiciary committee, it could not be excused on the specious ground that the photographer had demonstrated extraordinary initiative in his pursuit of the story.

Another controversial case put a temporary blot on the escutcheon of the prestigious paper *The Sydney Morning Herald*. It also illustrates the dangers of editors and journalists relying on the public interest as a justification for duplicity.

The case came to public notice on 15 September 1988 when the New South Wales Minister for Education and Youth Affairs, Dr Metherell, attacked journalist Tony Hewett for posing as a high school student to obtain information for a series of articles titled 'Classroom: The Inside Story'. Metherell also accused the newspaper of conniving in what he called 'a tawdry exercise'.[13]

Replying to a question in the New South Wales parliament, Metherell said that on 10 August that year Hewett had approached the principal of a government high school to enrol as a Year 11 student. Hewett indicated that he had recently arrived in New South Wales from Western Australia where he had been a student at Kalamunda High School. He told the principal that his parents' marriage had broken up and that he had moved to Sydney to live with his married sister.

Dr Metherell said the principal had spoken at length with Hewett about his broken family, his career prospects and the difficulties of changing to another school system. That interview was 'the beginning of a trail of deceit'. Hewett had filled in an enrolment form at the school indicating that his date of birth was 13 March 1971, making him 17 years old. The form showed an address in Jones Street, Ultimo — which, said Metherell, was about the closest Hewett came to the truth regarding his identity.

Hewett had claimed not to have any other papers of identification because of the complication of his family break up and having to leave Western Australia, but he assured the school principal that they would be forthcoming. Subsequent checks showed no record of any Anthony Hewett being enrolled at Kalamunda High School in Western Australia.

The enrolment form was signed by Hewett's alleged sister, a Mrs Margo Kingston, as his guardian. Margo Kingston was the name of another journalist at *The Sydney Morning Herald*.

Dr Metherell said it was clear that Hewett was not solely interested in his studies. According to teachers he was regularly late for some classes, talkative, uncooperative and disruptive. Rumours abounded of the money he spent buying drinks for his Year 11 mates. He seemed to have an unusually large expense account for an average Year 11 student.

Dr Metherell said Hewett had deceived the principal, teaching staff and students. He had obtained the trust of his classmates by lying to them about who he was, how old he was, where he came from and where he was living. He had lied about why he had returned to school, about where he got the money to buy drinks for students and why he was spending time with them.

'One can imagine how the students would have felt when they read the story and had their trust betrayed by Mr Hewett', Dr Metherell said. 'He has taught them a sobering lesson on the ethics, or lack of them, of some members of the media. He has taught them that some will dispense with the truth in the pursuit of a story'.

Dr Metherell said that by encouraging a journalist to lie to the school principal, to provide false information to the Department of Education and to mislead teachers and students *The Sydney Morning Herald* had shown 'an extraordinary contempt for the truth' and 'an appalling lack of integrity, judgement and commitment to acceptable levels of professional ethics'. He said the newspaper had lied and deceived not once but repeatedly and should admit that its desperation for a story had allowed its ethics 'to be perverted and distorted in a most serious and damaging way'.[14]

Replying to Metherell, the newspaper's editor-in-chief, John Alexander, said *The Sydney Morning Herald* had not taken lightly the decision to have a journalist pose as a student. He refuted the minister's assertion that it was an attempt by the paper to get one more big education story.

Alexander said the newspaper's overriding aim was to promote a discussion of what a representative group of high school students were thinking, the sorts of issues they regarded as important, how school life had changed and what their hopes were for the future. In the past there had been a number of 'orthodox attempts' by news organisations, including *The Sydney Morning Herald*, to carry out such an exercise, which had produced an artificial result. 'Unfortunately, having a journalist pose as a student was the only way we believed a truly accurate picture could be drawn.'

Pointing out that the overriding principles of the AJA's code of ethics were respect for the truth and the public's right to information, Alexander said: 'This particular exercise, we believe, fell within those boundaries. It was never our intention to name the school involved, nor its teachers and students, but merely to select and accurately describe in print what we believe to be a typical high school situation in New South Wales.'[15]

The first article in Hewett's series appeared in *The Sydney Morning Herald* the following day despite Metherell's request that it not be published. Subsequently, a complaint by Metherell was upheld by the AJA judiciary committee in New South Wales and Hewett was fined for unethical conduct.[16]

Hewett could justifiably plead in mitigation that he acted with the full knowledge and support of his superiors at the newspaper. However, the union has power to discipline only its members, not senior executives or media proprietors. Hewett therefore became the scapegoat. The real problem, nevertheless, was that the newspaper's executives overestimated the freedom of action that would be permitted under the ethics code.

Cases of reporters impersonating other people to gain information are rare in Australia. However, journalists have occasionally got away with it either because the facts could not be proved or because no one thought the circumstances serious enough to make a complaint. For example, the article which earned the national Walkley Award (best feature section) for Michael Gawenda of *The Age* was based on information which he obtained by undercover means.

Gawenda had been assigned to do a story on the social problems of living in high-rise Housing Commission flats in the Melbourne suburb of Richmond. These concrete monoliths housed hundreds of families, many of them too poor to live elsewhere. They had been in the news because of outbreaks of violence and hooliganism on the estates, and occasional suicide by despairing residents who had jumped off balconies.

Gawenda decided that the best way of finding out what conditions were really like in high-rise blocks was by living there. He wanted to observe quietly what happened around him while tenants went on with their everyday routine. So one of the Housing Commissions's tenants was moved to a hotel, his expenses paid by *The Age*, so that Gawenda could live in a commission flat for 11 days.

Strictly speaking, as Gawenda and his superiors at *The Age* knew, he was technically in breach of the AJA rule that journalists should properly identify themselves and their employers before obtaining an interview. In fact, Gawenda had reservations about what he had done, later describing the operation as 'a bit dicey'.[17] However, although Gawenda conversed with other tenants in the high-rise flats he was careful not to pry into their personal affairs, and avoided taking notes while in their company. His article mentioned no names, nor any of the intimate details some people had volunteered about their lives. Moreover, Gawenda had the backing of *The Age* editor, Creighton Burns. As Burns pointed out, Gawenda later went back to the high-rise block to identify himself to the tenants, and explain the purpose of the article. And none complained.[18]

Taping Without Telling

A more serious case of deception was investigated by the AJA's South Australian branch judiciary committee in May 1983. The committee heard a complaint by the federal government's information director in South Australia, Maurice Dunlevy, that private off-the-cuff comments which he had made to journalists during the federal election campaign of February 1983 had been surreptitiously tape-recorded in Adelaide and later played on Derryn Hinch's radio program on Melbourne Radio 3AW.

The incident occurred late in the afternoon of 24 February when journalists and camera crews were waiting to be taken by minibus to a restricted area of Adelaide airport tarmac for a press conference with the Prime Minister, Malcolm Fraser.

Dunlevy overheard several of the journalists discussing comments which had been made the previous day by the South Australian Liberal senator, Don Jessop, who had criticised the Liberal Party's election campaign. Dunlevy joined in the conversation and made a number of disparaging remarks about Jessop, at one point describing him as 'a fuckwit'.[19]

Dunlevy had been talking off the record so believed he could afford to be frank. But the next day Hinch put Dunlevy's remarks to air and identified him as the speaker.

Several days after the broadcast Dunlevy was informed by another government aide that his future 'could be in some doubt' if Senator Jessop chose to pursue the matter. The following day Dunlevy offered his resignation on the grounds that he could not continue as federal information director without the full support of the government. However, as a result of high-level ministerial discussions his resignation offer was rejected.[20]

Dunlevy complained that the taping of his conversation with the journalists had been done deliberately and mischievously to damage his professional reputation, and the broadcast to one of Australia's largest radio audiences had jeopardised his employment and caused him considerable personal distress and embarrassment.

He told the judiciary committee that under no circumstances could his remarks have been interpreted by journalists as any form of briefing. They were simply 'part of a perhaps unwise but nonetheless "chatty" conversation on the political issue of the day'.

Although sympathetic to Dunlevy the committee was unable to say who was responsible for the incident. In a report to the AJA federal executive the committee said that no case had been made out against an Adelaide radio journalist, who had denied responsibility, and that Dunlevy was unable to be certain who had taped his comments.

Expressing its 'extreme concern', the committee said that making the taped conversation available to an interstate radio station 'notorious for its willingness to live dangerously' was 'totally despicable' and a clear breach of the code of ethics regarding fair and honest methods of obtaining news. It added: 'If reporters and political aides are unable to talk privately, "off the record", among themselves without the possibility of such disgraceful disclosure then political journalism as well as journalistic ethics will be the poorer.'

The committee said that if it had been able to establish the identity of the person who had taped and passed on the conversation the maximum fine or even expulsion from the AJA would have been the appropriate penalty. It urged the AJA federal executive to issue a warning that 'such conduct should not be repeated by any member, even as a joke or stunt, because it could so easily backfire'.[21]

Although editors and journalists worry about the ethics of surreptitious taping very few would rule it out in all circumstances. In some situations, they say, it may be the only way of obtaining crucial information about fraud, corruption or mismanagement by people in public life, or the truth about other matters which are concealed from public view.

They also argue that by taping telephone conversations with their sources journalists can ensure accuracy of reporting and also more easily protect themselves against charges that they have misquoted people. As one news executive put it: 'The most efficient and foolproof way to make sure that a news reporter can prove the accuracy of an important interview is to have made a tape — with or without the consent of the person whose conversation was recorded.'[22]

Others point out that it is usually people with something to hide from the public who object to their comments being recorded. If their voices are not on tape they believe they are free to lie about what they have told reporters. They can claim that their comments were distorted or that the remarks attributed to them were invented. A tape is living proof, however, of the veracity of what a newspaper or broadcaster has made public.

Some journalists argue that taping without telling is no less ethical than taking a clandestine shorthand note of a telephone conversation, or silently keying it word for word into a computer. They say they have no special obligation to tell sources how or in what form information from an interview is being recorded. As one commentator puts it:

> If sources do not know they are being interviewed the deception is a consequence of keeping secret the reporter's role as a reporter; the deception is NOT a consequence of keeping secret the use of a tape recorder. In short, secretly recording an interview may be part of a larger strategy to deceive a source, but secretly recording an interview is not by itself an act of deception.[23]

Such reasoning does not allay the concerns of editors about the morality of surreptitious news gathering. Although hidden recording devices are used mainly to obtain information that is not easily available by orthodox means, they are still not convinced that the practice is justified. Because of their doubts some editors prohibit even telephone taping of interviews unless the journalist has received the permission of the interviewee. Others occasionally say yes to secret taping but only when they are convinced the circumstances warrant unusual methods.[24] By and large editors believe the media should be as open in their conduct as they insist people in public life should be.[25]

Cases arbitrated by the Press Council and other tribunals give some clues about the circumstances in which clandestine methods of news gathering will be tolerated. Although the Australian Broadcasting Tribunal, the predecessor of the Australian Broadcasting Authority, and the New South Wales Privacy Committee generally disapproved of surreptitious filming they at times turned a blind eye to the practice or openly sanctioned it.[26] The Australian Broadcasting Tribunal's program standards required stations to inform people whose words and images were being broadcast. However, as the associate professor in communications at Bond University, Peter Putnis, pointed out, the Australian Broadcasting Tribunal's standards did not prevent the use of outright deception in some situations. For instance, no action was taken against the Hinch program in 1991 when it used a hidden mini-camera and a microphone installed in a pot plant to record an allegedly corrupt policeman accepting bribes, and in another case the New South Wales Privacy Committee sanctioned the surreptitious filming of a 'scalper' selling rock concert tickets on the ground that it was 'justified in the public interest'.[27] The self-regulatory codes of practice, introduced under the 1992 Broadcasting Services Act, did not cover the matter.

The Press Council tries to balance the interests of the news media and the interests of the community, without always finding them incompatible. The council has frequently dismissed complaints about photographs being taken surreptitiously at the scene of this or that disaster on the ground that the events occurred in a public place and were of considerable public importance. It did not matter that the people concerned were unaware of being filmed and were not asked for their permission. The importance of the information to the community generally was seen as overriding the interests of the individuals involved. However, at other times the council has come down firmly on the side of the complainant.

In one case the council admonished *The Age* newspaper for publishing a photograph of a woman that had been taken without her knowledge and against her will while she was being interviewed at her home in Victoria's Wimmera district. The woman, who had given birth to quadruplets, had answered a reporter's questions but had said twice during the interview that she did not want photographs taken while the children were still in hospital. She was not told that a photograph of her had already been taken from a car parked in the driveway of her home.

The Press Council acknowledged that the birth of quads was a matter of public interest but said that neither that fact nor the acceptance of some publicity by the hospital and the husband deprived the mother of her right as a private individual to enjoy her home in her own way without being subjected to the un-welcome publicity of a press photograph.[28] What is notable about the ruling is that the council failed to differentiate between matters that were of interest to the public and those that were in the public interest: that is, matters the public needs to know.

Image Manipulation

The 'staging' of news photographs and manipulation of tele-vision news film generate as much controversy as the use of hidden cameras and tape recorders. Both techniques have at times been condemned as forms of deception. Staging usually involves the photographer making changes at the scene of the photograph to obtain a sharper, more exciting picture. If props or people are used to fake a scene but the photograph is passed off as a true reflection of reality the viewers have been cheated. In fact, reality has been distorted

Views differ about what degree of manipulation is permissible. Photographers have always manipulated lighting, studio settings, external props and people to achieve a variety of artistic effects that do not accord exactly with the objective view of reality. There is a case for artistic recreations of parts of life in journalism, especially in magazine journalism. However, the news photo-grapher has an obligation to the audience to provide a represen-tation of actual, not imaginary, events. He or she betrays the trust of the audience if the picture is merely a mock-up, or represents something other than he or she claims it to be.

Is all 'staging' unethical or does it depend on the extent to which manipulation of the content of the photograph has occurred without the knowledge of the audience? What if the manipulation has embellished but not radically changed the central story that the photograph or piece of videotape was meant to tell?

The two following situations show how photo staging can alter reality. In case one Maurice Wilmott of the now defunct *Daily Mirror* in Sydney exercised a little bit of artistic licence to construct a photograph which earned him the 1956 national Walkley Award for the year's best news picture.[29]

Wilmott had been asked by his editor to get an unusual Anzac Day picture — something different from the hackneyed photographs of VIPs laying wreaths at the cenotaph, or bemedalled veterans striding four abreast past the saluting dais. So early on Anzac Day, while wandering the streets looking for an idea he saw a war widow planting hundreds of small crosses in the garden of St Andrew's Cathedral, Sydney. It was a good scene but Wilmott decided he could improve it. What he needed to complete the picture was a wounded ex-soldier. So he walked the streets again, this time looking for a veteran to stand in the foreground of his picture, and he found a one-legged man drinking from a bottle with a couple of his mates.

Wilmott offered the man a couple of quid if he would pose for the picture. The man, leaning on a crutch, agreed to be in it on condition that Wilmott would not show his face in the picture. Wilmott tactfully positioned the 'veteran' with his back to the camera, looking down at the kneeling widow as she tended the crosses of remembrance. Picking up his camera gear Wilmott then asked the man whether he had lost his leg in the first or second world war. Neither, he was told. He had lost it in a tram accident in the centre of Sydney many years ago.

It was not what Wilmott had expected to hear, and he felt slightly put out. However, he reasoned that the widow and the crosses were really the focal point of the picture and the one-legged man simply supported the main theme. Next morning the photograph appeared with the caption 'A nation's look in a mother's eyes'. It seemed to represent the mood of Anzac Day.

Did it matter that the one-legged man was not the wounded veteran readers may have imagined him to be? Should they have been told? Did that fact materially change the nature of the story? Wilmott believed not. The picture was meant to evoke memories, and did so, whether or not it exactly mirrored reality.

In case two, the staging of a school photograph resulted in *The Australian* newspaper being admonished by the Press Council.[30] The photograph was published during a period of industrial action by teachers in Queensland. It showed a boy and a girl with their backs to the camera holding onto the closed gates of a school as though they had been shut out. A placard propped against the gates read 'No oversize classes'.

The Toowong State School Parents and Citizens Association complained to the Press Council that the photograph was 'stage managed'. They said that on the day before the picture was published teachers at the school saw two men and two children arrive. One man closed the gates and placed against them a placard left over from a demonstration. The two children, who did not attend the school, were positioned against the gates and a photograph was taken. The association said the photograph portrayed children apparently barred from entering the school when in fact it was open and teachers were in attendance.

The Australian replied that whether the photograph was posed was 'a peripheral matter'. It said that the real issues were that the photograph did not distort facts so as to mislead readers and publishing it had not been unfair to anyone.

The Press Council disagreed. It said that although posing photographs was not in itself necessarily undesirable the newspaper had gone too far in this case. It added: 'The clear suggestion of the photograph was that the children in it were barred from their school but, not only were no children barred from their school, the children were not even pupils there. Such a photograph was grossly unfair to the teachers.'[31]

As everyone in the news business knows, television film can also be manipulated to distort reality. For example, a picture of poverty can be created by filming only the dilapidated parts of a generally well maintained residential housing area, and a person's character or institution's credibility can be tarnished by focusing the cameras only on the negative aspects. The authenticity of the images viewers get depends on the integrity of the journalists and camera crews involved in the filming, scripting and editing. Cases of blatant dishonesty are either rare, or rarely reported, though the staging of some scenes for news and current affairs is quite common.

Some media critics, notably Stuart Littlemore, acerbic compere of the ABC's television program *Media Watch*, have also criticised artificial interviews in which questions asked by studio news presenters are matched up with pre-recorded 'answers' taken from reports by overseas correspondents.[32]

Politicians and their minders have at times also expressed concern about the technique of freeze framing and magnifying sections of television film to show up the details of 'confidential' documents that would not normally be visible at a distance from the naked eye. Is it unethical, or is anything that happens in public fair game? If not, what things are 'off limits' to the cameras?

These issues came to the fore in August 1990 when Channel Nine Journalist Laurie Oakes was at the centre of a controversy over the filming of a confidential memo in the possession of the then federal Treasurer, Paul Keating.

A Channel Nine cameraman standing behind Keating filmed the memo while it was on a lectern in front of the Treasurer at a Canberra press conference. The memo summarised a conversation between senior advisers to Keating and the then Prime Minister, Bob Hawke, on the sensitive issue of proposed reforms to Australia's telecommunications system. The contents, if made public, could be interpreted as evidence that Keating and Hawke were prepared to ride over their own party's policy to bring about changes to Telecom and the Overseas Telecommunications Commission.

Publication of the memo could be embarrassing to the government. Keating was therefore furious when Channel Nine freeze framed and magnified film of the memo for Laurie Oakes' news report that evening. Later that evening he telephoned Oakes to give him a piece of his mind.

Keating's advisers also complained that filming the memo was 'an invasion of privacy'. One of them, Tom Mockridge, said: 'Obviously the safest thing to do is to make sure you do not have anything embarrassing in front of you, but that does not mean you can dismiss private documents as "fair game" just because they are held in public forum.'[33]

Oakes later denied that any subterfuge was involved. 'Quite often the camera picks up things you are not aiming for,' he said.

> I don't think there was any breach of ethics. It wasn't deliberate. The problem was that what Keating was saying seemed to be the opposite of what he was doing. Our crime was to expose that. We were absolutely open about what we did. It was only after the event that the general ethical issue came up.[34]

It was not the first time that Oakes had obtained a 'scoop' by freeze framing and blowing up the contents of a confidential document. In 1990 his camera operator had filmed a document protruding from a file held by the public opinion pollster, Rod

Cameron, soon after Cameron had talked to Prime Minister Hawke about the best time for a federal election. Freeze framing and sharp focusing of the video segment showed that the document was offering advice about when an election should be called.

Was Cameron careless, or was he entitled to believe that no one would be filming the documents he carried? There could be no doubt that the information in the document was of very considerable public interest but did that justify the method of obtaining it?

That question was reopened when Keating complained about the freeze framing and public exposure of his memo and, according to Oakes, Channel Nine then decided not to do that sort of thing again. But this leaves open the question of whether television channels would always be as scrupulous if they saw the advantages of filming confidential material.

Finally, the question should be asked, why should private documents not be filmed if politicians and other public figures are silly enough to flash them around in public? There are sometimes good grounds for arguing that the television cameras are too intrusive. Nevertheless, street-smart politicians like Keating know that very little of what public figures do in public life goes unnoticed by the media. As Treasurer, Keating was always careful to ensure that only the previous year's budget papers were on his desk when photographers arrived to take preview pictures on budget eve. He must also have known that hiding confidential memos from view was equally a matter of good housekeeping. If he temporarily dropped his guard he had himself largely to blame.

Advances in technology have made deception easier because clandestine methods of news gathering are now more difficult to detect. Pictures can be taken surreptitiously with improved zoom lenses and miniature cameras and conversations can be picked up by listening devices as small as a cockroach or by easily concealed suction microphones.

Furthermore, computers have revolutionised the means of manipulating news photographs and videotape. Retouching of photographs by hand was, of course, quite common even before the advent of computers but it was clumsy and easily detectable. It was also discouraged in many newsrooms, except as a means of occasionally tidying up small blurred sections of pictures. Through the process of digital retouching it is now possible to change the contents of pictures without the slightest risk of detection.

Digital retouching equipment now in use by some American newspapers and on its way to some Australian papers can be used to add to or remove parts of pictures to make them visually more exciting or more relevant to the stories they are meant to illustrate. But the changes may also result in a distortion of reality, producing, in effect, photographs that lie, or tell a half truth. As one American editor put it: 'This new technology has the potential of undermining our faith in photography as a reflection of reality'.[35]

Electronic manipulation of pictures tends to make nonsense of terms like 'photographic proof' and 'seeing is believing'. Here are a few examples of how reality can be changed by digital retouching.

In February 1982, through electronic retouching, *National Geographic* moved one of the Great Pyramids at Giza so that a photograph which was originally shot in a horizontal format would fit the vertical shape of the magazine's cover. The photographer complained and the subsequent controversy caused the term 'moving a pyramid' to become the new slang for manipulating a photograph by using pixel technology.[36]

An editor of the *Asbury Park Press*, third largest newspaper in New Jersey, USA, removed a man from the middle of a news photograph and filled the space by 'cloning' part of an adjoining wall. The incident led the paper to establish a policy prohibiting electronic tampering with photographs.[37]

In July 1993 the Fairfax magazine *Good Weekend* ran a cover photograph of an apparently naked Victorian Premier, Jeff Kennett, addressing a public meeting. The manipulated image was an eye-catching way to illustrate the magazine's cover story about digital retouching equipment. It was arresting enough, along with some other cases, to prompt the editor-in-chief of the Herald and Weekly Times Limited, Steve Harris, to formulate a policy on image manipulation which required all images not generated by conventional photographic techniques to carry a tag identifying them as computer-generated or photo illustrations.[38]

Investing in the new technology is attractive to publishers largely for economic reasons. As Lassica points out, newspapers and magazines are using computers to achieve huge savings in labour and materials as well as to enhance the quality of colour photo reproduction.[39] However, the potentialities for misuse of the technology are also a cause of growing concern among editors. Some of the questions that need to be considered are: what changes to the content of news photographs, if any, are justifiable on artistic grounds and at what point does tampering with a picture become unethical?

Some commentators are pessimistic about the new trend. According to Reaves, the technology will ultimately lead to a shift away from photography as irrefutable evidence of a story to photography as a changeable story illustration. She argues that eventually, as the public realises that photographs can be and frequently are electronically altered, photographs could lose their 'moral authority'.[40]

The controversy over digital retouching has already raised doubts in the public mind about the integrity of news pictures. It was this concern which caused *National Geographic* to review its attitude to digital retouching after it had moved the pyramid. The magazine's former associate art director, Jan Adkins, said:

> At the beginning of our access to Scitex (digital retouching equipment) I think we were seduced by the dictum 'If it can be done, it must be done'. If there was a soda can next to a bench in a contemplative park scene we'd have the can removed digitally. But there's a danger there. When a photograph becomes synthesis, fantasy rather than reportage, then the whole purpose of photography dies. A photographer is a reporter — a photon thief, if you will. He goes and takes with a delicate instrument, an extremely thin slice of life.
>
> When we changed that slice of life, no matter in what small way, we diluted our credibility. If images are altered to suit the editorial purposes of anyone, if soda cans or clutter or blacks or people with ethnic backgrounds are taken out, suddenly you've got a world that's not only unreal but surreal.[41]

Other commentators claim that the critics are making a mountain out of a molehill, and that the advantages of digital retouching — especially the cost savings, the increased speed of photo-processing and improvement in photo quality — far outweigh the potential disadvantages. Whether the new technology is beneficial depends on how it is used by the people in the news media. As one commentator remarks: 'Machines aren't ethical or unethical. People are.'[42]

Manipulating Questions and Answers

The journalist's job is not easy. Condensing an event or a process into a few hundred words or 60 seconds of airtime is a daunting task, especially if the journalist values fairness and accuracy. To overcome the formidable difficulties of compression, journalists have developed various presentation techniques that aim to produce a comprehensive news story without distortion. The selective use of direct quotations in print stories, the use of reverse questions and so-called noddies in television, and a host of editing techniques in both print and broadcast media are all perfectly proper in themselves. Sometimes, however, they can be used to deceive, even if unintentionally.

Audiences, ignorant of such techniques, are misled into believing that what they read, see or hear is the literal truth. We have discussed above the deliberate use of dishonest tactics in news gathering and presentation. Here we are concerned with more subtle ways that a news item can convey the wrong impression.

John Hulteng in *The Messenger's Motives* says that 'in the handling of quotations, a staple of journalism, the reporter's integrity as a gatekeeper is put to more frequent and more severe tests than in almost any other aspect of the work'.[43] Despite the occasional admonition — such as that of *The Springfield Republican* which instructed its staff '[when] people are quoted, the paper is placed in the position of assuring its readers that the quoted passages were literally spoken . . . [and] inaccuracy in quotation is unpardonable'[44] — the press in the United States generally operates an openly flexible system in relation to direct quotations. House rules vary but a code proposed in 1993 for the American news agency Associated Press said:

> While some newspapers may impose a stricter standard, there may be little or no actual harm in altering quotes in the following limited circumstances:
> (1) Correcting grammar that could make the statement confusing or would make the speaker appear foolish;
> (2) Avoiding dialect that is not essential to the story.[45]

The Australian Press Council has been firmer in its pronouncements on direct quotations. In an early adjudication it tackled the problem. The National Front of Australia had complained about an article in Melbourne's *Sunday Observer*, alleging among other things that its chairwoman, Rosemary Sisson, had been misquoted. The paper quoted Sisson as saying: 'We have been well trained in the use of guns and explosives if we have to defend ourselves against political opponents'. Sisson denied she had made the statement and the council established that 'the quoted remarks were in fact a composite of remarks allegedly made by Ms Sisson at various times and at various places'. The council continued:

> Even though the original report had been reduced by two-thirds to fit the space requirements of the newspaper, the paper clearly was at fault in presenting remarks as a direct quotation when this was not the case. Readers are entitled to believe that direct quotes are what they purport to be and those misquoted in such circumstances are entitled to the protection of the Press Council.[46]

Even if it is acceptable to edit quotations to make them neater — so long as they still reflect the speaker's intent — a problem remains. Who is to decide whether a quotation honestly reflects what the speaker said? The reporter or the interviewee? The safest way is to work by the grammatical rules of punctuation that dictate that quotation marks, or inverted commas, must contain only the exact words spoken. The conventions say that if changes are made to clarify the sense they should be indicated by square brackets and omissions should be signposted by the use of dots. But a source's words, particularly when spoken, are not always as clear or succinct as a journalist would want. Rendering a direct quotation snappy enough for a short news sentence might result in an ugly confusion of dots and brackets. Using reported speech, or the indirect quotation, is one alternative technique. But newspapers, particularly popular newspapers, are wedded to the vibrancy of the direct quote, as the *Sunday Observer* case shows.

Another ethical dilemma arises if the reporter does not tidy the quotes of some people. If the interviewee is someone whose first language is not English, for example, should the reporter reproduce understandable grammatical errors or ungainly phrasing? Might this not hold the interviewee up to unnecessary and unfair ridicule? Does the context of the story require the 'true' voice of the speaker, even if the speech is in the vernacular or less than fluent? The Herald and Weekly Times' policy allows for adjusting quotes to avoid ridiculing a source. But it remains true that any tidying of direct quotations has the potential to mislead and is a technique that must be used with the utmost caution if a reporter is to uphold the value of accuracy.

The problem of rendering intelligible what people actually say, within the constraints of a news report, is not confined to the print media. Television and radio suffer similarly. One of the aims of the report is to produce the best possible sound quality or vision so that the story runs smoothly. Yet good editing conceals itself. The astute listener may recognise that a sentence in a voice grab in a radio story has been cut before the sentence is complete because of the inflection of the person's voice; but inflection is not an infallible indicator of editing.

As viewers become more sophisticated in their understanding of television techniques, they may detect when a reporter's reverse question has been inserted to allow neat editing of the interviewee's reply. But what they cannot tell is whether the wording of the reverse question was exactly the same as that originally put. An ABC television interview on 4 March 1987 with the then Prime Minister, Bob Hawke, demonstrates the problems that editing can create. The award-winning expatriate journalist John Pilger interviewed Hawke for 22 minutes, but the ABC imposed a nine-minute limit on the item. Fair enough: that is often the way things happen. But the interview had not been a happy one and Pilger's editing drew the Prime Minister's wrath.

The day after the interview, the Prime Minister's press secretary, Barrie Cassidy, wrote to the ABC deputy chairman, Wendy McCarthy, raising four complaints about the interview as telecast on the *7.30 Report*. Cassidy said that Pilger's claim in his closing remarks that Hawke had admonished him at the end of the interview were untrue. He disputed that Pilger had asked a question about Aboriginal affairs that Hawke had refused to answer and complained that Pilger had reframed and recorded his questions and his introduction after the interview.[47]

Nearly two weeks later, the ABC's managing director, David Hill, said that an investigation by ABC management had found the interview 'fell short of professional standards'.[48] Pilger countered with claims that political pressure had been applied to the ABC because the corporation's controller of news and current affairs, Bob Kearsley, had at first rejected complaints about the handling of the interview. He said he had 'never before been aware of such overt and unjustified hostility'[49] as he had encountered with the Prime Minister.

Mike Harris, reviewing the *brouhaha* in *The Bulletin*, said that what had gone to air was 'one of the most awkward interviews' he had seen. He continued:

> Nothing seemed quite right about it, and it was clear that Pilger had taped some of his questions after the interview. Now, this is a perfectly acceptable practice in television. The question that was asked may not quite prompt the answer you got, but the answer that you got was too good to lose and so, to create the semblance of continuity, you do the question again when the interview is over.
>
> What Pilger did was to retain the substance of his questions but re-phrase and tighten them, ostensibly the better to set up the Prime Minister's answer. But in one case he dropped in a bit of emotive language that Cassidy says the PM would certainly have reacted to, and thus changed the texture of his answer to the original question.
>
> Pilger also topped and tailed the piece in such a way that the inference could be drawn that the PM refused to answer a question on the plight of the Aborigines. And that is the crux of the controversy: Pilger never got to ask the question because the interview ran out of time and the ABC ran out of tape.[50]

Harris introduces a new idea about reverse questions: that they are useful to patch over a situation where the answer was not what was expected, but too good to lose. His explanation of reverse questions shows the extent to which a television story must look good, irrespective of its content.

The whole Pilger–Hawke incident was riddled with claim and counter-claim about the original arrangements and time set aside for the interview as well as the editing matter. The televised segment and the unedited tape show extensive use of reverse questions which is natural because the final version was less than half of the original. But it was the ending that was the most controversial. The vision of the unedited version shows Hawke pointing to his watch. The words were:

PM: And I'm sorry John . . .

Pilger: . . . I want to ask one about the Aborigines. Would you allow one question about them?

PM: You have had your time. You took up a . . . lot of time on an issue on which you were obviously wrong . . .

Pilger: . . . It was an important [one] about . . .

PM: Then if it was correct . . . You were given the proposition of the time. You could have easily got a question about

Aborigines. I'm sorry you didn't get it in. I haven't (inaudible)[51]

The audience saw none of this exchange. What was inserted was an ending in which Pilger summarised. He said:

That interview was concluded with Prime Minister getting up and leaving, but before he left he admonished me for taking up too much time in asking questions about inequality and poverty and concentration of media ownership. I asked him if I could ask one question about why so many Aboriginal people, the first Australians, now felt betrayed. And what he would be doing for them in 1988 to effect an historic reconciliation. He said he couldn't answer that question. He didn't have time and he left.[52]

Later Pilger wrote an article for *Australian Journalism Review* in which he expressed his amazement at the primitive conditions under which ABC interviews were conducted. The absence of a second camera or a playback mechanism so that he could record word-for-word reverse questions were not the conditions he would have expected from a national broadcaster.[53] Had they been provided, the controversy may have been averted. Pilger also made the point that the Prime Minister's office had implied there was something sinister in the use of re-recording questions when it was standard practice. He was right. It is standard practice. But it is what may be changed in the re-recording and editing that raises ethical questions about misrepresentation.

Deceitful methods of gathering the news and deceptive methods of presenting it pose some of the greatest ethical dilemmas for the media. If full disclosure is a principle to be upheld, then logically deception in news gathering is always unethical. But, if the public interest is served by deceptive means, then perhaps there is some justification. If editing, whether of vision or words, is faithful to the intent of the original, then there is nothing amiss. But who is to judge? Only careful examination of the facts of the particular case can give guidance to the journalist who is concerned to do the right thing.

CHAPTER 9

The Power of the Purse: Paying for Information

Journalists tend to be ambivalent in their attitudes to paying for information, the practice known as chequebook journalism. Generally they do not like it but few would argue that it is never justified. Yes, they admit, paying for stories does sometimes encourage greed on the part of the seller and a frantic, unseemly scramble between buyers to outbid their rivals. Nevertheless, if the story is important enough, and the only way of telling it is by paying for it — well, yes, they might seriously consider making an offer for it.

Another more brazen rationale is put forward by the people who are regularly to be found in the marketplace: on the one hand, the 'story brokers' with celebrities' tales to sell, and on the other, the people with open cheque books, usually the mass circulation women's magazines and the commercial television channels. Their self-justifying claim is that buying and selling information, or 'infotainment', is a perfectly legitimate business activity. Those who object to it are merely fastidious fuddy-duddies.

There can be no doubt that the practice is now widespread in

Australia. Some newspaper editors have expressed concern that more people are expecting, in some cases demanding, to be paid for information, especially for 'human interest stories' or articles detailing the private lives of celebrities. Drawing attention to this tendency, the editor of *The Sunday Age* in Melbourne, Bruce Guthrie, commented:

> I don't think cheque-book journalism will ever get to the level it has in England because the market here is not big enough, but there are signs that it's getting worse. The mass circulation women's magazines and some sections of commercial television are the catalysts. Some people are now automatically asking for money. That's what worries me. Even before the news media make any offers there seems to be an expectation that something will be paid. Some subjects are demanding it before they will open their mouths. My concern is that it may affect the way good journalists go about their business of gathering information.[1]

By implication we live in a 'greedier society', though it is clear that the financial acquisitiveness of which Guthrie and others complain is partly the result of the willingness of the women's glossies and television to pay for exclusive rights to stories. The practice has got worse because of the intensification of the circulation war between magazines like Kerry Packer's *Woman's Day* and Rupert Murdoch's *New Idea* and the competition for ratings between commercial television stations. 'They do it to sustain their success or to get in front', says Guthrie, 'and they've created a monster they can't stop.'[2]

It is a moot point whether people are greedier than they used to be or whether they are now putting out their hands more often because sections of the media are becoming bigger spenders; and they are told they can earn money by people who make commission on the sale of stories, pictures and other kinds of material. Certainly the industry in buying and selling information is big enough to spawn a number of very successful 'story brokers' or, as the agents sometimes call themselves, 'celebrity person handlers'. Some of these celebrity handlers, like Harry M. Miller, better known as a theatrical agent, are reluctant to say much publicly about the kind of deals they negotiate for their clients. Likewise, some magazine editors and television executives seem inordinately shy about admitting that the stories they promote as scoops to their audiences were actually bought for cash. If there is nothing wrong with the practice, there ought to be no problem in admitting that it happens. The fact that the buyers rarely do admit it, unless caught doing it, and never state the price they paid for the information, suggests that they are rather shamefaced about it. Or perhaps they do not want their readers or viewers to know that their 'exclusive stories' had a lot to do with the power of the purse and little to do with journalistic endeavour.

Some editors argue that chequebook journalism is good for business, and unavoidable. Thus, Nene King, editor of *Woman's Day*, told television reporter Iain Gillespie:

> The end of the line is how much you want to pay. It's important to get readers the best story — and the money doesn't come out of their pockets. It's the way of the world nowadays. You don't get anything for nothing. It comes out of my beloved chairman's [Kerry Packer's] pocket.[3]

Predictably, King was supported by Richard Walsh, managing director and publisher of Kerry Packer's Australian Consolidated Press, which publishes *Woman's Day*, *The Australian Women's Weekly* and a number of other magazines. Walsh was defending the payments made by *The Australian Women's Weekly* and the Nine Network program *60 Minutes* to Mrs Margaret Hewson for interviews she gave to them about her divorce six years earlier from the federal Opposition Leader, John Hewson. Walsh was quoted as saying that chequebook journalism was 'just a fact of life in the big city' and added: 'The truth of the matter . . . is that all major stories in Australia today are paid for'.[4]

This assertion was refuted by Peter Manning, controller of ABC news and current affairs programs, who said it was quite wrong for Walsh to suggest that chequebook journalism was an industry standard. 'It might be a Channel 9 standard but it is not the industry's', Manning said. Pointing out that it was the ABC's policy not to pay for stories, even personality stories of the kind Walsh was referring to, he added: 'There is clearly a conflict of interest if you pay people to tell a story. How do you know and how do you check if what someone is telling you is true if you are paying them?'[5]

Similar concerns were later expressed by Steve Harris, editor-in-chief of the Herald and Weekly Times Limited, and Bruce Guthrie, editor of *The Sunday Age*. Declaring his dislike of chequebook journalism, Harris said:

The only chequebook journalism that takes place at this newspaper is buying extracts from books and I can't avoid that. But generally I don't believe in paying for news stories or other information. Basically I think it gives journalism a bad name. It puts people in the role of entertainers, and once you open the door to paying them it leads them to say things they would not otherwise say because their motive is the money rather than the truth. I think journalists and people on magazines and television in particular need to think very hard about paying money for information. It doesn't reward journalistic endeavour. It simply rewards the size of the cheque. There are unscrupulous people who are willing to pay a lot of money to conceal or manipulate the truth. When it becomes clear that the media are prepared to pay money more people will get in the queue. Where will it stop? There are journalistic standards to be upheld. Beyond that, in purely pragmatic terms, once you go down that road it begins to happen more often and there is no going back. Where do you draw the line?[6]

Guthrie was as forthright:

I think that once you pay someone for a story it calls the facts into question. I think there is an expectation that the seller will earn their dough and it's hard to be sure whether they're embellishing the story because of the dough. And maybe pressure will also come from the buyer because the expectations from that side are too high. If I paid $20,000 for a story and I didn't think that what I got was all that hot would I go back and say to the informant 'Can't you do a bit better?' The problem is that when the stakes are high there seems to be an unspoken invitation to people to embellish the facts to earn their money.[7]

The daily newspapers are generally not very interested in the kinds of stories that sell to the women's magazines. Guthrie acknowledged that people will continue to demand money for putting their private lives and emotions on show. Nevertheless, he said, 'most of our best stories come from good investigative journalism where no money changes hands. We don't have any whistle blowers asking us for money. We believe that the wit and guile and other skills of our journalists can overcome any demand for dough.'[8]

Making Exceptions

Although Harris and Guthrie opposed chequebook journalism on principle neither would go so far as to say they would never be involved in it. As Guthrie explained:

> If I had a telephone call from a journalist I trusted about a hot story that had the potentiality to bring down the government and the only way I could get it was by paying $10 000 I would seriously consider it. But I would need to be convinced that we had properly checked all the facts, that the sources were credible and that the story was right. It's the same with deception. I know that the ethics of the profession say that a journalist should not deceive. But if I could not get a story except by deception and the story was clearly in the public interest I probably would, particularly if the wrong committed was less than the wrong corrected.[9]

Another consideration is that chequebook journalism is sometimes counter-productive. Instead of winning the story it antagonises the potential source of information and undermines the credibility of the journalist or editor involved. Guthrie recalls how *The Sunday Age* benefited because it deliberately avoided becoming involved in the bidding for a man's story about his wife's death from a shark attack. The man was pestered for days by television channels and magazines, all offering him money for the story. He recoiled in pain and disgust. But later he agreed to talk to *The Sunday Age's* Caroline Wilson when she approached him in a straightforward and sympathetic manner and asked for an interview. Two days later he telephoned to thank her for the sensitivity she displayed in gathering the facts and writing the story. Parts of the story were also read out at one of the memorial services. The newspaper did not need to offer any money and none was paid. Their success in getting the story, said Guthrie, was a victory for the courteous, old-fashioned approach to news gathering.

Although chequebook journalism has become a term of opprobrium in some quarters, there is nothing inherently wrong in the purchase of information from willing sellers. We live in a society which says that buying and selling knowledge is a legitimate commercial practice. Newspapers and magazines regularly pay for serialised memoirs and excerpts from biographies of celebrities. The more provocative they are and the more sensational the disclosures they contain, the better it is for circulation. Is there any difference between paying former politicians for their recollections, the truth of which may be coloured by their wish to enhance their own reputations and demean their enemies, and paying a similar amount to pop stars and sex symbols for titillating tales of their private lives? How far should we concern ourselves with the motives of the people who sell their own stories or stories about other people? Does the size of the cheque encourage honesty or dishonesty on the part of the seller? Will the public value the information less, or more, if they know that it has been paid for, and should the media tell them what information has been bought, and from whom it was obtained, so that they can make judgements about its worth?

These questions agitate the minds of people across the spectrum of the media. How often they are prepared to pay, and how much, depends largely on whether they see themselves in the news or 'infotainment' business. Not many newspapers buy news, and those who do do not do it very often. The women's magazines do because they are driven by intense competition to outdo their rivals with each week's cover story. In the 1990s the prices being paid by Australian Consolidated Press (ACP) for personality stories usually range from $2000 to $20 000 though the occasional story fetches a lot more. For instance, ACP paid $150 000 for clandestine pictures of Princess Fergie cavorting with a friend in France after it had become clear that her marriage to Prince Andrew was on the rocks.[10] The story was strongly criticised on the grounds that it was an invasion of privacy, that the pictures had been obtained by underhand means and that publication of them was in poor taste. Walsh justified publication on the ground that there was an obvious public demand for the pictures, as illustrated by the fact that the circulation of *Woman's Day* went up by about 250 000 in the week of September 1992 when they appeared.[11]

The boost in circulation or ratings usually more than compensates magazines and television channels for the high prices paid for exclusive stories. Walsh also justifies chequebook journalism on the basis that people are entitled to be paid for telling stories of their misfortune or endurance under great stress. It is, he says, sometimes a compensation for the pain they have undergone or the financial loss they have suffered. If the media profit by showing the anguish or vulnerabilities of people in the news, why should those people not have a share of the proceeds.[12]

Similar arguments were advanced by the editors of English newspapers in evidence to the British Press Council about payments made or offered for information concerning the Yorkshire Ripper murders. The editor of the *Daily Mail*, Sir David English, told the council that it was the right of any newspaper to use its financial resources to buy exclusive rights to political, sporting or general stories, except for the memoirs of violent criminals. He gave two examples of his newspaper having been involved in what he considered legitimate chequebook journalism.

In the first case it had bought the story of the only survivor of the Pottery Cottage murders after her family — and later the murderer — had been killed, and in the second it had paid for exclusive rights to the story of the first test-tube baby. He asked why a woman in a terrible position should not acquire capital to assist in rebuilding her life, and why, in the second case, the baby's parents should not take advantage of a once-in-a-lifetime chance to transform their lives.[13] Another newspaper, the *Daily Star*, argued that payments were sometimes necessary to expose facts which the public needed to know. It added: 'Chequebook journalism is all around us. Policemen and judges, politicians, pop stars, university professors, sportsmen, victims of crime are all paid by newspapers for their memoirs, their pictures, their time. In fact, in many cases they DEMAND to be paid . . .' The *Daily Star* said that in their inquiries into the Yorkshire Ripper murders many of the people they had questioned had demanded money — for time lost at work, for the anxiety of being cross-examined by journalists, and sometimes for greed. It said newspapers were justified in making some payments, as long as the money did not go to criminals, or to people who were likely to give any part of it to criminals.[14]

Paying Criminals

If chequebook journalism can be justified in commercial terms, what, then, are the ethical grounds for objecting to the practice? One of the strongest objections is to the payment of large sums for the memoirs of convicted criminals or for interviews and stories which allegedly contribute to the 'glamorisation of vice'. The issue came to the foreground of public attention in Britain following protests about payments made by the *Sunday Pictorial* for the memoirs of former spy, William Vassall; by *The Sun* for the memoirs of Ronald Biggs, who had escaped prison after being sentenced for his part in the Great Train Robbery of 1963; and by the *News of the World* for the memoirs of prostitute, Christine Keeler, who had been implicated in a scandal that had rocked the Conservative government in the early 1960s.

Reviewing these and other cases the British Press Council unhesitatingly condemned as immoral 'the rewarding of criminals for disclosure of their nefarious practices by way of entertainment'.[15] It was unimpressed by *The Sun's* defence in the Biggs case that the newspaper should escape censure because payment had been made, not to Biggs, but into a trust fund for the benefit of his children. Rejecting this argument, the council commented: 'It is particularly harmful for the press to allow itself to be used as a vehicle for criminals who are under sentence but at large and thereby enable them to enrich their dependants or friends.'[16]

The council warned that payments for revelations by notorious criminals could encourage others to seek similar profit from their own crimes. It stated: 'To some people the prospect of wide publicity and a monetary reward being obtainable for details of their illegal exploits could be a vivid and compelling inducement to criminal activity. . .'[17]

The scope of the council's declaration on chequebook journalism was extended in 1983 to cover the family and associates of criminals after it was revealed that thousands of pounds had been paid by newspapers to the wife and acquaintances of the Yorkshire Ripper. There was general outrage that the wife of the murderer had been compensated while the victims' families had received nothing. The council echoed that view. It declared:

Just as it is wrong that the evildoer should benefit from his crime so it is wrong that persons associated with the criminal should derive financial benefit from trading on that association . . . The practice is particularly abhorrent where the crime is one of violence and payment involves callous disregard for the feelings of victims and their families.[18]

Sections of the Australian media have also been criticised for making or offering payments to criminals and their associates, although the evidence so far is that they are not as free with their money as their English counterparts, partly because they cannot afford to be. One of the few cases to receive a public airing involved the payment of $12 000 made by Channel Seven to former rugby league star, Paul Hayward, for exclusive rights to the story of the 11 years he spent in a Bangkok gaol after being convicted of drug trafficking. The money was paid to Hayward when he was reunited with his family in Sydney in April 1989. It provoked an angry reaction by Channel Seven viewers and callers to radio talk-back programs, some of whom said they had children who had died after using drugs.[19] The New South Wales Premier, Nick Greiner, was also outraged and promised to introduce legislation to make it a criminal offence for media organisations to pay money to convicted criminals for stories about their crimes. Among the media critics of Channel Seven were Radio 2UE announcer, John Laws, the host of Radio 2GB, Mike Carlton, the ABC Radio's Andrew Olle, and Channel Seven's own current affairs personality, Derryn Hinch. A consistent opponent of chequebook journalism, Hinch had reportedly been infuriated when Channel Seven had inserted an interview that had been paid for into Hinch's own program. An executive of George Negus's production company had paid National Safety Council boss, John Friedrich, for the interview and Channel Seven had bought it.[20] Now they were at it again, and Hinch could only lament how 'disgraceful' it was that his employers seemed to be helping crims.[21]

The Sydney Morning Herald columnist and television compere, Peter Luck, was one of the few journalists to defend publicly the payment for Hayward's story. He pointed out that Hayward was sick with AIDs and would not live long, and that he would not receive any of the money. Part of it would be paid to Hayward's family and the rest would go to drug rehabilitation. Secondly, Luck argued that Hayward had already paid his debt to society by serving about twice the sentence an average criminal got for raping a nun or blowing up a kindergarten. Should his family be begrudged the pittance that was now offered? And would the payment have been justified, he asked, if Hayward had pointed the bone at the Mr Big who had put him up to drug running in the first place. This, he conceded, was a somewhat bizarre suggestion, bearing in mind that if Hayward had done so he would have been signing his own death warrant. In any case he could not have done it legally, and even if he did the media would not have had the guts to run it.[22]

Luck endorsed the comments of Channel Seven's news chief Bob Johnson, who condemned the hypocrisy of some of his colleagues claiming that Seven was being made the scapegoat for 40 years of chequebook journalism. Johnson asked why publication of a story was morally defensible if no money was paid and immoral if money was involved. He argued that the story was an 'object lesson, particularly to young people, who might otherwise be lured by the prospect of easy drug money', and needed to be told with or without money.

Johnson's argument seemed to miss the point that if the story was worth telling — and Channel Seven and Hayward had really believed they were performing a public service — they could have told it without any money changing hands. Secondly, as one drug rehabilitation worker pointed out, there were better ways of teaching young people the dangers of drugs than paying a drug runner for his story. There was no compelling evidence that the story was justified by some overriding consideration of public interest. And as one commentator noted, no one had bothered to ask the question of whether Hayward's story could be absolutely relied upon and was being honestly told.[23]

Competition for stories leads to strange behaviour by some of the people who brandish the cheque books. An illustration of this was offered by Melbourne journalist Tess Lawrence in her column in the *Sunday Press* on 15 November 1987. Lawrence had obtained an interview with the *de facto* widow of Robert Trimbole, who had been sought for years by police for questioning in connection with the murder of anti-drugs campaigner Donald Mackay. At considerable personal expense Lawrence produced a video tape of her interview with Trimbole's *de facto* partner, Ann-Marie Presland, and offered it to Channel Nine, at a price.

She told her *Sunday Press* readers that while she was negotiating the price Channel Nine wrote to Presland, offering her $10 000 if she would re-do the interview with a better known member of the Channel Nine staff. She refused and Lawrence then sold the tape to Channel Two.[24]

The understandable concern about the ethics of paying money to criminals and their relatives and associates does not mean that it is never justified in any circumstances. During the British Press Council's inquiry into chequebook journalism, the chairman and editorial director of the Mirror Group Newspapers, Anthony Miles, noted that in an ideal world one could sympathise with the contention that no one related to or connected with a criminal should benefit from his or her crime by being paid by a newspaper. But, said Miles, an editor sometimes had to balance the undesirability of paying money to an undeserving person against his or her duty in the public interest to keep his readers properly informed.[25] The point was underlined by Ranald Macdonald, ABC radio public affairs commentator and former managing director of *The Age*, in an article in the *Australian Press Council News*. Macdonald stressed that criminals sometimes had important information which, regrettably, could only be obtained by payment. He argued that a prisoner with hard evidence of drug trading in jails, criminals prepared to document claims of police corruption or harassment, prostitutes (with prison records) telling of illegal immigration rackets organised from within government departments, or criminals prepared to finger leaders of the Mafia or the Mr Bigs of the drug trade would all withhold their stories if they would not gain financially by telling them. 'Obviously editors and news directors do not want to pay for news and, unless costs have been incurred, it is a concern to have to resort to paying criminals', Macdonald noted. 'However, in the end, the greater good (or the public interest) could well be served by cash changing hands.'[26]

Other journalists have argued with equal force that payments to criminals or their associates may sometimes be the only way of getting information which the public has a need to know. The British Press Council also acknowledged that there could be occasions when 'the activities of newspapers are affected by overriding questions of public interest, such as the exposure of wrongdoing'. It added that no code of ethics could cover every case, and satisfactory observance of basic principles depended on 'the discretion and sense of responsibility of newspaper editors and proprietors'.[27]

Another of the objections to chequebook journalism raised by judges and other members of the legal profession is that payments made by the media to actual or potential witnesses could seriously interfere with the course of justice in criminal or civil court proceedings. The main danger, as they see it, is that witnesses could be tempted to 'colour' their evidence, or even withhold parts of it, if offered a sufficiently attractive price for their stories. Typically such an offer would be made to a witness before or during a trial, and payment would be made conditional upon the outcome of the case. As the former associate professor in journalism at Deakin University, John Avieson, explained, this could have a strong influence on the way a witness gave evidence. Avieson cited a typical 'worst case' scenario — a court case in which a media organisation made a deal with witnesses to pay them a certain sum for an exclusive story if the accused was convicted and a lesser sum if the accused person went free. He argued that if the witnesses were being paid by a media organisation they would have reason to 'forget' some of the facts and to present their stories in such a way as to drive the price up.[28]

Avieson applied the same reasoning to payments by the media for other kinds of stories. If courts believed that chequebook journalism could tempt witnesses to tell fanciful accounts, would not the power of the purse encourage other story tellers to embroider or distort the truth for financial gain? Undoubtedly that is sometimes the case, but then money is not the only reason why people embellish their stories, as Australian Consolidated Press publisher Richard Walsh was quick to point out:

> We don't need money to corrupt the process of memory. Memory is selective anyway. Politicians are not usually paid for their stories by the media but what they say is 50 per cent bull-shit. Anyone who has led any kind of public life tells their own version of the truth. People often tend to colour information whether or not it's paid for. Of course there are dangers but I don't think journalists work any less at finding the truth nowadays than they ever did. They are aware of the temptations and good journalists will be very much on their guard to ensure that they are not fed a whole lot of rubbish.[29]

What Walsh says is, of course, partly true. People do have other motives for embellishing the facts or telling lies to the media, not the least of which is the wish to create a good impression of themselves. They may merely want to make a mediocre story seem more interesting. It is also no secret that some sections of the media sometimes 'beat up' stories for extra dramatic effect, to the dismay of their more fastidious colleagues. However, these realities do not change another basic fact of human nature — that the lure of money is a powerful corrupting influence. The offer of money is an inducement to tell the best possible story, and that may not always mean the most accurate story. The bigger the cheque the bigger the temptation to colour the facts or stretch them a little further so that the buyer will not be disappointed. Why let a few awkward facts get in the way of a good story — and the $20 000 to $100 000 that goes with it?

Harmful Side Effects

One of the regrettable side effects of chequebook journalism is the grossly irresponsible behaviour it sometimes induces among the media people pursuing exclusive rights to a story. Competition for stories has sometimes led to rowdy public arguments and street brawls between rival news organisations and also to harassment and intrusion into the privacy of the people with stories to tell. The hounding of the relatives of the Yorkshire Ripper's victims, described in evidence to the British Press Council, is one of the worst examples of this. The accused man's wife, Mrs Szurma Sutcliffe, also had grounds for complaint. She reported:

> Hordes of reporters clambered one over the other banging at the door, window and letterbox, shamelessly yelling that they would pay more than the next man or woman for my story. The scene was akin to a frenzied auction, with wild attempts to outbid each other in shouts of 'I will topple any sum the rest of you care to name'. In the process of the ongoing disgraceful behaviour three back windows were broken. This pantomime used to continue until midnight when one reporter in particular. . .hammered at the front door, and in spite of the hour, insisted that he be let in because he had travelled all the way from London.[30]

Another objectionable feature of the practice is 'body snatching' — the term sometimes used by journalists to describe the extreme steps taken to ensure that a bought source of information will not talk to anyone other than his or her paymasters. This has included keeping people in hiding or under guard in hotel rooms where they cannot be 'got at' by the opposition until they have told their stories and earned their money. There is as yet little evidence that journalists in Australia have often resorted to such tactics, though other methods have been used to discourage the opposition from talking to the sellers of stories. Either the sellers themselves, or their solicitors, or their agents, have told other media — sometimes politely, sometimes abruptly — that interviews or pictures or other kinds of information are out of the question while they are under contract. The deal often does not become apparent until journalists turn up at a public function to take a few pictures and ask a few simple questions. Thus, when Australian Test cricketer, Merv Hughes, married pre-school teacher, Sue Kelly, the media were prevented from entering the church or talking to the couple. Hughes explained that he had sold the rights to their story to *Woman's Day*.[31]

So did it really matter? Probably not, since Merv's marriage was soft news, or entertainment, rather than information which the public needed to know. Why, then, should some sections of the media want to make a fuss about it, unless it was the chagrin at having been outbid in the auction for the story? That is one possibility. Another reason is that some journalists find it offensive that news of any kind is rationed on the basis of who has the power to pay for it. Information is supposed to be available to all who want to hear or read about it, not merely to the readers of one newspaper or viewers of one television station. The critics argue that the power of the purse takes the element of 'fairness' out of normal, healthy competition between journalists of roughly equal abilities. It gives the advantage to the news organisation with the greatest financial resources, not to the most astute or hardworking journalist. Acknowledging the validity of these criticisms the British Press Council stated that the power of money to deny competitors legitimate access to news or facts that the public ought to know was 'a grave matter'. The limits it placed on the circulation of news was 'at the heart of the anti-social side of chequebook journalism'. The council emphasised: 'If the public good requires that news shall be generally known it is completely unethical for any newspaper, by exercise of the power of the purse, and for private gain, to block dissemination.'[32]

But in one sense this only begs the question of what kinds of news the public good requires should be made generally known. The story of Merv Hughes's wedding and most of the other candy floss stories that are regularly bought for cash by the mass circulation magazines are demonstrably of considerable interest to the people who read them, or presumably they would not continue to buy them, but it would be hard to establish that they are essential to the well-being of the general public. Since they are a form of entertainment rather than news that is important enough to warrant general circulation does it matter if most of us miss out? If not, does it matter that the information was bought rather than obtained by normal journalistic means?

Journalists answer such questions tentatively, partly because of their confusion about the difference between stories that are largely for entertainment, or simply interesting, and those that are primarily for the purpose of keeping the public properly informed. Even though there is a clear distinction, this is not to say that a story 'of public interest' may not also be 'in the public interest'. And as even the critics of chequebook journalism reluctantly admit, it is not easy to say that they would never buy a story, even if by doing so they prevented important information from going into general circulation. In some situations the only way of publishing a story of significance to the public would be by paying for it.

Some editors argue that in most circumstances it is not necessary to pay. Bruce Guthrie of *The Sunday Age* says his newspaper never has to pay 'whistle-blowers'.[33] Other editors argue that the reputation of the newspaper and its journalists and the range of its contacts are what attracts the best stories, not the power of the purse. Even if more people are asking for money, as Guthrie and others suggest is now the case, not many are paid. The consequence may be that newspapers and broadcasting stations with a general policy against chequebook journalism sometimes occasionally miss stories because others will buy them, although as one news editor commented, 'I'm prepared to endure that loss'.

There is in fact very little evidence of Australian newspapers paying large amounts for news stories of major significance. One of the exceptions was the undisclosed but reportedly substantial amount paid by *The Age* in the mid-1980s for information about alleged political corruption in New South Wales and based on clandestine police tape recordings — the so-called 'Age tapes'. However, a great many other stories about political corruption and other forms of incompetence and chicanery have been obtained over the years by the more conventional methods of investigative journalism, including the series published by

The Herald in Melbourne in 1975 on the Khemlani affair, which helped to bring down the Whitlam Labor government.[34] Fortunately for journalists, and for the general public, many people are prepared to divulge important information to the media, sometimes by clandestine means, for motives other than money, although this causes different ethical problems as we saw in Chapter 7.

Stories that fall into the category of 'entertainment' rather than 'hard news' are usually the ones that find ready buyers in the media. These 'human interest' or personality stories are not essential reading; that is, it is not absolutely vital that the public should know about them. Nevertheless, as we have pointed out elsewhere in this book, providing entertainment as well as hard news — a serving of souffle to go with the meat — is a legitimate function of the media. The pop star who makes a comeback after being addicted to drugs, the parents of newly born quins, the politician's wife who wants to put the record straight about a failed marriage and the people who have made 'miraculous recoveries' from normally fatal illnesses or survived extraordinary hardships at sea, in the desert or in the Himalayas are nowadays usually aware, or are soon told by story brokers, that they have something very useful to sell. There is nothing new in the phenomenon. The women's magazines were competing for exclusive rights to stories decades ago. For instance, Kay Keavney's 'exclusive' story for *The Australian Women's Weekly* in 1968 about the birth of quads to an Aboriginal woman, which won her the prestigious Walkley Award for journalism that year, was obtained with a cheque paid by her employer, Sir Frank Packer, and negotiated with the help of a priest at the mission where the mother stayed.[35] What *is* new about the practice is that more people know that money is to be made and more people are around to do the bartering on their behalf.

If a story needs telling because it is in the public interest, it could be argued that the source and the media have a duty to tell it without any money changing hands. However, few of the people who sell stories, or the agents who act for them, argue their case on the grounds of necessity and the public *need* to know. What they do claim, and usually on good commercial grounds, is that the story is demonstrably 'of public interest' because the circulation or ratings figures prove it. Simply by giving the public what they want, they assert, is performing a valuable public service. The critics argue that this rationale merely confuses 'needs' and 'wants'. Simply because it can be shown that some people want dross, pornography or dangerous drugs does not justify the circulation of them by the mass media. The usual response is that it is not the role of the media to be censor or to control the agenda for public discussion, even if that, in effect, is sometimes what they do in the process of news selection and distribution. The argument tends to be circular, and the story brokers rarely get involved in it. So far as they are concerned if there is a story worth telling it should be sold.

Journalists are often spared anxiety over the ethical issues by the fact that story brokers bypass them and usually negotiate with middle or senior management. Max Markson, managing director of the Sydney-based firm of celebrity management consultants, Markson Sparks, says he does business mainly with editors or publishers' personal representatives, and journalists sometimes do not get to know about the deal until the story has been bought and is about to appear. What journalists rarely hear about, except through rumour, is the price. As to prices, Markson laments that they are not nearly as generous as in England. 'You don't get much money from newspapers here. They're prepared to pay up to £50,000 in England. Here they may give you $100 for a photo. But the magazines here will pay from $1000 to $50,000, depending on the value of the story.'[36]

It was Markson who negotiated the sale of Margaret Hewson's story to Channel Nine's *60 Minutes*. His other clients include celebrities as diverse as Olympics swimming gold medallist Duncan Armstrong, tennis player Pat Cash, triple world boxing champion Jeff Fenech, author and raconteur Thomas Keneally and magazine publisher Ita Buttrose. He stresses the importance of acting quickly in bringing a story sale to a conclusion: 'If the story is good enough a lot of magazine and television people will come chasing for it, but the business has to be done while the story is still hot. When it's no longer hot the price quickly goes down.' Markson admits that it is partly the competition and partly salesmanship that forces the price up.

If I have a good story and everyone rings up wanting to cover it I say 'Sorry, but the story is obviously of major news value and therefore if you want it you're going to have to pay.' I might suggest to a magazine that they can have an exclusive for, say, $25,000. And if they agree they get a scoop and add another 50,000 to their circulation that week. They win. We win.[37]

He rejects the notion that story tellers and their agents exaggerate stories to get the price up.

Sure, stories get embellished but the media do that every day in the news business, whether or not it's a story about the Prime Minister or the Queen or another member of the Royal Family. The media are in the entertainment business and you have to provide entertaining material but it's up to the editor of the publication how the story comes out. It's the media who hype up stories — not the story tellers.[38]

Selling Sport

David Emerson, who acts as a story broker for a number of test cricketers, including David Boon, Merv Hughes and Dean Jones, through his family company, Competitive Edge Sports Management, offers a slightly different view. Emerson says he does not have to try the hard sell because the cricketers he acts for already have a very high public profile through reporting of their exploits on the field and more and more women want to read about them. 'The women's magazines show a lot of interest in their private lives but it's up to the cricketers whether they want to talk about things like that. We don't hang out for money. They [the media] set the price more than us.' However, Emerson says there are also some management companies which tend to beat up stories: 'They tend to think that selling is more important than the stories themselves'. He also suspects, as some other agents do, that the amounts that are sometimes reported to have been paid are deliberately inflated with the aim of keeping prices at that level: 'Some companies talk bull-shit. The information they give about deals is wrong. The figures are escalated for image and to get more business, and so that the other business they do is for around the same price.'[39] Wearing his other hat as marketing manager for the Victorian Cricket Association Emerson says there is no case for charging newspapers and television sports shows for interviews about what happens on the field. Nevertheless, he defends chequebook journalism in sport as a means of helping players to set aside money for the time when they will be past their top and no longer able to continue. Seen in that way, the media payments to players are a form of retirement benefit.

To Pay or Not to Pay

If, as the story brokers and some editorial executives assert, there is nothing inherently wrong with chequebook journalism, why is it that people in the media are often either very reticent about it or slightly shamefaced about it? Usually a news organisation will admit paying for a story only after it has been caught in the act by an envious or morally righteous rival or by its own journalists. Sometimes the buyer will brazen it out. Thus, when *The Courier-Mail* in Brisbane was discovered to have paid $30 000 for exclusive rights to the story of the sacked Queensland Police Commissioner, Sir Terence Lewis, who had been charged with corruption, and journalists at the newspaper protested to the proprietors, the managing director of Queensland Newspapers, Ron Richards, replied tersely: 'Other sections of the media wanted the story. We got it and we make no apologies.'[40]

The reluctance of some editorial executives to admit to paying for stories, and the intensity of their denials when they are accused of it, seems to be a tacit acknowledgement that there is something dishonourable in the practice. They would rather not be seen buying information when the opposition has striven to obtain it by the usual journalistic means. Journalists, too, are somewhat abashed about admitting that their own news organisations do it. They feel that information that has been bought cannot be as worthwhile as information obtained by painstaking research, probing interviews and cross-checking of sources. Somehow, paying for stories seems to devalue journalistic skills.

Some critics argue that the real losers are the general public, who are misled into believing that what they see, hear and read is brought to them by honest, investigative and independent journalism and not through a simple cash transaction.[41] This raises the question of whether the public would value the information any less if they knew it had been bought. Would the source lose credibility once it was known that his or her chief motive for making the story public was monetary gain? Would the audience wonder, for instance, whether the prospect of a big cheque had induced the seller to exaggerate the story or to withhold some of the inconvenient facts in order to obtain a better price?

These are understandable concerns but there are no easy answers. As a number of commentators have noted, people may have all sorts of reasons for exaggerating or lying, quite apart from cash, including the enhancement of their own reputations and the damage which misinformation may do to their enemies. Money alone will not distort the truth if the newspaper is determined to get at the truth. In fact it could be argued that in return for large amounts of money fastidious editors might expect a lot more of the facts and deeper levels of the truth. They would certainly want their reporters to check and double check the more dubious parts of purchased material. Nevertheless, members of the public are surely entitled to know whether or not a story has been paid for so that they can make their own judgements about its worth. This is consistent with the principle of full disclosure which must be weighed when making ethical decisions. One of the strongest proponents of this kind of disclosure, the ABC's public affairs commentator, Ranald Macdonald, argues:

> It is important to know whether a news item has emanated from a leak, prepared statement, interview or has had to be paid for. One way of developing the media's credibility is for us to reduce secrecy. Why are we so reluctant to admit mistakes and to tell the public about our operations and activities? [42]

One of the risks of disclosure is that a section of the public may come to believe that the value of each story depends on how much has been paid for it. Yet as most journalists know, the most expensive stories are not necessarily the most important. Another of the possible consequences would be that the magazines regularly involved in chequebook journalism would have constantly to justify doing it. Yet that is possibly better than the pretence that all exclusives are obtained by hard-nosed journalistic inquiry. The editor of *The Sunday Age*, Bruce Guthrie, saw merit in the idea, arguing:

> Hopefully it would make the press more accountable. If we had to pay for a story that brought down the government the

newspaper would have to come clean about its sources long before it was asked to do so. If that meant admitting that we had to pay for some information I could not see any problems with it. I would not feel we were any less of a newspaper for admitting it. I think we in the news media sometimes under-estimate the ability of people to understand and accept the processes of news gathering and journalism.[43]

The principle of disclosure has also been accepted by the Herald and Weekly Times Limited in Melbourne. Late in 1993, as a result of the influence of its editor-in-chief, Steve Harris, the company introduced a comprehensive professional practice policy, covering all its editorial staff. Section 11 of that policy, dealing with chequebook journalism, stated that as a general principle, payments or offers of payment or any other induce-ment for stories, pictures or other kinds of information should be avoided unless publication was demonstrably in the public interest and there was no alternative to payment. Any payment had to be authorised by the editor, and the policy laid down that 'readers should ideally be informed of the fact of payment' although disclosure was to be 'at the discretion of the editor'.[44]

CHAPTER 10

Serving Many Masters: Conflicts of Interest

Ethical decision making requires rigorous thinking about one's loyalties. Many journalists have conflicting loyalties. We have already alluded to the tug of loyalties journalists have to their employers and to their audiences. Conflicts of interests, and related loyalties, continually crop up in debates about media conduct. Of particular concern are so-called freebies, or gifts and other benefits, outside employment and a journalist's participation in community affairs and public life. These conflicts pose the risk that a journalist's independence and integrity may be compromised.

Freebies

Most journalists have at one time or another been offered freebies or other favours by publicity seekers. Some have politely refused the offers. Many others have accepted them, in full or partial knowledge of what the givers hoped to gain.

Both the donors and recipients of freebies have frequently argued that there is nothing inherently wrong or sinister in the practice. It is said that journalists often entertain their news contacts to lunch or dinner so why should not the hospitality sometimes be returned? Journalists also send cards and gifts to their contacts at Christmas — usually at company expense — so what is the objection when their seasonal goodwill is reciprocated? And if it is acceptable to buy a journalist a free lunch or send him several bottles of wine what can be wrong in giving a cheap holiday or a free trip?

The critics reply that journalists who accept freebies and other favours place themselves under an obligation to those who distribute the largesse. As a result they lose, or are in danger of losing, their independence, and the freedom to report without fear or favour the kinds of news that the public needs to know. The primary duty of journalists is to tell the news as it is, good or bad. They might be reluctant to tell the bad news if they felt indebted to a source because of favours, such as junkets.

The chief motive of the people who make junkets available is to obtain favourable publicity for themselves or to avoid bad publicity. At the very least they hope to keep journalists 'on side'. Rarely are strings attached to the benefits they confer, and seldom is it explicitly stated that they want something in return. Rather, it is suggested that the real aim is to provide a good story, and the junket is merely to assist the media to do the job with the minimum inconvenience. Journalists might privately acknowledge that freebies are a subtle attempt to buy their goodwill, but not to their hosts. And seldom do they admit that they have been influenced by such gifts, or that their independence has been compromised in any way.

There is an important difference between the journalist who entertains his or her contacts and the journalist who accepts freebies. In the first place the journalist who buys a contact a lunch usually is trying to obtain information of interest, perhaps of vital interest, to the public. Those who wine and dine the media have no such aim. They act out of self-interest and the information they hope to put before the public may put a gloss on their own activities or deliberately conceal a part of the truth.

By accepting freebies and favours journalists lay themselves open to the suspicion that they may have sold out and become subservient to sectional interests. Even if they are innocent they may find it difficult to convince the public that they are under no obligation to the benefactor if the connection comes to light. The fact that they have taken the gifts may be enough to convey the impression that they are open to influence. Once that happens, they are in danger of losing their credibility as objective reporters and interpreters of public affairs.

There is another problem. Journalists are usually told early in their careers not to get too chummy with their contacts. The risk of getting too close is that they may not be able to write the unwholesome truth if one of their closest contacts becomes involved in a scandal about which the public needs to be informed. The journalist may easily be tempted to shield a contact who has been the source of useful information over the years, and the temptation may be much greater if the contact also happens to have provided freebies.

Freebies come in various guises — free travel and holidays, free accommodation, free meals, complimentary theatre and cinema tickets, Christmas gifts and free goods and services distributed at other times of the year. They are now so readily available that some journalists have come to regard them as a perk of the profession. Indeed, as a former member of the Victorian branch committee of the then Australian Journalists Association (AJA), Margaret Simons, pointed out, offers of free trips and junkets are often passed on by editors to reporters in lieu of a pay rise and as a reward for work well done.[1]

It is no exaggeration to say that if freebies were banned at short notice by the journalists' section of the Media, Entertainment and Arts Alliance the news media would have to do without millions of dollars of free largesse a year. This would have a considerable impact on the budgets of media organisations and would probably reduce their willingness to cover certain kinds of news. An obvious example is travel stories. Either the media would have to pay for their own travel or not send reporters on travel stories.

Obviously there would be alternative ways of covering assignments if freebies were banned. Instead of employing their own tourism specialists, for instance, newspapers might come to rely on brochures and other handouts distributed by the travel industry. That would be a cheap way of doing it but it is not the best alternative from the public point of view. Travel agencies paint rosy pictures for their clients. Independent travel writers, on the other hand, are under an obligation to the public to describe places honestly, without overdoing the superlatives.

The best of them see beyond the idyllic scenes and puffery of the travel brochures, knowing full well that not every palm-fringed resort is the paradise it is made out to be. They are sharply observant, and criticise the second rate and the substandard.

However, if the experts themselves continue to take advantage of freebies they should at least acknowledge who paid for their trips. Some newspapers, such as *The Age* in Melbourne and *The Sydney Morning Herald*, do so, usually putting a footnote on travel stories saying who hosted the trip. It is not a foolproof way of ensuring that journalists tell the unadulterated truth, but at least readers are under no illusions about how the story was obtained and can judge for themselves whether the journalist might have been influenced by the hospitality.

It should be said that, while the travel industry is perhaps in the best position to offer free jaunts, there are many other sectors of business which see advantages in entertaining the press. For many years firms have tried to win friends and influence people in media circles. Bottles of whisky or wine with a decanter or set of wine glasses, cartons of cigarettes, hampers of food and other gifts have been delivered to journalists' offices or homes at Christmas with seasonal greetings from the donors. More expensive gifts sometimes go to those whose status in the media seems to warrant special attention.

No explanation is offered and none is needed. Nor is there any obligation to accept what is offered. The recipient can give them to charity, return them or throw them away. If he accepts, nothing is said about a quid pro quo. Any such suggestion would be unsubtle, ill-mannered and unfair. Everyone involved knows how to play the game.

The same unspoken rules apply to other favours. The company which offers an all expenses paid trip to show off its new Asian or European plant or which throws a lavish party to launch its newest product, perhaps with a free sample or two for those who attend, may hope to obtain generous coverage. But usually it has the good sense not to demand anything in return. Journalists react badly to suggestions that they can be bought, so if that was the intention behind the freebie, it is left unsaid.

Governments and government departments also spend considerable amounts of public money to win over journalists or keep them on side. Governments invite journalists to lunch or dinner to put across information that will help their cause. The food and wine put the guests in a more receptive mood, it is believed, and helps them to digest the information about government policy more easily. Opposition parties try the same tactic, though without recourse to public funds they may not be able to spend as freely on entertainment of the media.

Hostile journalists, or those who ask awkward questions, may find they are left off the invitation lists for these intimate, informal occasions. Politicians confer their favours on those they believe will help them the most. Thus, they frequently employ what is known as the 'stroke or punish the media technique'.

One of the most obvious examples of media stroking was the twice-yearly dinners which former Prime Minister Malcolm Fraser gave at The Lodge in Canberra for groups of newspaper editors to demonstrate to senior media executives that the prime minister was not as cold and aloof and unpleasant as their publications sometimes made him out to be. The information given at these dinners was on a background basis, but sometimes an editor would telephone a quick story from the phone out in the hall.[2] Fraser never quite overcame his image as a dour, headmasterly figure; news photographs of him frowning and Ron Tandberg's cartoons in *The Age* saw to that. Nevertheless, The Lodge dinners illustrated what governments will do to get the media on side.

The Fraser government also employed the 'punish the media technique'. Early in 1980, for instance, Anne Summers, political correspondent for *The Australian Financial Review*, was denied a seat on the VIP plane carrying Fraser, his retinue and a party of journalists overseas.

Despite a protest from the Canberra branch of the AJA, Fraser publicly claimed there was 'no room' on the plane for Summers but privately it was made clear to her editor that if the paper wanted to send another person room would be found. Summers followed Fraser around by commercial aircraft but towards the end of the trip he relented and allowed her on board his VIP plane.[3]

It should be said that the bite-back technique is not exclusive to one political party. The incident involving Anne Summers was matched during the 1980 election campaign by complaints from two News Limited journalists that they had been excluded from the VIP aircraft for the Opposition Leader, Bill Hayden. It is clear that leaders on both sides of politics and some of their advisers have come to regard VIP trips as a privileged form of travel — as freebies — to be given or denied to journalists according to the kind of publicity they receive. So far Summers and other journalists have shown, to their credit, that they are not prepared to submit to that kind of pressure.

The AJA has occasionally expressed concern about the widespread acceptance of freebies but has never said they should be refused in all circumstances. In fact, the journalists' code of ethics is unspecific and somewhat vague about the issue. Clause 5 of the code says that journalists 'shall not allow their professional duties to be influenced by any consideration, gift or advantage offered and, where appropriate, shall disclose any such offer'. It is left to the judiciary committees which hear complaints about breaches of the code to decide whether or not journalists have been influenced and when it would have been 'appropriate' to disclose the offers.

The reality is that the AJA turns a blind eye to most of the freebies that are accepted and there is no record of any journalist being penalised for allowing himself or herself to be influenced or for failing to disclose an offer. It is assumed that in most cases journalists would not allow a freebie to influence what they write, and few have felt it necessary to declare to the AJA what gifts and junkets they have received. Yet freebies of various kinds are so easy to obtain that journalists joke about them.

What journalists do about freebies is left to their own consciences and common sense. But the main question for some commentators is not simply whether journalists *have* been compromised but whether, by accepting free trips and the like, they lay themselves open to the risk that they could be compromised.

The moral absolutists argue that even the risk should be avoided. They say that it is always better to say no. The more pragmatic view is that the element of risk is minimal in most cases and that journalists can be trusted not to barter away their independence.

This argument sometimes turns firstly on the nice question of whether the freebie was intended as a bribe and secondly on whether the value of the gift is likely to undermine the journalist's integrity and self-esteem. Thus, it is suggested that only a fool or a knave would place his or her journalistic career in jeopardy by rendering a service for a bribe, especially a small bribe. One flaw in this assumption is that neither the fool nor the knave expects to be caught. Another is that it is seldom possible to tell what price will buy one man and not another. Would a journalist sell out for a free trip but not for a bottle of wine? For a holiday in Fiji, perhaps, but not for a box of chocolates at Christmas? And would the amount of favourable publicity depend on the size of the gift or the cumulative value over time of other favours? Simply, there can be no definite answer, human nature being so variable. We can only make reasonable guesses.

The first guess is that most journalists would strongly deny that they have ever been suborned or that they would allow themselves to be influenced by freebies. The second guess is that only the most foolhardy donor would offer a journalist an outright bribe or demand a quid pro quo. What we know is that freebies are sometimes offered in the expectation that the recipients will *feel* favourably disposed towards the donor. There is no compulsion to do anything in return, but a sense of obligation to the donor may arise out of acceptance of the freebie.

The fact remains that freebies are now so common that they are almost taken for granted. Some journalists worry about them but do nothing to stop them. While so many of their colleagues are accepting what is offered it seems churlish to refuse. Better to take what comes, and ask no questions. Those who object to the practice and publicly complain about it are likely to be accused of envy, of dobbing their colleagues in, and of making a mountain out of a molehill. Why complain at all if the price of ethical purity is unpopularity?

Travel writers accept a lot of freebies on the rationale that they could not do their jobs properly if their organisations had to bear the cost of their travel and accommodation. Certainly they would not be of much help to the travelling public if they simply stayed close to home and rehashed travel brochures. Even so, critics are entitled to ask whether travel writers always tell the unvarnished truth since their bills are paid by the people who profit from tourism.

In theory, it is harder to seduce the well-travelled writer on his fifteenth freebie than the goggle-eyed *ingénue* on her first overseas trip. The experienced scribes may believe they are untainted and, if challenged, would assert their immunity from the whole gamut of subtle and not so subtle corporate ploys. Nevertheless, it remains a moot point whether they are subconsciously influenced to write uncritically about the services laid on by their hosts. At the very least, one suspects, the all expenses paid jaunt to a sun-kissed Pacific resort would tend to induce that warm inner glow of gratitude towards the donor. At worst, the trip might anaesthetise the writer's critical faculty and result in puffery. There's no easy answer to the problem. The safest way for journalists to avoid the risk of being compromised is to refuse the offers. Some American newspapers such as the *New York Times*, the *Chicago Tribune*, and the *Boston Globe* and travel magazines such as *National Geographic Traveller* and *Travel and Leisure* have rejected freebies.[4]

There is not much evidence that Australian newspapers and magazines are prepared to pay their own way, largely because of the huge expenditure involved. And even if one organisation were highly principled enough to try, would its competitors follow suit, or continue to take what comes?

The problem does not stop with travel writers. Motoring writers, fashion writers, food and wine writers, television writers, film and theatre critics, computer and video equipment writers and other journalistic specialists are also courted and entertained by companies in the industries they cover.

Motoring writers are loaned cars for test drives, and sometimes for much longer periods, and at Christmas there will probably be something for them gift wrapped. If they buy a new car a special deal may be offered by the manufacturer — again with no strings attached. 'It's all part of the service mate — don't mention it.' Fashion writers, too, are liberally entertained, their trips sometimes paid for, and at Christmas there may be free perfume. Wine writers get trips to wineries and samples, not as a bribe, but in the hope that they will say something nice about the stuff.

Wining and Dining

Wine companies spend large amounts to keep the top wine writers happy, flying them around the country to various vineyards, accommodating them, wining and dining them. Mark Shield, a columnist for the Melbourne *Herald*, says his refusal to accept hospitality from wine companies had earned him a reputation as the 'mad monk' of the wine writers corps. He said: 'I could go out every day of the week for lunch and probably three nights out of seven for dinner.' But he reckons that the meals are not really free. 'They're trying to get you obligated.'[5] Some wine columnists do not write about wines they do not like, preferring to say nothing if they cannot say anything complimentary. But Shield argues: 'I reckon you should write about the bad wine, because it's the punter, the poor dickheads who are putting the money out, who get saddled with it.'[6]

A potentially more serious ethical problem arises from the fact that some wine columnists also act as public relations and marketing consultants for, or have a financial interest in, the companies whose wines they review. The question arises of whether they can be objective in what they write or broadcast. The question was put by journalist Jane Cadzow when she interviewed some of the wine experts for an article in Fairfax's *Good Weekend* magazine. Among them was Leo Schofield, a well-known restaurant reviewer and columnist for *The Sydney Morning Herald*, who had a marketing and promotions firm representing the wine company, Lindemans. Schofield featured in Lindemans radio commercials, in which he interviewed winemakers. However, he assured Cadzow that he scrupulously avoided giving free publicity to his clients. He added: 'You'd have to comb my column for the last five years and you'd be pushing to find three or four name-droppings.'[7]

Likewise, Tony Baker, wine and food columnist for Adelaide's *Sunday Mail*, also acted as a public relations consultant for Ryecroft and Burge wines and was the author of *The Orlando Way*, commissioned for the firm's 150th anniversary. Baker told Cadzow that his financial arrangements with wine companies had never compromised his independence as a writer. He said: 'You have to go out of your way to make sure that other wineries get a fair run.'[8]

Cadzow reported that John Fordham, wine columnist for *The Sunday Telegraph* in Sydney, also ran his own public relations firm, and that the Wyndham Estate wine group was one of his clients. She noted that in the March 1989 issue of *Ita* magazine, in which Fordham published a list of 'some of the best chardonnays I have tasted this summer', two of the seven labels named were members of Wyndham Estate group, and that in the May 1989 issue he devoted half a page to a glowing report on the export performance of 'the Hunter Valley's exceedingly successful Wyndham Estate wine group'. Fordham saw no conflict of interest. He said: 'It's only a conflict of interest if it's abused. In many fields there are conflicts. Some people handle them ethically and professionally; other people abuse them.' He said he only wrote about Wyndham Estate wines when a story was genuinely warranted, and then only after checking with his editors.[9] Others in the industry are worried about the trend. For example, Wayne Jackson, group managing director of Thomas Hardy and Sons and deputy chairman of the Australian Wine and Brandy Corporation, said it was disturbing 'from any objective viewpoint' that wine writers received payment from wine companies. He was not suggesting that writers indiscriminately praised the products of the companies they represented but 'you never see them can their own wines, for example'.[10]

Addressing a wine industry conference in Melbourne in 1988, Huon Hooke, columnist for *The Sydney Morning Herald* and *Wine & Spirit*, said readers expected a wine writer to be 'objective, unbiased, not working for a wine company, nor moonlighting as a publicist to supplement his income'. However, he said that traditionally the wine writers had sided with producers rather than with consumers, adding: 'There has been a tradition among wine writers . . . that they don't criticise, they don't mention poor wines or poor value, they don't expose producers for using questionable practices, they don't probe or investigate matters about which the producers are sensitive'.[11]

The general attitude of the AJA has been succinctly stated by its federal secretary, Chris Warren. He says that columnists should declare their interests and that readers have a right to know which writers were paid by wine companies. Similarly, the New South Wales branch of the Public Relations Institute of Australia has adopted a policy that public relations consultants who write columns 'should not promote their clients or organisations without disclosing their interests'. It has asked newspaper and magazine editors to support this policy.

Some newspapers are stricter than others. Cadzow reported that late in 1988 editors at *The Age* learned that wine columnist Jeremy Oliver had a public relations business whose clients included Delatite, Saltram, Mount Avoca and Dominique Landragin. Oliver was moved to another column, The Educated Drinker, in which he wrote in general terms about wine but did not recommend or compare labels.[12]

Food writers are subject to the same kind of temptations as wine writers and they, too, have different ways of dealing with the problem. Some accept hospitality from restaurants they review. They say free meals will not change their opinion of the food and service, and the host knows in advance that they may be criticised or praised. Others say there is no such thing as a free lunch and will not take the risk of being compromised. Their newspapers pay for their meals, they go incognito to restaurants they are about to review and since they have taken nothing free they cannot be accused of puffing up restaurants for personal gain. But problems arise for journalists when management offers advertorials — stories in the news columns in return for paid advertisements — which we will discuss at greater length in Chapter 11. In such arrangements defects are glossed over and the public gets a less than complete picture of the quality of the fare.

Editors of the food pages are targeted by food companies. As well as invitations to dinner or lunch, they are offered junkets linked with food conferences, overseas food tours and free samples to coincide with Christmas or product launches. No favours are asked. The companies simply hope that the brand names of their products will appear somewhere among the recipes and other helpful tips that fill the space between the supermarket ads or that a new food processing plant or kitchen gadget will get a favourable mention somewhere on the business pages.

The competition for publicity has increased with the rapid development of the catering industry over the past two decades. Hundreds of restaurants in the major cities, offering many varieties of national and international cuisine, now vie for precious newspaper space and many make generous allowance in their budgets for media freebies of various kinds.

Investigative journalist Ben Hills is one of the veterans who disapproves of the trend. Hills was one of the two original Epicure writers for *The Age* in the 1970s and co-author with Peter Smark of the first issue of *The Age Good Food Guide*. Hills says:

> In those early days a lot of restaurants didn't know much about cooking and we didn't know much about eating. The new writers are part of a food Establishment and tend to get a lot more invitations. There are more goodies in Santa Claus's stocking than there used to be. I never accepted a free lunch as a food writer or a free anything. I was a trappist monk in that respect. For about two years we had a Christmas gift box at the Age into which a number of journalists put all the presents they received. Everything in it would go to charities like the Brotherhood of St. Laurence or St. Vincent de Paul. When I returned from a tour of duty overseas that practice

had been stopped — I never found out why. The attitude of media managers and journalists to freebies seems to be a lot more lax nowadays. I'd like to see it tightened. In an ideal world journalists wouldn't accept anything. But obviously we don't live in an ideal world.[13]

Hills admitted that he once accepted a free overseas trip but in line with the policy laid down by the newspaper's then editor, Graham Perkin, he publicly acknowledged which airline made it available. 'That way', he says, 'the readers can judge for themselves whether it's wrong.'

He does not know of any straight cash bribes of journalists and states that 'It's much more subtle than that'. But he does recall a party of journalists coming away from the launch of a new product with gifts of portable typewriters. 'I thought that was a bit over the top', he says, though he was glad to learn that *The Age* journalist was too proud to accept.

The AJA has no evidence of journalists taking straight bribes and if it had any the offenders would be disciplined by the judiciary committee. Allegations of bribery are rare. One occurred during the trial of a former Rothmans tobacco company executive, John Ernest Scott, who was charged in the Sydney District Court on 9 February 1990 with having fraudulently converted $263 180 of the company's money. The prosecution alleged that Scott diverted cheques from Rothmans to a bank account in his own name with the help of two Commonwealth Bank employees, both of whom were also on trial but denied being accessories.

Scott had been employed by Rothmans as a community service executive responsible for promoting sporting events such as horse racing and snooker championships. He was, among other things, the company go-between in relations with the media and television stations. His defence was that Rothmans's bosses knew how he was spending the money. During the trial another former Rothmans executive, Martin Tauber, said the company had a group of 'apostles', including media people, who were rewarded for their friendship.

Tauber said he had advocated the $60 000 sponsorship of the Australian Horse of the Year awards in 1982. That had included the payment of a $10 000 retainer to the Australian Racing Writers Association. Scott's defence counsel, Charles Waterstreet, suggested to him: 'You knew that was payments in cash to members of that Association to achieve their good offices.' Tauber replied: 'No'. He testified that a list of apostles included media people who were known to mention Winfield favourably in their reports. The reward was cigarettes, he said. He denied a suggestion that Scott paid the apostles in cash.[14]

Scott was found guilty of misappropriation and sent to gaol after Judge Herron had told him that he did not believe his story about how the money was used. But one of the questions which the trial again brought to the fore was whether the general acceptance by the media of gifts and freebies has any more moral justification than the acceptance of monetary bribes. Of course the answer hinges partly on whether the media offer anything in return. If, or when, they do, the moral taint is the same, whether payment is in cash or in kind.

But there is another question. The media consider themselves the public watchdog, and profess their concern about corruption. Should they not, then, live according to the rigorous moral standards which they set for others? Stereotypes die hard: how can 'the world's greatest bunch of freeloaders' with nothing on their minds except the next scoop, the next deadline or the next junket be expected to behave like paragons? But the question needs to be asked. Can journalists fulfil their responsibilities to the public if they are under suspicion of impropriety? And can they, for all their declarations of good intent, avoid the appearance of impropriety if they continue to accept gifts from sources? In the minds of some media critics it is appearances that matter, even when no deals are made and no legal wrong is done.

Ralph Otwell, a former managing editor of the *Chicago Sun-Times*, put the problem thus:

> In the performance of our journalistic jobs there is more than a conscience to be served; it is not enough to know down deep inside that you are not being bought or influenced, that the 'freebie' has not dulled your critical senses or lulled your watchful vigilance. The conflict of interest might not be felt on the inside . . . but it may be imagined or perceived on the outside. And there is the rub . . . the point where self-image and self-confidence end and public confidence begins. The so-called 'appearance of impropriety' is a condition which we in the media invoke against politicians, judges and even preachers — it is one which we must be on guard against also.[15]

A few Australian journalists have expressed similar concerns. Explaining why she no longer accepted any freebies, a journalist with *The Age* and member of the AJA's Victorian branch committee of management, Margaret Simons, argued that the media could not afford to be smug about their responsibilities and vulnerability to compromise when they condemned people in public office for accepting favours of the same kind. Pointing out that in 1986 the Governor of Victoria, Sir Brian Murray, was sacked and public servants and policemen were rebuked by the media for accepting free trips on Continental Airlines, Simons stated:

> No one has proved that ex-Governor Murray and those policemen were actually compromised or corrupted by those free air tickets. All that has been said is that they may have been open to compromise. And we are just as open to compromise. Certainly, we are not politicians or governors, but we do hold positions of power. In some ways we are not unlike policemen. They, too, are badly paid and get few perks. If junkets are wrong for them, they are wrong for us as well.[16]

Simons was not impressed by the argument of some of her colleagues that they could not do their jobs properly unless they accepted company-sponsored trips. She said:

> Companies like Yamaha and BMW do not fly journalists to other countries just to show them equipment. In most cases it would be cheaper for them to fly the equipment to the journalists rather than the other way round, and if all journalists refused to take free trips, doubtless they would do this. The companies know that by getting a party of journalists together they establish friendly and personal contacts with the writers. Even though the reporters may make it clear that they don't consider themselves under any obligation to the manufacturers, the company has gained the ear of the reporter. When friendship becomes involved as well, the hazy line of independence becomes even harder to draw.[17]

Journalists who leave themselves open to compromise risk losing first their independence, then their integrity, then their credibility. Do they really have the right to censure freeloaders in other fields? There is another danger. Journalists on the make and the take may grow lazy in the chase for real news, and indifferent to the needs of people whose voices rarely reach the media but deserve to be heard. An associate editor of the *Washington Post* argued that it was the first responsibility of the independent journalist to listen to the voiceless. The journalist who gathered information through junkets, he said, was likely to spend less time listening to the often irritating voices of dissatisfied consumers.[18]

The interests of consumers tend to be overlooked when journalists accept at face value the press handouts designed to promote the sales of new products, the quality or reliability of which has yet to be proved. Flattered and cosseted and liberally entertained, journalists may be led to see only what the company wants them to see. The danger is that the elaborately prepared media kit may tell only half the story, and the views of the Standards Association, the Consumers' Association or independent experts are passed by. The media promotion of so-called wonder drugs in the United States further illustrates the point.

In 1982 American journalists gave a lot of favourable coverage to a story about a new drug called Accutane that was said to cure a disfiguring skin disease, cystic acne. Almost all drugs have potential side effects and reporters noted that the main problem with Accutane was that it caused chapped lips. However, a much graver risk — known from the start of the selling campaign by the manufacturer, Hoffmann-La Roche — was the possibility of birth defects among children born to women who had taken Accutane. Some reporters mentioned this near the end of their stories; others said nothing about it.[19]

By the summer of 1983 some mothers on the drug were giving birth to children with blindness, deafness, brain injury, defective hearts, facial disfigurement, abysmally small heads, cleft palates and other deformities. In March 1984 the American Food and Drug Administration warned all blood banks not to accept blood from patients being treated with Accutane and by September that year the number of deformed 'Accutane babies' had reportedly reached at least 25, and more than 75 pregnant women who had taken the drug had elected to have abortions.[20]

As one American journalist, Jim Sibbison, commented, the media had been the vehicle for fantastic over-promotion of the drug. Relying largely on drug company and the American Food and Drug Administration evaluations of the product, reporters had played up Accutane's benefits and minimised the hazards. By failing to warn women of child bearing age adequately of the danger, the news media 'unwittingly shared responsibility for the casualties'.[21]

The Accutane case was not unique. The media continues to be vulnerable to drug companies' publicity campaigns though it is equally true to say that the quality of reporting on science and health matters has improved in recent years and that journalists are now very much on their guard against company hype. Australian health reporters, like their American counterparts, tend to go well beyond press releases and test company claims against the information supplied by scientists and federal and state health administrations.

It is easy to give the impression that journalists are readily seduced into writing flattering drivel about freebie donors when in fact many of them are far too cynical to be sucked in. A Western Australian journalist, Peter Laud, told of a facility trip laid on by the British Army in Gibraltar in the hope that the press would write glowing accounts of the idyllic life enjoyed by 'our boys on the rock'. The public relations campaign went badly wrong. The troops loathed the place and told the visiting media how they pined for home. When the stories appeared, the public relations officer erupted: 'As a result of what you stinkers have written heads are going to roll. And one of them is going to be mine!'[22]

The incident illustrates that the freebie does not always buy what it is meant to buy. Still, as Laud admits, the donors try hard, though some of the gifts would not buy much. As a television writer, Laud has had his share of free trips and has collected a clockwork bear, an Alf doll, a brown beret said to be similar to that worn by French Resistance fighters and holidaying Channel Seven executives, enough books to stock a library, Appealathon and Telethon T-shirts and a small Japanese TV set which functioned only intermittently. He admits that he has been compromised and asserts that freebies are wrong:

> The risk is that they turn journalists into little more than entries on corporate advertising budgets and blunt the pens of those supposedly independent-minded souls who are paid (often quite reasonable sums) to review cars/holidays/television programs and wine, though to be fair I do remember the withering criticism of one motoring writer who complained that it was quite impossible to wear a cap in the back seat of the fuel-injected Triple XXX Fandango, which had an alarming effect on subsequent sales.[23]

For all that, Laud tends to the view that freebies are now so much a part of the system that all journalists can reasonably be expected to do is to accept them and at the same time raise the flag of self-pride and independence. 'The trick', he says, 'is to steer the middle course — and keep an eye out for the drinks waiter. And at crowded functions, that's a trick in itself.'[24]

Other journalists are also pragmatic. Some freebies, they claim, pose such a threat to the journalist's independence they have to be refused. Others are of such limited value they would not suck anyone in. It is simply a matter of knowing where to draw the line.

Those who insist that nothing of any value should be accepted tend to overlook the fact that for many years it has been standard practice for newspapers to receive gratis the many books that they are asked to review. It could be argued that the journalist who receives a free hardback edition of a new best seller might be influenced to give the author a flattering review. But this is far from the case, as we know from observation of what the reviewers write. The books are as likely to be panned as praised, irrespective of whether they are bought or given to the people who write about them.

Examples of journalists seemingly being compromised by their acceptance of free goods or services are not easy to locate or substantiate. Stuart Littlemore, the acerbic compere of the ABC-TV *Media Watch* program, suggested one example when he pointed the bone at *The Australian's* golf writer, Tom Ramsay. It turned out that Ramsay had written some very complimentary comments about a Queensland golf course resort for which he also happened to work as a paid public relations consultant.[25] It looked very much as if he was being paid twice to extol the virtues of the one place. There was no proof of that being so. Nevertheless, it would perhaps have been wiser had *The Australian* told its readers of Ramsay's connections with the resort company. As we have said elsewhere, full disclosure at least gives people the opportunity to make their own judgements about the value of the information they are being offered and whether the writer is presenting an unbiased view.

Trading Shares

Business and financial journalists place themselves in a particularly awkward position if it is discovered that they are accepting shares or other concessions from the companies about which they are expected to write. Some business editors discourage their reporters from trading in shares because of the conflicts of interest that may arise. Moreover, the Corporations Act requires all business and finance journalists to complete a register of their current financial interests. The register is held at the offices of newspapers and radio and television stations and may be inspected at any time by officers of the Australian Securities Commission (ASC), although neither the ASC nor its predecessor, the National Companies and Securities Commission, have had cause to investigate possible breaches of the Act by journalists.[26]

This does not mean there have never been cases of unethical behaviour by journalists reporting business affairs; according to some commentators it means only that they have not been caught doing it or have not been reported. According to sources quoted by Peter Grabosky and Paul Wilson, co-authors of the book *Journalism and Justice*, some finance journalists have compromised themselves by accepting offers of low-price shares in newly formed companies. Having a vested interest in the company's success they are naturally tempted to give the company favourable coverage so as to boost the share price. One business journalist they interviewed commented:

> During the nickel boom of the late 1960s and early 1970s there were numerous instances of journalists getting favourable treatment in the floats of companies. Only a fortnight ago I was offered 10,000 shares in a new gold float. As you know, gold has been going berserk in the market over the last few days. I knocked it back. I'm satisfied that those twenty cent shares will come on at forty and even more. It's very common for journalists to be offered favourable treatment in new floats. The promoting broker may see some advantage to himself. I think the trap is that you become their tool. They've got something on you.[27]

A senate select committee which investigated the regulation of Australian securities markets in the early 1970s also inquired into alleged cases of journalists using privileged access to information to inflate share prices, especially during the preceding mining boom. The committee handed down its report in 1974 but was unable to show conclusively that journalists had been involved in insider trading, although several of the finance editors who gave evidence said that they had heard of instances which they could not substantiate.[28]

So far, despite the occasional scuttlebutt about some journalists being on the make, there have been no spectacular cases of business reporters in Australia being involved in insider trading. However, research by associate professor Julianne Schultz and professor Zoltan Matolcsy, based on a survey of 105 business and finance journalists, suggests, in their view, that such practices 'are not as unusual as the lack of prosecutions may indicate'.[29] More than 80 per cent of the journalists surveyed thought that they could be put in a difficult position of being tempted to seek financial gain because of their privileged access to information. Two of those surveyed felt that succumbing to this temptation was widespread; 12 per cent thought that using privileged access to information for personal gain was reasonably common, and a further 14 per cent thought this behaviour was quite usual. Those working on magazines were most likely to expect this behaviour.[30]

Divided Loyalties

Gifts, share offers and other kinds of freebies are not, of course, the only means by which a journalist's independence can be compromised. Some commentators argue, for instance, that journalists should not stand for public office or accept any paid part-time jobs or become actively involved in political or social causes because of the conflict of interest problems that might arise. They suggest that journalists who hold public positions or are emotionally committed to one side of an issue cannot be relied on to write impartially about the organisations in which they are involved.

We can think of obvious cases where it might be a problem, for instance if a political correspondent was privately acting as a paid consultant to a political party or a real estate reporter was on the payroll of a developer whose projects he was describing or the local government reporter also happened to be married to the mayor. Questions could legitimately be asked about whether their connections allowed them to write without fear or favour and tell the public all they needed to know. But again, where should the line be drawn? Is it sensible, or practicable, to impose an embargo on all outside activities by journalists simply because of potential conflicts of interest? Should the environment reporter be transferred to other assignments because he is also president of the Save the Forests League, or the minerals and energy reporter be shifted because she campaigns actively against the mining of uranium? Or should a journalist be asked to stand down from the local council because he or she also reports council affairs for the local newspaper? No, according to the Press Council, not unless it can be demonstrated that the reporter has misused his or her position as councillor.[31]

Nevertheless, some employers are extremely anxious to avoid apparent conflicts of interest. For instance, during the by-election for the federal Victorian seat of Wills in May 1992 the Independent candidate, Phil Cleary, was unable to continue in his role as Victorian Football Association commentator for the ABC. From the moment he decided to stand the ABC refused to let him appear in any of the programs he had previously worked on because it might appear that the ABC were supporting him.

Common sense would seem to demand that journalists should declare any outside interests which could conflict with their duties to their employers and to the public. But as two American commentators note, there is a danger that in their zeal to demonstrate their purity some news organisations might reach too far into the personal lives of their employees by over-regulating outside activities that pose no real conflict.[32]

The problem has not so far sparked much discussion in Australian journalism and the AJA judiciary committees have not yet had to deal with one conflict of interest case. However, the issue has aroused a lot of controversy in the United States where some news organisations are very strict, others relatively permissive, in their attitudes to political and community involvement by journalists. Some American newspapers like the *Chicago Tribune* tell their reporters not to run for public office, the *NBC News* says it will discipline employees who speak publicly on controversial issues, and editorial staff of the *Philadephia Inquirer* were once warned against wearing anti-war badges at public rallies. On the other hand, the *New York Times* allows staff to do 'creative, community or personal work and to earn additional income in ways that are separate and distinguishable from their work at the newspaper', while journalists at the *Boston Globe* need written permission to run for office but are generally free to engage in political activities.[33]

Most journalists are sensible enough to avoid activities that would lead to their impartiality and integrity being challenged. However, many object strongly when codes of ethics or individual employers stipulate how they should conduct their private lives. What they do in their own time, they say, is not their employers' business. Others say there are positive virtues in being directly involved in community organisations, arguing that it makes them better informed citizens and, as such, better journalists.

Against this it is argued that the observance of a code of ethics requires the sacrifice of some freedoms and that journalists who are prevented from being involved in politics or other community roles are not being asked to surrender their rights, only to suspend temporarily the exercise of those rights.

But some journalists are not easily persuaded by that kind of argument. They point out that many newspaper proprietors serve as directors, patrons or officials of companies and community groups that are often in the news. This could easily influence their attitudes to the way those organisations are covered in their own newspapers. Indeed, they have more power to determine what is fit to print and whether favouritism should be shown. The same holds true of senior management and some editors. As Hulteng notes:

> If reporters know that one of the owners of the paper is a board member of the local community theatre, or a director of a major corporation with plants in the paper's circulation area, the reporters' coverage of theatre productions or a strike at the plant is almost certain to be affected to some degree. There is no need for a smoking-gun directive from on high; awareness of the involvement of the top brass seeps out by a kind of osmosis and tends to tinge the publication's treatment of news.[34]

Not surprisingly, then, journalists sometimes argue that bans on outside activities, if necessary at all, can only make sense if they apply to everyone in the news organisation, not just reporters. They are prepared to admit that outside jobs, paid or unpaid, can in some circumstances conflict with their role(s) as journalists. Nevertheless, they are not easily convinced that the rules of ethical behaviour should be any different or any less rigorous for management.

CHAPTER 11

The Pressures of Business

Conflict of interest comes in many forms. In the preceding chapter we examined the problems that arise when individual journalists are beholden to several masters. Now we look at the contentious issue of conflict of interest of media owners and managers. The dual nature of the news media — as businesses and social institutions — makes actual and perceived conflict inevitable, but the damaging effects on right conduct may be mitigated by reliance on the principle of full disclosure. The House of Representatives Select Committee on the Print Media acknowledged the conflict difficulty in its report *News & Fair Facts*:

> The key issue . . . is the separation of the legitimate business interests of the proprietor or management to run a business for profit from the editorial process of the fair selection and presentation of news. Such separation, however, may not be entirely possible. Owners and managers have a say in the general editorial direction of the paper, and select editors who in turn have responsibility to maintain or increase circulation figures.[1]

The committee was talking specifically about the press, but the same can be said about the broadcast media. One might also add that there is an imbalance in the claims of the two parties, management and editorial staff. Australian finance law imposes a fiduciary duty on directors of public companies to conduct company business in the interests of shareholders. No similar general legal duty requires editors and their staffs to produce fair reports in the interests of the audience, although defamation and other such specific laws apply to the interests of news makers.

In any ethical discussion, the introduction of material things such as money tends to confuse the issue. Many people assume that money automatically taints right conduct. This is not so; but the transfer of money does change the components that must be taken into account in the process of ethical decision making. Money can change loyalties and obligations and, consequently, the final decision.

The inherent conflict of interest between business considerations and independent editorial judgements manifests itself in three ways. The first is the influence of advertisers on the editorial content of a news outlet. The second is the cross-promotion of a media business within the editorial pages or in a news bulletin. The third, and perhaps the most controversial in Australia because of the country's high level of concentration of ownership of the news media, is the impact that owners' outside business interests might have on the reporting of those interests in the owners' news outlet.

Paying the Piper, Calling the Tune

For well over a century, since the advent of privately owned newspapers dependent on advertising revenue for survival, Australian news organisations have faced the predicament of deciding whether to bite the hand that feeds them and publish stories or adopt an editorial stand that runs counter to the interests of the advertisers who largely foot the bill.

In the late 1860s David Syme — who had taken over *The Age* in Victoria from his brother and had built it into a thundering advocate of liberal values and protectionist trade policies — faced an advertising boycott from the colony's freetrader merchants. Syme countered by dropping the paper's price from threepence to a penny and succeeded in trebling its circulation, thus off-setting the financial impact of the boycott.[2] In 1986, businessman Alan Bond withdrew advertising lodged by his extensive business concerns from John Fairfax publications because he objected to *The Sydney Morning Herald's* coverage of his activities. The ban lasted a year and, according to one report, cost Fairfax several million dollars in revenue.[3]

Usually such boycotts are relatively short-lived, largely because advertisers derive benefit from being able to advertise their products and a long-term boycott can affect sales. They can, however, be devastating for smaller media organisations. A former associate editor of *The Age* and Press Council member, Peter Cole-Adams, spelt out the implications in an address on censorship and self-censorship:

> Advertising being the lifeblood of commercial publishing, major advertisers are in a position of some potential power, particularly in relation to smaller media enterprises. Country and suburban newspapers and local radio stations are typically dependent on relatively few advertisers for their bread and butter. It is a brave, arguably foolhardy, country editor who consistently runs an editorial policy that threatens the interests of the blokes in the Rotary Club. A sustained advertisers' boy-cott could spell ruin for the paper and unemployment for the editor.
>
> Metropolitan newspapers and electronic media are much less vulnerable to such overt and crude pressures.[4]

If larger organisations are less vulnerable, it may be that they are often part of conglomerations with non-media interests that can tide them over the hump, in itself a problem as we have noted. No such internal subsidy is possible for the one-person bush paper where the editor often operates as advertising manager, desktop publisher and chief reporter.

However damaging commercial advertising boycotts may be, more sinister are the occasional attempts by governments to bring renegade news media to heel by similar means. In the early 1980s, two state governments decided to stop placing lucrative classified advertising orders with newspapers which had appar-ently offended them. The Australian Press Council, commenting on the decision by the New South Wales Premier's Department not to lodge classified advertisements with *The Sydney Morning Herald*, saw the decision as a possible threat to the freedom of the press. The department had said a review had found that transferring the advertising to the rival newspaper, *The Daily Telegraph*, would achieve significant cost savings. But in the light of the New South Wales Premier's strong criticism of reports and comments in John Fairfax publications, the council was sceptical.

> The withdrawal of government advertising is an established method of discouraging or punishing criticism of the government in a number of overseas countries. Examples have occurred recently in Mexico, Bolivia, India and under the military regime in Argentina.
>
> . . . the Press Council is not able to determine whether the transfer was politically motivated, although it does consider that the government might reasonably have been expected to justify its decisions in more detail than it has chosen to do.
>
> The situation is thoroughly unsatisfactory.[5]

The council also noted a similar ban imposed by the Bjelke-Petersen government in Queensland. Although 'unsatisfactory', government attempts to muzzle fair report and comment are likely to come to grief in Australia because of the news media's vehement defence of their role as watchdogs of government.

Government bans do not happen often, fortunately. Much more common and more insidious in terms of the tainting of information presented to the public as independent journalism is the nexus between the advertising and editorial departments that may develop inside individual news organisations. Cultivated closeness between the two arms of the enterprise gives birth to the 'advertorial', an item in the editorial pages which reads exactly like surrounding news items and is presented as news but which has won its place in the paper in return for an advertiser buying space.

Some newspaper organisations, such as the Isaacson suburban newspaper group in Melbourne, ban advertorials outright. Others do not. In a study which looked partly at the effects of the 1990s recession on advertising pressure on editorial content in the Victorian media, Georgina Griffin found evidence that reports were linked to advertising. Tony Wells, a sub-editor and member of the Victorian judiciary committee, told her:

> We're one of many local papers that runs articles where the only reason they get a guernsey in the paper is because Joe Bloggs advertises . . . We did an article about a bloke in

Williamstown who runs a chicken shop. It got in the paper because it was the only way to get him to advertise with us. And I think that's appalling.[6]

Some, while not so open about encouraging the quid pro quo of advertorials, have weekly meetings between advertising and editorial staffs so the two groups can bounce ideas off each other.[7] Other groups, big and small, publish advertorials but label them as such.

The problem with advertorials is that they can contain information of genuine interest to the audience. Griffin cites the example of a man who advertised a diet and health seminar in *The Footscray Mail* in suburban Melbourne. He asked if the paper would run a story on him and the editor agreed because he believed the item was 'beneficial to the community'.[8] But who among his readers would have known that the decisions to run the story was made on its editorial merits, not its advertising link? A nearby advertisement must surely have made them think twice about the item's claims to news value.

The recognition difficulty is compounded by increased service journalism in modern newspapers. The advent of lifestyle pages in daily newspapers during the late 1970s and lifestyle programs on commercial television in the early 1990s has confused matters. The days are long gone when the women's editor of *The Sydney Morning Herald* at the time of World War I could refuse to report the names of ballrooms in which dances were held for fear that people might perceive the news to be tainted by commercial considerations.[9] Today quantities of newsprint are devoted to product news of various forms, much of it, as we saw in Chapter 2, written by publicity or public relations practitioners, not journalists. How do the readers determine whether such information has been selected by the same news criteria as the rest of the paper? The answer is, they cannot. They can only trust the media to do the right thing.

Accommodating the wishes of advertisers is not restricted to the press. Television news bulletins yield examples in which commercial considerations appear to colour news selection. In September 1993, the ABC's *Media Watch* program took one of its commercial competitors to task for its advance coverage of the Australian launch of the Nissan Bluebird.[10] On 22 September, the Channel Ten news bulletin in Sydney, Melbourne and Canberra extolled the car's virtues, claiming its design was partly modelled on a jet fighter. Its speedo reading was reflected onto the windscreen, 'a safety measure enabling drivers to check speed without taking their eyes off the road'. The following evening, the Sydney bulletin ran another laudatory story on the Bluebird, this time showing a reporter test driving the vehicle. No other television news network covered the story. On 26 September, an ad aired during the Channel Ten news announced: 'Tonight's edition of *Eyewitness News* is proudly brought to you by the fully imported Bluebird by the new Nissan'.

Earlier in the year, *Media Watch's* presenter, Stuart Littlemore, castigated Channel Ten for a news story in which a media release outlining the merits of the introduction of 24-hour banking by the St Georges Bank — a large advertiser with the Ten Network — was incorporated almost word for word in the reporter's story. He also questioned the news judgement behind Channel Nine's decision to run a three-minute interview with the new managing director of the McDonalds hamburger chain on the *Today Show* when the non-commercial channels seemed to have missed the story.[11]

The Press Council has had no time for advertorials either, consistently asserting the need for editorial matter and advertising to be delineated clearly. In 1978 it heard a complaint from a candidate in municipal elections for the City of Oakleigh, a Melbourne suburb. The candidate said that the local paper, the *Chadstone Progress*, had told him the paper's policy was not to publish editorial comment from candidates unless they inserted several advertisements. The candidate maintained he could not afford to advertise and sought the council's ruling on what he considered a discriminatory practice. The paper's editor said it was true that all political and municipal candidates were required to take out minimal advertising so that they might submit 100 words of their policy for publication in the issue before each election. The policy was a long-standing one but the complainant had been misled; candidates were only required to take out one advertisement which could cost as little as $7.80. Resisting the temptation to point out to the *Chadstone Progress* the press's public duty to publish information about candidates during an election, the council said merely: 'The Press Council cannot support the policy of a paper in stipulating that a policy statement cannot be published unless accompanied by paid advertising'.[12]

Six years later, the Advertising Standards Council asked the Press Council to issue a statement on advertorials and their use. The statement made the essential distinction between advertorials and regular features and supplements which contain related advertising material.

'Advertorials' are defined as stories providing direct support for particular advertisements, conditional on the paid advertising appearing.

The Press Council believes 'advertorials' presented in the guise of news reports are misleading.

Readers of a newspaper are entitled to expect that news will be presented in good faith.

It is a breach of good faith when news is contrived so that stories appear that are conditional on paid advertising and are an integral part of such advertising. Such practices must result in a lowering of public confidence in the integrity and independence of newspapers. They are also an affront to proper standards of journalism.

The Press Council believes where such advertisements occur, the entire material should be regarded as an advertisement and clearly identified as such, by the use of such labels as ADVERTISEMENT and SUPERCAR SUPPLEMENT.

However, the council recognises there are many occasions when products or services are the proper subject of news reports. This applies particularly where the products or services are of direct relevance to the publication's readership, such as news about home improvement or gardening products, or services in publications directed to readers interested in those subjects.

The council also believes there are legitimate regular features and supplements which attract related advertising content.

Such features, sections and supplements should, to avoid any possible confusion, be labelled with such words as COMPUTER SUPPLEMENT, MOTORING SECTION, REAL ESTATE NEWS.

The dividing line is crossed where direct editorial support for a specific product or service is provided conditional upon paid advertising space.

The council believes that readers are entitled to expect on all occasions that journalists are free to write objectively without pressure or influence because of advertising considerations.[13]

The Press Council's counsel of perfection does not completely resolve the issue. While it is a simple matter to label material that is conditional on paid advertising with a banner or strap heading announcing an 'advertising feature', it does not cover the grey areas in which a story, such as the diet and leisure seminar case mentioned above, is of some independent value. Nor does it deal with those countless pages of restaurant reviews and such that are published in local papers, seemingly to provide an independent service to the readership.

The journalist, assigned to write such reports or reviews, may well be less rigorous in the questioning and more generous in the writing. But, at least, the council's statement spells out the dichotomy that many in the industry recognise. If the idea for a story or supplement comes from editorial staff and is treated like any other news item, it is editorial material. When the impetus comes from the advertising department, whatever the story's final form, it is advertising.

Identifying when a news story in the broadcast media has independent merit is even less easy, because advertisements are aired during non-news programming and are thus divorced in time from news bulletins, even though their influence may be felt.

Some news editors of metropolitan television channels assert there is a clear division between the advertising department and the newsroom. John Gibson, news editor at Channel Seven in Melbourne, says: '[I] don't think that we're deliberately kept separate but I just don't think we're interested in their sort of area and I don't think they're very interested in us'.[14] But the division seems less marked in regional television. As the news director at one Victorian regional television station said: 'The advertising staff do walk in frequently. They always have and always will. They say: "We've got a client, can you do this and this". If there's a story there, we'll do it, but it's got to be newsworthy.'[15]

Pressure from advertisers can be applied to make so-called news favourable to the advertiser. It can also be used to suppress unfavourable information. A former editor of *The Australian*, Adrian Deamer, recounted an instance to the New South Wales Council for Civil Liberties in 1972. It concerned the now-defunct department store company, Waltons, which was a big advertiser in the *Daily Mirror*, a stablemate of *The Australian*.

> When [Waltons'] annual report was due in 1969, the assistant editor of the *Australian*, Alan Ramsay, who was acting editor of the paper while I was down at Canberra, was called around to the chairman's office and told that the *Australian* was to give Waltons' report a 'good run' in the paper and to handle it gently. For some reason, and, knowing the assistant editor at the time, I think probably just out of anger, the message was

not passed on to me or the finance editor. The story was run and treated as it would normally have been, under the heading 'Waltons profit rate drops'. The first I knew that anything was wrong was when the chairman was on the telephone . . . He wanted to know why we handled the story the way we did. I said I thought it was a normal way, and, why, what was the trouble? And he said it was an absurd way to handle it, especially as 'You put it next to the report from David Jones which you didn't handle much better' . . . I didn't know whether the chairman had been asked by Waltons to treat them favourably, or whether he did it on his own initiative because of the advertising tie-up with the *Mirror*. The *Australian*, of course had no Waltons' advertising. But the result of this, although it failed at that time, succeeded in the next year. We knew without being told how to handle the Waltons story, and we made sure that the story wasn't next to David Jones and the heading was a straight-forward thing like 'Waltons profit'.[16]

Deamer's story is now old but it remains telling evidence of how the needs of advertisers can pervert the news. It is difficult to gauge how often pressure is exerted because few news executives are as willing to go on the record as Deamer was.

Most news organisations, both print and broadcast, have a policy not to allow critical stories about advertisers to appear next to their advertisements. The deputy news director at Channel Nine in Melbourne, Richard Allen, explained the rationale behind such a policy:

We get a copy of what advertisements are in the news each night and if we've got a story that conflicts in any way [with the advertisements] we just get onto the traffic department (who do the scheduling) and get them to change it. If we've got a story on Ford being car of the year and Holden is the first ad up in the next ad break you might move it just out of that place because it's going to make you both look a bit silly.[17]

Shifting the placement of an advertisement to save face is not unethical, simply realistic. What would be of concern is if the news story's placement were changed to accommodate the advertiser. If a negative news story deemed worth a position on page three, for instance, were buried back in the paper to avoid conflicting with a page-three advertisement, then the value of the story would be compromised.

The news media do themselves a disservice and weaken their credibility if they claim to be fearless and independent in their selection and treatment of news and are then seen to be succumbing to pressure from advertisers to bend the rules. But the public is sensible about such matters. People realise advertising is essential to the continued dissemination of news in a capitalist system. If material is published or broadcast that has an advertising component and is acknowledged as having it, then public confidence is not betrayed. It is the slanting of stories to favour advertisers' interests and the hidden advertisement that, justifiably, attract charges of unethical conduct.

Promoting the Enterprise

In-house promotions and circulation boosters, such as games and competitions, present similar problems for journalists and news executives as outside advertising pressures do. As far as the public is concerned, however, such promotions are usually obvious and the audience can easily discount their intrinsic news value.

The widespread promotion of newspapers and periodicals for anything other than their news and information content is a relatively recent phenomenon in Australia. It was not until the late 1960s that newspapers began to seek sophisticated ways of enhancing their public image. Of course, during the 19th century and the first half of the 20th century, individual papers and owners sponsored singing contests, rifle competitions, art shows and so on. It was a perfectly acceptable way to be part of the community. But it was fairly low key and sporadic.

Today, the news media seek to promote their product vigorously, by publishing non-newspaper material, sponsoring community programs to monitor pollution or spot sharks off popular bathing beaches, and arranging public events such as literary luncheons. Most of these events are acknowledged for what they are: pure puffery. Others are a little slower to announce their real intent.

Take a random example. On 11 October, *The Australian* carried a picture story across five columns with the headline

'McCullough writes off debate on republic'. The story was an interview with author Colleen McCullough who had, according to the reporter, 'written three novels about the Roman republic and has planned another three'; the latest title in the series was *Fortune's Favourites*.

The interview appeared topical, for community debate on an Australian republic was running hot. McCullough's views on political moves for a republic took up the first third of the story. The reason for publication, however, was not McCullough's authority on republicanism, albeit of the historical variety. The final two paragraphs of the 23-paragraph 'news' story read:

> McCullough will speak about Fortune's Favourites during a series of literary lunches sponsored by *The Australian* and Myer/Grace Bros.
>
> Lunches will be held in Sydney on October 13, Melbourne on October 14, Adelaide on October 18, Perth on October 20 and Brisbane on October 22.[18]

Such manipulation of news value is common, although the Press Council has expressed muted concern about the practice. In April 1985 it heard a complaint about an item headed 'Thesaurus begin as a 12km list', which had appeared on a news page of *The West Australian*. The complainant's objection was that the article was nothing more than an advertisement, yet it was presented as a news article. It was deceptive because the reader was led to read what purported to be a news item, only to discover the real purpose at the end when the story said: 'The Macquarie Thesaurus is available from WA Newspapers book department in Newspaper House and our Fremantle office in Highgate Court for $29.95. Mail orders are welcome'.[19]

In its adjudication, the council noted that the editor had pointed out that the use of promotional material of this kind was a fairly common practice among newspaper publishers in Australia.

> He said that the information was of genuine interest to readers, was accurate, and was not deceptive because the interest of the publisher was made clear. These points are well taken in the context of current practice and the council does not see the occasion as calling for any condemnation of the newspaper.[20]

Although it absolved the paper of misconduct, the council took the opportunity to restate its position on advertorials and promotional material.

The [advertorial] policy is directed to ensuring that readers are not misled by assuming that what appears in the news columns is the objective work of journalists when in fact it is written for promotional purposes. When a newspaper promotes its own retailing, there is no question of paid advertising, but there is equal need to distinguish between material which appears in the paper as the result of the independent professional work of journalists, and that which is inserted for advertising purposes. The Press Council considers that the true character of promotional material should always be made obvious to the reader.[21]

Cross-promotion is not, of course, restricted to newspapers and magazines. Television news bulletins often contain items that relate favourably to other programs shown on the channel. When the long-running television serial *A Country Practice* ceased production in 1993, Channel Seven news carried a story about the cast party after the final episode; rival stations which did not screen the series ignored the story, although it was of clear interest to at least some viewers. During the Channel Ten news bulletin on Melbourne Cup Day in 1993, vision of the famous horse race was replayed several times; the fact that the channel's sports department had the rights to telecast the Cup meeting was obvious.

As long as in-house promotion is clearly identified, it does not cross the boundary into unethical behaviour. But journalists should resist the temptation to embellish such stories to meet news judgement criteria when such criteria do not apply.

Reporting the Boss's Business

In the mid-1980s, a feeding frenzy began in the Australian media. Established media owners such as Rupert Murdoch and relative newcomers — including Robert Holmes à Court, Alan Bond and Christopher Skase — began carving up Australia's newspaper empires and television networks as if playing a Monopoly game. Properties changed hands, deals were done, the rules on media ownership were rewritten. Then Warwick Fairfax Junior, the 26-year-old scion of the Fairfax clan which had ruled a newspaper empire since 1841, entered the lists. In August 1987, he launched a bid for the shares in the Fairfax group, aiming to privatise the company. To raise the cash, he had to slice away lucrative parts of the empire. He promised a rich prize, *The Australian Financial Review*, to Robert Holmes à Court, one of the superstar business entrepreneurs of the money-crazy decade, as part of a package which was to raise $475 million. Before the deal was finalised, the stock market crashed and hit Holmes à Court hard. The deal was cancelled, leaving *The Australian Financial Review* in the Fairfax stable.

The implications, however, were profound for those who were concerned about free and fearless reporting of business news. Commenting the next year on the aborted sale, the then editor of *The Age*, Creighton Burns, spelled out the ramifications clearly:

> When Mr Robert Holmes à Court appeared to be on the point of acquiring control of the only national financial daily, *The Australian Financial Review*, there was considerable head shaking in the business community. No matter what Mr Holmes à Court said or did, would it be possible to attach the same credibility to the financial reports and analyses in the newspaper if it was owned by one of the nation's then leading speculative investors and financial managers.
>
> The same questions must be asked, the same reservations made, of Messrs Murdoch, Packer and Bond who between them effectively control over three-quarters of the national daily circulation.
>
> . . .
>
> Mr Bond has substantial interests in brewing, coal mining, gold mining, real estate and property development and communications, including . . . a share in the telephone system of Chile. If one were editing a newspaper for Mr Bond, imagine the anguished soul-searching that would be involved in writing an editorial on a budget which substantially increased the excise on beer, or the recommendation of a Royal Commission into a tax on gold, or national elections in Chile. And if one's editorials deplored the increase in the excise on beer, opposed a tax on gold and acclaimed the re-election of General Pinochet, imagine the problems one's readers would have in deciding whether one's opinions were entirely disinterested.[22]

Burns could also have added that Skase owned, among other things, tourist resorts and property developments, or listed Murdoch's interests in transport and film distribution companies and numerous other non-media enterprises.

Holmes à Court's death and the bankruptcies of Alan Bond and Christopher Skase removed those three players from the media game. But the potential for distortion of news about the non-media business interests of media owners remained of considerable concern to media critics and many within the industry.

Business journalists themselves are aware of the constraints. A 1992 survey of 105 economic, finance and business journalists by the Australian Centre for Independent Journalism found that one-third agreed they would 'not pursue a story that was potentially damaging to [their] employer's commercial interests as actively as a story about an unrelated company'. Another third absolutely rejected the proposition.[23]

A year earlier, the House of Representatives Select Committee on the Print Media heard conflicting evidence on the degree to which the non-media businesses of media owners were favourably reported. The committee noted that there seemed to be general agreement that 'the editor should ensure that reporting of the business interests of the proprietor is done fairly. However, in a situation of increasing levels of concentration of ownership, the fear exists that this will not always be possible . . .'[24]

In particular, the committee heard competing claims about the coverage of the 1989 airline pilots' strike. Julianne Schultz of the Australian Centre for Independent Journalism told the inquiry that the centre's research 'pointed toward there being a particular sort of coverage of that dispute which was not incompatible with the corporate aims and the nature of News Limited, which owns part of Ansett'.[25] The editor-in-chief of *The Australian*, Paul Kelly, rejected the claim as a 'slur on our professionalism'[26] and News Limited tendered the findings of a study it had commissioned which 'concluded that in both news stories and editorial coverage there were no statistically significant differences between Fairfax and News Limited papers in their coverage of the pilots' dispute'.[27] The last word appeared to lie with Gerard Noonan, editor of *The Australian Financial Review*, who told the committee that it had become something like folklore that Ansett got a better run in *The Australian* but that he could not detect any such bias. The committee noted that, because Noonan was editor of a rival publication, he 'would presumably have an interest in "exposing" any such bias'.[28]

Noonan, however, was less forgiving when he commented to the inquiry about the publication in *The Australian* of an article about News Limited from *The Economist*. *The Economist* article had been altered — by the non-publication of a caricature of Murdoch, the changing of cross-heads and headlines and alterations to the text — in such a way as to present 'an image that is a little more favourable to News Corp', Noonan said.[29] Kelly again countered, saying that his newspaper covered 'the activities of our own company in the same way in which we cover those of other companies'.[30]

In October 1993, Kelly restated his position in reply to the allegations of media critic Stuart Littlemore that *The Australian* had published 'sycophantic and unbelievably lengthy' interviews with Murdoch and given favourable treatment to News Limited proposals to issue 'super shares'. Errol Simper, *The Australian's* communications writer, detailed his editor-in-chief's rejection of Littlemore's claims.

> It was a completely proper and professional interview. The questions were completely proper and appropriate. It was the first interview [the paper] had published with Mr Murdoch for quite some time. We sought the interview; we were very pleased to be given the interview.
>
> . . .
>
> We report our own affairs, in terms of company affairs, the same way as we treat other companies.
>
> As a commercial story, one of the realities is that the share price has increased somewhat remarkably over the course of the last 18 months. So the commercial story in relation to News has been a story of success.
>
> In the period before that, when the share price collapsed and the company was in severe financial difficulty, these facts and events were reported and analysed in *The Australian* in considerable detail.[31]

Traditionally allegations of bias in reporting media owners' business interests have been met publicly with a 'you did, you didn't' response. Anecdotal evidence and the very real constraints of self-censorship suggest, however, that the public does not always get a totally impartial coverage of such stories. Even if it did, the fact remains that rightly or wrongly — as Creighton Burns pointed out — the credibility of the news media is undermined.

Whatever the truth of the matter, the journalist and the editorial executive are faced with a range of difficult ethical decisions whenever the business face of the news media confronts its indivisible twin, the publicly accountable social institution.

CHAPTER 12

The Challenge Ahead

In 1989 *The Bulletin* — a periodical that has been around in different guises for longer than Australia has been a modern nation — asked why our media were 'on the nose'. *The Bulletin* sought the answers from the country's editors, leading journalists, politicians and businessmen. Had it asked the people, they might have answered: 'Because they smell of hypocrisy. They say they work on our behalf. They say they tell the truth. But what they really do is give us half the truth. They sensationalise things, just to get us to buy their papers and watch their shows. They talk about how they fight corrupt politicians and crims but they'd sell their grandmothers for a good story. They barge in whenever they want to without so much as a by-your-leave. You could be injured or half-dead and they still won't leave you alone. They reckon they are the voice of the public. But when we complain, they don't want to listen'.

The news media claim that they do listen: they have developed codes of practice to meet public criticism and have established mechanisms to deal with people's complaints. On the face of it, that is true.

The union representing journalists, the Media, Entertainment and Arts Alliance (MEAA), has its 10-point code of ethics that sets standards of conduct for all its members and, in 1993, announced it would review the code to make it more effective. The broadcast media peak bodies, the Federation of Australian Commercial Television Stations and the Federation of Australian Radio Broadcasters, published codes of practice laying down principles of responsible broadcasting, binding on all their member stations. The Australian Broadcasting Corporation revised its editorial policy to set up an independent complaints review panel to hear complaints of serious bias, lack of balance or unfair treatment in its programs. The Australian Press Council, midway through its second decade of operation, pledged itself to become more visible and vigorous in its handling of public grievances.

This flurry of activity and apparent willingness to lift standards of conduct was partly in response to perceived concerns about the implications of concentration in media ownership and to a deregulatory environment for the broadcast media. But it was also a reaction to the constant stream of findings by public inquiries which concluded that the news media shared some responsibility for Australia's social and political problems. Adverse comment came, for instance, from the Royal Commission into Aboriginal Deaths in Custody, the Fitzgerald Inquiry into political corruption in Queensland and the National Inquiry into Racist Violence.

The news media's traditional antagonist, government, also entered the fray in the early 1990s. Sensing the public mood of disquiet, the federal parliament established bipartisan House of Representatives and Senate inquiries into the operations and ethics of the media.

While the media were prepared to cooperate, government attention was the last thing they wanted. The intervention of government has always been seen as a profound threat to the freedom of the news media to fulfil their professed role as guardians of democracy. Their claim to special authority is based on their ability as an independent institution to curb the excesses of government and provide citizens with the facts they need to make informed choices about the sort of society they want to live in.

Unfortunately, these high-sounding ideals are inevitably modified by the need of the media to survive in a competitive, commercial environment. Much of the public disenchantment results from the tensions between the public service role and the profit imperative. It is possible to meet both objectives; however, it is not easy.

Reasons for Past Failures

Why have the Australian news media's previous attempts to demonstrate their accountability and good intent failed to convince the public? How can news organisations repair their relationship with their audience, without being subjected to the unacceptable alternative of government controls?

The media's past response to public criticism has been fragmented and incoherent. Different parts of the news industry have put forward different solutions. The press has stood aloof from broadcasting. Publishers and working journalists have looked for guidance to two separate self-regulatory bodies. In-house rules are rarely codified and live only in a hazy collective memory or are expressed in random editorial memos.

The trouble with the application of the MEAA journalists' code of ethics is that it covers only the conduct of its members, and excludes proprietors, publishers and senior editorial executives who shape the product and sometimes exert strong pressures on their staff to behave unethically.[1] It does, however, have the advantage that it covers journalists in both print and broadcast media. But, for the first 50 years of the code's operation, breaches were adjudicated in private by the defendant's fellow members only, sitting as an elected judiciary committee. There was virtually no publication of either the evidence, the results or reasoning behind the committees' decisions. The wording of the code dealt with the central issues of truth, fairness, honest dealing, respect for individuals and the public's right to information; but without a body of interpretation and clear precedents it remained too vague to help a journalist in daily decision making.[2]

The number of alleged breaches heard by judiciary committees is minuscule and, in most years, can be counted on the fingers of one hand. Further, despite the provision for reprimands, fines, suspension and expulsion of errant members, the penalties are so rarely invoked that they have no deterrent effect. A clear illustration of this was the failure of the Victorian branch of the union to enforce payment of a fine of $500 imposed on the producer of a Melbourne television program by the branch judiciary committee. For four years, the committee pressed both the branch leadership and the federal executive of the union to take action to recover the fine, but without success. In the view of several committee members, the failure rendered the judiciary system impotent and the code a dead letter because members could now treat the code contemptuously and with impunity.[3] The chairman of the committee, Maclaren Gordon, resigned from the chair and the union because Australian Journalists Association (AJA) judiciary committees could 'no longer effectively perform the function of taking appropriate disciplinary action when there are proved breaches of the Code of Ethics'.[4] He had been an AJA member for 50 years.

The problem with the Australian Press Council is that, as its name implies, it has the authority to deal only with complaints against newspapers and periodicals and not against the ubiquitous influence of television and radio. The council hears complaints against a publication, rather than the individuals responsible for the publication. While it brings publishers and editorial executives within the scope of its judgement, the responsibility for unethical behaviour is never directly apportioned so that transgressors are not seen to take personal responsibility for their conduct. Adjudications are strewn with general phrases such as 'the newspaper erred' and 'the paper might have done more'.

The council's representation does include members of the public; but industry representatives form the majority. Further, since the AJA withdrew from the council in 1987, those industry representatives come almost exclusively from the ranks of editors or editorial managers. However hard the council strives to convey a public impression of independent judgement, it continues to be labelled, with some justification, as a publishers' poodle.

The council operates on the principle of the public disclosure of misdemeanour and, in recent years, the number of its adjudications — adverse or otherwise — published in defendant and other publications has greatly increased. Some stigma certainly attaches to exposure of this kind and the council often asserts that publicity has a salutary effect on media standards. Publication also provides a measure of case law — although the council's adjudications are frequently erratic and narrowly based. The council looks at the specifics of cases, without conceding the validity of broader criticisms of media images. The adjudications are rarely placed in context.

Ultimately, however, the council must be judged on whether its decisions have had lasting impact on publishers and journalists. Public disaffection with the press suggests the council's moral authority has been only marginal and there is no overt evidence from within the industry that, without the power to punish, it is much feared.

The self-regulatory procedures for the broadcast media, which came into being with the 1992 Broadcasting Services Act, will take some years to test. As the present codes of practice stand, self-regulation does not require public participation, nor are the powers of the final 'court of appeal', the Australian Broadcasting Authority, made clear. Complaints that go as far as the Australian Broadcasting Authority will not be dealt with at the time. They may, however, be taken into account when the allegedly offending station's broadcast licence is up for renewal.

The Act was a deregulatory move that took away some of the punitive powers exercised by the earlier Australian Broadcasting Tribunal. If the tribunal precedent is anything to go by, the Australian Broadcasting Authority will have little impact on ethical standards. The tribunal rarely found broadcasters in breach of its broadcast standards, and in at least one case where it did so, it imposed no sanction.[5]

Prescriptions for Change

We have argued that a piecemeal approach to ensuring adherence to ethical standards does not satisfy the needs of the industry or the public. The nature of moral reasoning dictates consistency, yet discussion about ethical matters when it does occur in the Australian news media is characterised by shoddy logic and heavy reliance on 19th century newspaper rhetoric. To win back public trust and support, the different branches of the news media must get their act together. This means change at three levels: for individuals, news organisations and the industry as a whole.

Change will require acceptance that ethical conduct really does matter to the survival of a free and robust media industry.

It will require more rigorous intellectual consistency than simply repeating the old catchcries. It is no longer good enough for the public interest to be invoked to defend unethical behaviour relating to news items that have no public interest component. Change may even require the creation of new channels for public access and scrutiny.

Ethical conduct cannot be imposed; it can be encouraged and celebrated. Here are some strategies for change:

- Individual news organisations should develop in-house policies that establish the boundaries of acceptable behaviour for their own journalists and systems to discipline those who offend. Such policies should be publicised as widely as possible.
- In-house commitment to change should include rigorous intellectual debate on ethical issues so that individuals, whatever their status in the news organisation, understand the components of ethical decision making. Opportunities for debate should be provided in formal training programs, informal seminars and discussions. Discussions about ethics should be regarded as essential as skills training.
- Individual organisations should also consider establishing regular lines of communication with their publics. The tactics will vary depending on the nature of the organisation and its resources, but should go beyond the traditional Letters to the Editor and other forms of tokenism. They may include: public forums on media issues sponsored by individual news media outlets or co-sponsored with outside organisations; the appointment of independent ombudsmen to mediate between the news organisation and its audience; the introduction, or expansion, of media commentary columns or programs.[6] All such initiatives have to be properly planned. *The Sydney Morning Herald's* brief experiment in employing George Masterman, QC, as an ombudsman, aborted in 1990 because of disagreement between management and the journalists' union over the scope of his role, shows the need for prior identification by all parties of an ombudsman's powers and obligations.[7]

Individual organisations can do much to build understanding and create confidence among their own audience. But the Australian news media must also be seen to be acting in unison to promote higher standards and accountability rather than putting up smokescreens to deflect criticism and protect their self-interest. The industry's credibility has suffered because the present systems of self-regulation have tended to shuffle the blame for wrong conduct to other parties. Union members say 'They forced me to do it'. Management says editorial staff are too demanding and do not understand the commercial realities. Television accuses the press of being holier-than-thou; the press blames television for declining standards; radio blames both. And the public says 'A pox on the house divided'.

A National News Media Commission

Branches of the media family should join in consideration of the benefits that might flow from the creation of a national news media commission. The objectives of the commission would be those of the Australian Press Council: to defend the freedom of the media and regulate standards of conduct. It would also shoulder a new responsibility of increasing public awareness and understanding of news media operations.

The commission would cover all news media, whether print or broadcast. It need not be cumbersome, either in its composition or its procedures. Each branch of the media can be adequately represented by a maximum of five members, which must include MEAA journalist members. Substantial public representation is essential to the commission's authority, however. Both the full commission and any complaints committee should have equal public and industry representation.

To be effective in raising standards of conduct, the commission would need more power than the Press Council's moral suasion. It would need to be able to reprimand or fine offenders, in addition to taking every opportunity to publicise transgressions. Government would need to confer a statuatory power to fine offenders, but that must be the limit of government intervention.

All parties who contribute to the production and dissemination of news and opinion would come under the commission's jurisdiction. Complaints could be lodged against individual journalists, editors, proprietors or against the publication or news program as a whole. The commission's responsibility would be to determine individual and/or collective culpability; the complainant should not have to identify either the exact nature of the alleged transgression or its perpetrator(s).

The commission would need greater and more reliable financial support than the Press Council has received to date. Funding options might include a levy on advertising revenue or annual profits and a levy on journalists' union members or some other form of direct industry contribution based on the size of media enterprises.

In meeting its educational responsibilities, the commission would draw not only on the knowledge and expertise of its constituent media and public members but on the resources of the whole community. It may, for instance, commission independent research on public perceptions of the media or develop industry-wide educational programs.

While we believe that our suggestions go a long way towards rectifying the failings of current methods of regulating media behaviour, the composition, objectives and powers of the commission can only be determined after the widest possible discussion between the various components of the news media and their publics.

In the end, whatever strategies the industry as a whole adopts to present a united and responsive face to the public, the future health of the profession depends on the willingness of every individual who is concerned with presenting news and opinion to the public to internalise the lessons of past failures and the wisdom of right conduct.

Exercises

There is no end to debate about ethics. Here are a few suggestions to keep you thinking about ethical journalism. They are grouped to relate to specific issues raised under the chapter headings and contain questions for class discussion and ideas for further individual study and research.

Chapter 1

Ideas for Discussion

1. The text identifies seven central goods or values of right conduct for the media. They are fairness, honesty, respect for the rights of others, keeping one's word, accuracy, full disclosure and respect for the needs of the community. Should the media take other values into account? If so, what are those values?
2. Is it possible to devise rules for journalists' conduct that can apply to every reporting situation without exception?

3. How do you distinguish between matters that are 'of public interest' and those that are 'in the public interest'? Or is there no difference?
4. The UK Press Complaints Commission defines the public interest as including exposure of crime or serious misdemeanour, issues of public safety, anti-social conduct or misleading statements. Are these categories sufficient?
5. What kinds of media behaviour are justified in the public interest?
6. How do you distinguish between matters that the public want to know about and those they need to know about? Does the difference between 'wants' and 'needs' result in different types of news story?

Ideas for Action
1. Devise a 12-point code of ethics for journalists, encompassing those values you believe are essential.
2. Gather a folio of stories over a period of time from a daily newspaper/radio or television news program that you believe meet the criterion of public need to know.
3. Analyse a single issue of a daily newspaper, a general interest magazine (including women's magazines), a radio news bulletin and a television news bulletin to identify which stories meet the 'need to know' criterion, which ones meet the 'want to know' criterion and which ones contain elements of both. What are the differences and similarities between the media?
4. Identify and develop two story ideas about events or issues in your immediate community about which the public needs to know. Do the same for two stories about which the public wants to know.

Chapter 2

Ideas for Discussion
1. What is meant by the term 'journalistic objectivity'? How true is it to say that there is no such thing as 'a good, objective journalist'?
2. Can you identify those elements that distinguish 'unconscious bias' from 'deliberate bias'?

3. Is media bias always unethical? If not, in what circumstances could it be ethical and justifiable?
4. Can you identify specific characteristics that distinguish 'factual reporting' from 'truthful reporting'? Could factual and/or truthful reporting sometimes be considered unethical?

Ideas for Action

1. Return to your code of ethics prepared for Chapter 1. Write a short briefing document explaining the reasoning behind your 'fairness and accuracy' clause for presentation to a training session of junior journalists on your local newspaper.
2. Interview the candidates who stood in your electorate during the last local, state or federal election about their perceptions of the media coverage within the electorate and generally. Using the material you have gathered prepare a class paper for discussion with your group.
3. Conduct 20 random interviews with voters in your electorate about their perceptions of the way the media covered the most recent election in your area, whether local, state or federal election or by-election. Can you identify any pattern of response, relating to age, sex, voting preference or occupation?
4. Identify a news article (not a comment piece or editorial) that you regard as biased. The article need not necessarily be about a strictly political issue; it could be about any divisive social issue. Rewrite the article to reflect the opposite view by changing the emphasis, positioning, word use, etc. You cannot, however, introduce new information or exceed the length of the original article.
5. Obtain a copy of a media release issued by any local authority or organisation in your area. Monitor the local media to see what use is made of the release and the information it contains. Identify any similarities in wording and content and any material in the story derived from sources other than the release.

Chapter 3

Ideas for Discussion

1. What do you believe are the images of women and their role(s) portrayed by the news media? Do images of women

differ between the different news media? What specific evidence can you find to support your opinion?
2. What are the main criticisms of media coverage of Aboriginal affairs? Is there any difference between the criticisms made by Aboriginal communities and those made by non-Aboriginal journalists and media commentators? To what extent are any of these criticisms justified?
3. What are the arguments for and against censoring news and views that disparage ethnic and religious minorities? In your discussion, consider the implications of self-censorship and legal sanctions imposed by such mechanisms as anti-vilification laws. In what way do public interest considerations enter this debate?

Ideas for Action
1. Examine the complaints about sexism in the last two annual reports of the Australian Press Council. Write a 1000-word article for publication in a news magazine, based on the adjudications of the council and the issues raised by the complainants.
2. Examine the complaints about racism and religious disparagement in the last two annual reports of the Australian Press Council. Write a 1000-word article for publication in a news magazine, based on the adjudication of the council and the issues raised by the complainants.
3. Write a 1500-word feature article about the mainstream media coverage of any identifiable minority group. Information for the article should come from a range of sources, including representatives of the identified group.
4. Write a 1500-word article about the development of specific media outlets for minority audiences, for example Aboriginal broadcasting, the gay press, radio for the print handicapped, ethnic newspapers or broadcasting, the religious press.

Chapter 4

Ideas for Discussion
1. Are there any circumstances in which a voluntary ban on media coverage of a threat to public safety is justified? In your discussion, consider the implications of a total ban, a ban on

some information only, a short-term or long-term ban, the relative competence of authorities and the media to judge the possible outcomes, commercial pressures on the media and the difference, if any, between the public need to know, the public right to know and public curiosity.

2. How do you think you would feel if your decision to reveal information in a story about crime or threats to public safety resulted in the death or injury of any participant in the event? On the basis of your feelings would you reassess your arguments about the circumstances in which a voluntary ban may be justified?

3. Crime, violence and trauma can affect everyone, irrespective of age, sex or social status. But is there any justification to treat children, as victims or witnesses, any differently from adults when reporting crime and disaster?

4. How much does communications technology influence the ethical decision-making process in the coverage of natural disaster, war or crime?

Ideas for Action

1. Write a 1000-word feature article about the effects of trauma on people, based on interviews with such groups as police, doctors, psychologists, ambulance officers, victims, etc.

2. Attend a coronial inquiry in your city and write a short news article.

3. Using the coronial inquiry, write an account of how you as a person felt about the evidence. This account is not for publication.

Chapter 5

Ideas for Discussion

1. Identify what you consider to be the essential elements of a person's private life.

2. Are there any circumstances in which the essentially private elements of a person's life should be made public?

3. You have been asked to provide a discussion paper on the introduction of a 'public figure' defence for the media reporting

on the private lives of people in public life. How would you define a public figure?

4. Discuss the impact of technological advances on reporting private lives.

Ideas for Action

1. Drawing from the information you gathered for your feature article about the effects of trauma as well as from other sources, set out brief but comprehensive guidelines for journalists interviewing people who are suffering from post-traumatic shock or grief.

2. Identify three television current affairs stories which may be regarded as intrusions into privacy. In 500 words for each example, put the arguments for and against the alleged intrusion.

3. Write a short discussion paper on the introduction of a public figure defence in Australian law.

Chapter 6

Ideas for Discussion

1. Identify the variables which may affect a person's judgement about whether a news item is in good or bad taste.

2. Is good or bad taste in the media seen only in the published or broadcast story or is taste something that can manifest itself in the process of news gathering?

3. Can the circumstances of a story — for example whether it is close to home or far away or about war or peace — influence the judgement about its taste?

4. The following exercise requires both individual thought and group discussion. Each person should separately identify — and write down — three examples of news stories or news pictures they consider to be `lapses of taste so repugnant as to bring the freedom of [the news media] into disrepute or be extremely offensive to the public'. As a group, compare the individual reponses and try to form a consensus about the type of material that is repugnant. What do the results of the exercise tell you about questions of taste?

Ideas for Action

1. As a group, develop a list of 12 words or phrases that the group generally agrees are distasteful. Develop another list of 12 images that are seen as distasteful.
2. Armed with the lists, ask 20 members of the public to nominate whether each item on the list is 'grossly offensive', 'offensive', 'inoffensive' or 'don't know'. Analyse the results to see if any patterns emerge, relating to the respondent's age, sex, education level and occupation. You may like to add other variables such as religious affiliation.

Chapter 7

Ideas for Discussion

1. Are there any circumstances in which journalists should be required to disclose publicly their sources of information?
2. Are there any circumstances in which journalists should be required to disclose their sources of information to the editorial executives and/or general management of the organisation for which they work?
3. Discuss whether there are dangers in journalists having an absolute right to protect their sources.
4. What effect does the absence of protection of sources have on the free flow of information in a community?

Ideas for Action

1. Working as a group, analyse one day's issue of a metropolitan or regional daily newspaper to determine the types of sources on which journalists have relied for their information. For instance, a pair of students may examine one page of the paper while other pairs do other pages. The group should then pool the findings to develop a list of categories of sources.
2. Working by yourself, select at least 10 examples of news stories from different parts of a paper or news magazine to discover what categories of sources are used. Is there any pattern you can see which matches types of story with categories of source?
3. Select at least 10 examples of television current affairs stories to discover the categories of sources used. Is there any difference in the type of source categories in television compared to

those in newspapers? If there is a difference, can you explain it?

Chapter 8

Ideas for Discussion

1. Discuss whether covert methods of obtaining information are ever justified.
2. Are journalists ever justified in breaking the law to obtain information?
3. Discuss the ethical implications of using hidden cameras or concealed sound recording devices.
4. If journalists agree to 'off the record' briefings, are they compromising the principle of the public's right to know?
5. Discuss whether there is a need for specific guidelines relating to the editing of interviews for radio or television.

Ideas for Action

1. Develop brief guidelines for journalists, defining the terms 'off the record', 'background briefing' and 'not for attribution'.
2. Develop an image manipulation policy for a daily newspaper or magazine.
3. Research current television technologies and, using the results of that research, develop an image manipulation policy for a television newsroom.

Chapter 9

Ideas for Discussion

1. If information in the modern age is a commercial commodity, why do some journalists object so strongly to chequebook journalism?
2. Discuss whether the handing over of money inevitably compromises the truth of the information provided.
3. Discuss the notion that chequebook journalism jeopardises the unfettered flow of information in a community.
4. Consider whether paying for information can undermine the principle of fair competition in the marketplace.

Ideas for Action

1. Develop an editorial policy on paying for stories for three separate media outlets: a metropolitan daily, a mass circulation magazine, a television current affairs program. Write briefing notes for the editorial staff to accompany each policy.

Chapter 10

Ideas for Discussion

1. Who should pay for lunch: the journalist or the contact?
2. What are the ethical implications of:
   (a) a music critic reviewing a band when she is living with the lead guitarist;
   (b) a general reporter asking a theatrical entrepreneur for free tickets to a forthcoming show;
   (c) a motoring writer accepting the free use of a four-wheel drive vehicle to use for a six-week holiday in Central Australia;
   (d) a finance writer being asked to prepare the annual report of a public company;
   (e) a reporter having a part-time job with a public relations consultancy.
3. Does the management of any news organisation have an ethical responsibility in relation to the acceptance of freebies or payola?
4. Should journalists be free to participate in community activity and/or join political parties?

Ideas for Action

1. Prepare a class discussion paper, based on an interview with one of the following: the publicity director of a theatre company; the media director of a sporting organisation such as a racing club; a music promoter; the marketing director of a fashion house or similar organisation, etc. The interview should aim to discover what benefits an organisation derives from providing free goods and services to journalists and media managers.

Chapter 11

Ideas for Discussion

1. Can a news organisation's need to survive be separated from its editorial content? Consider the relative size of the news organisation in resolving this question.
2. Discuss the ethical implications for journalists who work for an organisation that has extensive non-media business interests or is part of a conglomerate with non-media interests?
3. How closely should the advertising and editorial departments of a media organisation work with each other? Consider the role of advertorials, advertising features, etc.

Ideas for Action

1. Interview the advertising manager and the editor or news editor of your local newspaper, radio station or television station to discover their attitudes to the relationship between editorial and advertising content and prepare a brief paper, summarising their conclusions.

Chapter 12

Ideas for Discussion

1. Discuss the validity of past and present criticisms of mechanisms for regulating the conduct of the Australian news media.
2. What are the arguments for and against government intervention of any sort in the working of the news media?

Ideas for Action

1. Draft the objectives and composition of a national news commission to regulate the conduct of all branches of the media.

The Media, Entertainment and Arts Alliance (Journalists) Code of Ethics

Respect for truth and the public's right to information are overriding principles for all journalists. In pursuance of these principles, journalists commit themselves to ethical and professional standards. All members of the Australian Journalists Association engaged in gathering, transmitting, disseminating and commenting on news and information shall observe the following code of ethics in their professional activities. They acknowledge the jurisdiction of their professional colleagues on AJA judiciary committees to adjudicate on issues connected with this code.

1. They shall report and interpret the news with scrupulous honesty by striving to disclose all essential facts and by not suppressing relevant, available facts or distorting by wrong or improper emphasis.
2. They shall not place unnecessary emphasis on gender, race, sexual preference, religious belief, marital status or physical and mental disability.
3. In all circumstances they shall respect all confidences received in the course of their calling.

4. They shall not allow personal interests to influence them in their professional duties.
5. They shall not allow their professional duties to be influenced by any consideration, gift or advantage offered and, where appropriate, shall disclose any such offer.
6. They shall not allow advertising or commercial considerations to influence them in their professional duties.
7. They shall use fair and honest means to obtain news, pictures, films, tapes and documents.
8. They shall identify themselves and their employers before obtaining any interview for publication or broadcast.
9. They shall respect private grief and personal privacy and shall have the right to resist compulsion to intrude on them.
10. They shall do their utmost to correct any published or broadcast information found to be harmfully inaccurate.

Australian Press Council Principles

1. Newspaper readers are entitled to have news and comment presented to them honestly and fairly, and with respect for the privacy and sensibilities of individuals.
2. A newspaper has an obligation to take all reasonable steps to ensure the truth of its statements.
3. Rumour and unconfirmed reports, if published at all, should be identified as such.
4. News obtained by dishonest or unfair means, or the publication of which would involve a breach of confidence, should not be published unless there is an over-riding public interest.
5. A newspaper is justified in strongly advocating its own views on controversial topics provided that it treats its readers fairly by
   - making fact and opinion clearly distinguishable;
   - not misrepresenting or suppressing relevant facts;
   - not distorting the facts in text or headlines.
6. Billboards and posters advertising a newspaper should not mislead the public.
7. A newspaper has a wide discretion in matters of taste, but this

does not justify lapses of taste so repugnant as to bring the freedom of the press into disrepute or be extremely offensive to the public.

8. A newspaper should not place gratuitous emphasis on the race, nationality, religion, colour, country of origin, gender, sexual preference, marital status or intellectual or physical disability of either individuals or groups. Nevertheless, where it is in the public interest, newspapers may report and express opinions upon events and comments in which such matters are raised.

9. A newspaper should not, in headlines or otherwise, state the race, nationality or religious or political views of a person suspected of a crime, or arrested, charged or convicted, unless the fact is relevant.

10. If material damaging to the reputation or interests of an individual, corporation, organisation or specific group of people is published, opportunity for prompt and appropriately prominent reply at reasonable length should be given by the newspaper concerned, wherever fairness so requires.

11. A newspaper should make amends for publishing information that is found to be harmfully inaccurate by printing, promptly and with appropriate prominence, such retraction, correction, explanation or apology as will neutralise the damage so far as possible.

12. When the Council issues an adjudication which wholly or partly upholds a complaint, the newspaper concerned should give appropriate prominence to the adjudication.

Complaint Procedure

If you have a complaint against a newspaper or periodical, you should first take it up with the editor or other representative of the publication concerned.

If the complaint is not resolved to your satisfaction, you may refer it to the Australian Press Council. A complaint must be specific, in writing, and accompanied by a cutting or clear photostat of the matter complained of, with supporting documents or evidence if any. Complaints must be lodged within three months of publication.

The Council will not hear a complaint subject to legal action or, in the Council's view, possible legal action, unless the complainant is willing to sign a waiver of the right to such action.

Address complaints or inquiries to:

Executive Secretary
The Australian Press Council
Suite 303
149 Castlereagh Street
Sydney NSW 2000

For information or advice telephone (02) 261 1930, and callers from outside the Sydney metropolitan area can ring toll free on (008) 025712.

A booklet setting out the aims, practices and procedures of the Council is available free from the above address.

Extracts from the Australian Broadcasting Corporation Code of Practice

1 Preamble

The ABC's place in the broadcasting system is distinctive because of its Charter, which gives the Corporation unique responsibilities, and because of other provisions under the *Australian Broadcasting Corporation Act (1983)*, which give the Corporation particular responsibilities, for example, the provision of an independent news service.

The ABC Act guarantees the editorial independence of the Corporation's programs. The ABC holds its power to make programming decisions on behalf of the people of Australia, for which it is accountable to Parliament, but in which by law and convention neither the Government nor Parliament seeks to intervene.

2 General Program Codes

The guiding principle in the application of the following general program codes is context. What is unacceptable in one context may be appropriate and acceptable in another. However the use of language and images for no other purpose but to offend is not acceptable.

The code is not intended to ban certain types of language or images from bona fide dramatic or literary treatments, nor is it intended to exclude such references from legitimate reportage, debate or documentaries. Where appropriate, audiences will be given advance notice of the content of the program.

2.1 Violence. The presentation or portrayal of violence must be justifiable, or else the material should not be presented. Particular attention should be paid to the portrayal of violence against women.

In news and current affairs programs, violent events should never be sensationalised or presented for their own sake.

. . .

2.3 Sex and Sexuality. Provided it is handled with integrity, any of the following treatments of sex and sexuality may be appropriate and necessary to a program:
- It can be discussed and reported in the context of news, information or documentary;

. . .

2.4 Discrimination. The presentation or portrayal of people in a way which is likely to encourage denigration of or discrimination against any person or section of the community on account of race, ethnicity, nationality, sex, age, physical or mental disability, occupational status, sexual preference or the holding of any religious, cultural or political belief will be avoided. The requirement is not intended to prevent the broadcast of material which is factual, or the expression of genuinely-held opinion in a news or current affairs program . . .

3 Specific Program Codes

. . .

3.3 Aboriginal and Torres Strait Islander Programs. Program makers and journalists should respect Aboriginal and Torres Strait Islander culture. Particular care should be exercised in traditional matters such as the naming or depicting of Aboriginal and Torres Strait Islander people after death.

4 News and Current Affairs

(a) Every reasonable effort must be made to ensure that the content of news and current affairs programs is accurate, impartial and balanced.

(b) Demonstrable errors will be corrected in a form most suited to the circumstances.

(c) Impartiality does not require editorial staff to be unquestioning; nor should all sides of an issue be devoted the same amount of time.

(d) Balance will be sought through the presentation, as far as possible, of principal relevant viewpoints on matters of importance. The requirement may not always be reached within a single program or news bulletin, but will be achieved within a reasonable period.

(e) Editorial staff will not be obliged to disclose confidential sources which they are entitled to protect at all times.

(f) Re-enactments of events will be clearly identified as such and presented in a way which will not mislead audiences.

(g) If reported at all, suicides will be reported in moderate terms and will usually avoid details of method.

(h) Sensitivity will be exercised in broadcasting images of or interviews with bereaved relatives and survivors or witnesses of traumatic incidents.

4.1 News Flashes. Care will be exercised in the selection of sounds and images and consideration given to the likely composition of the audience.

4.2 News Updates and News Promotions. News updates and news promotions will not appear during obviously inappropriate programs, especially programs directed at young children. Due to their repetitive nature, there will be very little violent material included in them, and none at all in the late afternoon and early evening.

. . .

8 Complaints

Complaints that the ABC has acted contrary to this Code of Practice should be directed to the ABC in the first instance. Phone complainants seeking a response from the ABC will be asked to put their complaint in writing. All such written complaints will receive a response from the ABC within 60 days from the receipt of the written complaint.

The ABC will make every reasonable effort to resolve complaints about Code of Practice matters, except where a complaint is clearly frivolous, vexatious or not made in good faith.

. . .

8.2 Independent Complaints Review Panel. The ABC has established an Independent Complaints Review Panel (ICRP) to review written complaints which relate to allegations of serious bias, lack of balance or unfair treatment arising from an ABC broadcast or broadcasts.

If a complainant making such an allegation does not receive a response from the ABC within 42 days or is not satisfied with the response, the complainant may ask the Convenor of the ICRP to accept the complaint for review. Further information can be obtained from the Convenor, Independent Complaints Review Panel, GPO Box 688, Sydney, NSW 2001 or by phoning (02) 333 5639.

If the Convenor rejects the complaint or if the complainant is dissatisfied with the outcome of the review and the complaint is covered by the ABC Code of Practice, the complainant may make a complaint to the Australian Broadcasting Authority about the matter.

8.3 Australian Broadcasting Authority. If a complainant: does not receive a response from the ABC within 60 days; or
• the complainant is dissatisfied with the ABC response; or
• the complainant is dissatisfied with the outcome of the ICRP review (as mentioned above); and
• the complaint is covered by the ABC Code of Practice;
the complainant may make a complaint to the Australian Broadcasting Authority about the matter.

8.4 Complaints Alleging Error of Fact or Invasion of Privacy. Complaints received by the ABC and referred to a Community Affairs Officer pursuant to section 82 of the ABC Act in so far as they allege:
(a) that an error of fact has occurred in a program, announcement or other matter broadcast or televised by the Corporation; or
(b) that an invasion of privacy has occurred in, or in connection with, the preparation of a program, announcement or other matter broadcast or televised by the Corporation;
shall not be construed as complaints on the grounds that the Corporation has acted contrary to this Code of Practice unless the Community Affairs Officer has, pursuant to section 82, declined to investigate the complaint.

Extracts from the Federation of Australian Radio Broadcasters Codes of Practice

Code of Practice 1 — Programs Unsuitable for Broadcast
Purpose: The purpose of this Code is to prevent the broadcasting of programs that, in accordance with community standards and attitudes, are not suitable to be broadcast.

. . .

1.3 A licensee shall not broadcast a program which:
(a) is likely to incite or perpetuate hatred against; or
(b) gratuitously vilifies
any person or group on the basis of ethnicity, nationality, race, gender, sexual preference, religion or physical or mental disability.

Code of Practice 2 — News and Current Affairs Programs
Purpose: The purpose of this Code is to promote accuracy and fairness in news and current affairs programs.

2.1 News programs (including news flashes) broadcast by a licensee must:
(a) present news accurately;

(b) not present news in such a way as to create public panic, or unnecessary distress to listeners;

(c) distinguish news from comment.

2.2 In the preparation and presentation of current affairs programs, a licensee must ensure that:

(a) factual material is presented accurately and that reasonable efforts are made to correct substantial errors of fact at the earliest possible opportunity;

(b) the reporting of factual material is clearly distinguishable from commentary and analysis;

(c) reasonable efforts are made or reasonable opportunities are given to present significant viewpoints when dealing with controversial issues of public importance, either within the same program or similar programs, while the issue has immediate relevance to the community;

(d) viewpoints are not misrepresented, and material is not presented in a misleading manner by giving wrong or improper emphasis, by editing out of context, or by withholding relevant available facts;

(e) respect is given to each person's legitimate right to protection from unjustified use of material which is obtained without an individual's consent or other unwarranted and intrusive invasions of privacy.

Code of Practice 5 — Complaints

Purposes: The purposes of this code are to prescribe methods (a) of handling complaints from members of the public about program content or compliance with codes of practice, and (b) of reporting to the Australian Broadcasting Authority (ABA) on complaints so made.

5.1 For the purposes of this Code, a complaint is an assertion made either orally or in writing to a licensee that the licensee has broadcast matter which:

(a) infringes a code of practice or a condition of the licence, and/or is of personal concern to the complainant; and/or

(b) in the opinion of the complainant is of concern to the community.

5.2 A licensee shall make appropriate arrangements to ensure that:

(a) complaints will be received by a responsible person or person in normal office hours;

(b) complaints will be conscientiously considered, investigated if necessary, and responded to as soon as practicable;

(c) a record of complaints will be kept in accordance with Clause 5.4.

5.3 Where it appears to the licensee that a complainant is not satisfied with the licensee's response and wishes to press the complaint, the licensee shall inform the complainant of his or her right to make a complaint to the ABA about the matter.

5.4 The record of complaints shall be kept in permanent form and shall include the date and time each complaint is received, the name, address and/or telephone number of the complainant (if provided), the substance of the complaint and the substance and date of the licensee's response.

5.5 The licensee shall cause an extract of the record of complaints, in a form agreed between the ABA and the Federation of Australian Radio Broadcasters (FARB), to be supplied to FARB upon 14 days' notice for inclusion by FARB to the ABA.

Note: In the case of commercial stations not being members of FARB, those licensees shall cause the extract of the record of complaints to be supplied direct to the ABA and in the same form agreed between the ABA and FARB.

Extracts from the Federation of Australian Commercial Television Stations Code of Practice

Section 2: Classification

Objective
2.1   This Section is intended to ensure that;

...

    2.1.5   News, commentary on current events, and serious presentations of moral or social issues are presented with appropriate sensitivity to the classification zone in which they are broadcast, but are not unreasonably restricted.

Classification of material

. . .

    2.3.1   *News, Current Affairs and Live Sporting Programs*: These programs do not require classification, but when broadcast in a 'G' classification period must comply with Clauses 2.6 and 2.7.

. . .

2.6   *News, Current Affairs and Live Sporting Programs*: These programs may be broadcast in 'G' classification periods, provided that care is exercised in the selection and broadcast of all material. News material broadcast outside reqular bulletins in 'G' classification periods must be compiled with special care, particularly when many children may be watching.

2.7   *Material Which May Distress or Offend Viewers*: Licensees may broadcast a news or current affairs program containing visual or aural material which, in the licensee's reasonable opinion, is likely to seriously distress or offend a substantial number of viewers only if there are identifiable public interest reasons for broadcasting the material and if adequate prior warning is given to viewers (See Clause 2.25).

. . .

Warnings Before Certain News, Current Affairs and Other Programs
2.25   Where news, current affairs, or other programs . . . include for public interest reasons material which is, in the licensee's reasonable opinion, likely to seriously distress or offend a substantial number of viewers, the licensee must provide adequate prior warning to viewers. The warning must precede the relevant segment in news and current affairs program and precede the program in other cases.

2.26   Warnings before the broadcast of material of this nature must be spoken, and may also be written. They must provide an adequate indication of the nature of the material, while avoiding detail which may itself seriously distress or offend viewers.

Section 3: Program Promotions
. . .
Promotions for News, Current Affairs, Sporting and Certain Other Programs
9.1   Promotions for news, current affairs and sporting programs, and for programs dealing in a responsible way with serious social or moral issues, must comply in every respect with the requirements for the viewing zone in which they are broadcast and, as far as is practicable, with the additional restrictions set out in Clauses 3.6 to 3.10.

. . .

Section 4: News and Current Affairs Programs

Objective

4.1   This Section is intended to ensure that:

4.1.1 news and current affairs programs are presented accurate and fairly;

4.1.2 news and current affairs programs are presented with due care, having regard to the likely composition of the audience at the time of broadcast (and, in particular, the presence of children);

4.1.3 news and current affairs take account of personal privacy and of cultural differences in the community;

4.1.4 news is presented impartially.

Scope of the Code

2.1   Except where otherwise indicated, this Section applies to news programs, news flashes and current affairs programs. A 'current affairs program' means a program focussing on social, economic or political issues.

News and Current Affairs Programs

4.3   In broadcasting news and current affairs programs, licensees:

4.3.1 must present factual material accurately and represent viewpoints fairly, having regard to the circumstances at the time of preparing and broadcasting the program;

4.3.2 must not present material in a manner which creates public panic;

4.3.3 must comply with Clauses 2.7 and 2.25 of this Code in selecting and broadcasting visual and/or aural material which may seriously distress or offend a substantial number of viewers;

4.3.4 must include only sparingly material likely to cause some distress to a substantial number of viewers;

4.3.5 must not use material relating to a person's personal or private affairs, or which invades an individual's privacy, other than where there are identifiable public interest reasons for the material to be broadcast;

4.3.6 must display sensitivity in broadcasting images of or interviews with bereaved relatives and survivors or witnesses of traumatic incidents;

4.3.7 must not portray any person or group of persons in a negative light by placing gratuitous emphasis on age, colour, gender, national or ethnic origin, physical or mental disability, race, religion or sexual preference. Nevertheless, where it is in the public interest, licensees may report events and broadcast comments in which such matters are raised;

4.3.8 must make reasonable efforts to correct significant errors of fact at the earliest opportunity.

4.4 In broadcasting news programs (including news flashes) licensees:

4.4.1 must present news fairly and impartially;

4.4.2 must clearly distinguish the reporting of factual material from commentary and analysis.

Media, Entertainment and Arts Alliance Guidelines for Reporting on Aboriginal Issues

- Members recognise the importance attached by the Aboriginal people to sacred sites, ceremonies and other practices associated with traditional Aboriginal culture.
- Members will endeavour not to film or televise Aboriginal sacred sites or ceremonies where it is likely to cause offence.
- Members will endeavour to respect other traditional Aboriginal customs, such as refraining from televising or naming recently deceased people where such action is likely to cause offence.
- When necessary, members will use qualified Aboriginal interpreters in communities where English is not a primary language.
- Copies of all material recorded in Aboriginal communities will be available at cost when requested by the community in advance.

Herald and Weekly Times Limited Professional Practice Policy

The professional activities of all editorial staff shall be guided by the principles of openness, fairness and commitment to accuracy and truth.

This policy of professional practice reflects the following basic principles of journalism:

- The primary purpose of gathering and distributing news and opinion is to serve society by informing citizens and enabling them to make informed judgements on the issues of the time;
- The freedom of the press to bring an independent scrutiny to bear on the forces that shape society is a freedom exercised on behalf of the public;
- Journalists are committed to ensure that the public's business is conducted in public, and must be vigilant against anyone who would exploit the press for selfish purposes or seek to restrict the paper's role and responsibilities;
- Good faith with the reader is the foundation of good journalism.

The public interest is the only test that may occasionally justify divergence from the standards of conduct set out in this policy. The public interest includes:
- detecting or exposing crime or serious misdemeanor;
- detecting or exposing seriously anti-social conduct;
- protecting public health and safety;
- preventing the public from being misled by some statement or action of an individual or organisation;
- detecting or exposing hypocrisy, falsehoods or double standards of behavior on the part of public figures or public institutions and in public policy.

The policy applies to all editorial staff, whether management or staff, union or non-union members, permanent and casual staff and contributors.

1.0 Accuracy

1.1   Take care not to publish inaccurate, misleading or distorted material and make every endeavour to get all sides of a story and present same fairly.

1.2   Always verify fact and quotations and corroborate any critical information.

1.3   If a significant inaccuracy, misleading statement or distorted report has been published, correct or clarify it promptly.

1.4   Always report fairly and accurately the outcome of an action for defamation or a judgement by the Australian Press Council, or other self-regulatory or regulatory body, to which the paper has been a party.

1.5   Give a fair opportunity for reply to inaccuracies to individuals or organisations when it has been called for reasonably.

1.6   In general, direct quotations should not be altered. There is, however, some justification for the deletion of offensive and gratuitous language or minor amendments to grammar that make the statement confusing or the speaker appear foolish, so long as the alteration does not fundamentally alter the meaning and context of the quotation. If in doubt that any such alteration goes beyond minor adjustment, seek advice from your editorial supervisor/s.

1.7   Subeditors should take care not to allow the subediting process to adversely affect the accuracy, context and fairness of a story.

2.0 Comment and Fact

2.1   To be impartial does not require our papers to be unquestioning or to refrain from the expression of editorial opinion; however, editorial material should distinguish clearly between comment, verified fact and speculation.

2.2   Editorials, analytical articles and commentaries should be subject to the same standards of factual accuracy as news reports.

3.0 Misrepresentation, Deceptive and Illegal Practices

3.1   Do not obtain or seek to obtain information or pictures through misrepresentation or subterfuge.

3.2   Do not remove documents or photographs except with the express permission of the owner.

3.3   Do not use a false name, either verbally or in writing, when seeking information for publication or gaining entry to any private or public institution in pursuit of information.

3.4   Do not use long range recording devices or cameras, or surveillance or bugging devices.

3.5   The above clauses may be waived only when the public interest justifies subterfuge. The use of any deceptive practice/s must be approved by the editor and any other relevant editorial executive/s after thorough discussion.

3.6   An editor confronted with a decision to authorise deceptive methods or subterfuge should meet these minimum conditions: the expected news story must be of such vital public interest that its news value clearly outweighs the damage to trust and credibility that might result from the use of deception; the story cannot reasonably be recast to avoid the need to deceive; all other means of getting the story have been exhausted. Those involved in the decision should ask themselves whether the decision to deceive has been discussed as thoroughly and broadly as feasible and whether readers and staff members will tend to agree that the story justified the deception.

3.7   The nature of any deceptive practices and the reasons for their use must be disclosed to readers at the time of publication.

3.8   As a general principle, the Herald and Weekly Times does not condone the breaking of any laws by employees acting on behalf of the company and the company does not accept liability for any such action.

4.0 Confidentiality

4.1　Unless there is a clear and pressing need to maintain confidences, sources of information should be identified.

4.2　Do not promise confidentiality or imply protection unless you are convinced that the information is in the public interest and the source is neither malicious nor mischievous.

4.3　If you promise confidentiality, you have an obligation to protect your confidential sources of information at all costs.

4.4　Make every effort to verify independently any material gained from confidential sources.

4.5　Tell your editorial supervisor/s whenever you have made a promise of confidentiality.

5.0 Harassment

5.1　You should not obtain information, documents or pictures through intimidation or harassment.

5.2　You should not photograph individuals on private property without their consent, unless the editor is convinced there is justifiable public interest.

5.3　You should not persist in telephoning, following or questioning individuals after you have been asked to stop.

5.4　You should not remain on a person's private property after having been asked to leave.

6.0 Discrimination

6.1　Avoid prejudicial or pejorative reference to a person's race, colour, religion, marital status, sex or sexual orientation or to any physical or mental illness or incapacity.

6.2　Avoid publishing details of a person's race, colour, religion, marital status, sex, sexual orientation, physical or mental illness or incapacity except when those details are directly relevant to the story.

6.3　You should avoid participation in and membership of clubs and associations which have discriminatory membership policies and should make any such membership known to your editorial supervisor/s.

7.0 General Privacy

7.1　You should avoid identifying relatives or friends of people convicted or accused of crime unless the reference to them is necessary for the full, fair and accurate reporting of the crime or subsequent legal proceedings, or is of direct relevance to the story.

7.2　Be aware that using identifying details, such as street names and numbers etc., may serve to enable others to intrude on the privacy of individuals, who have become the subject of news coverage, and their families.

8.0 Grief and Trauma

8.1　All people, including public figures, should be treated with sensitivity and courtesy during times of grief and trauma.

8.2　Ordinary citizens caught up in newsworthy events are ignorant of journalistic practice and that ignorance should not be exploited.

8.3　When seeking permission to interview or photograph a victim or bereaved person, make every effort to make the initial approach through an intermediary, such as family member, friend, counsellor etc. Make a direct approach to the subject only if no intermediary is available.

8.4　If permission is refused, do not persist. (You may, however, leave a contact number or card so the person may reconsider the request at a less stressful time.)

8.5　Do not enter non-public areas of any institution charged with caring for, and counselling, victims and their families (such as hospitals, welfare institutions, funeral parlours or chapels, churches etc.) without identifying yourself to a responsible official or without the express permission of the affected people, their intermediaries or their medical/welfare/legal advisor or guardian.

8.6　A victim or bereaved person has the right to terminate an interview and/or photographic session at any time and should be made aware of this right before the interview/photographic session begins.

8.7　If a subject breaks down during an interview, offer to terminate the interview.

8.8　Conduct all interviews with the utmost sensitivity to both the distress likely to be caused by the interview itself and the possible impact on the interviewee that publication of information given in times of stress may have.

8.9　If you feel at any time that ordinary citizens may not be aware of the import of what they are saying, discuss this with them and give them the opportunity to withdraw any such remarks.

8.10   Draw your editorial supervisor's attention to any material or image that may be particularly sensitive or to any circumstance that may have led you to omit material from your copy.

8.11   Photographs of victims or grieving people should be published only following due consideration of sensitivity and privacy.

8.12   Any restrictions placed on the use of photographs supplied by the immediate family or an intermediary should be honoured.

8.13   Distressing or gratuitous reference to the state of a victim's body or to body parts should be avoided.

8.14   Care should be taken when republishing any material on the anniversary of a trauma or crime not to cause undue distress to victims or their families.

9.0 Reporting Destructive and Self-destructive Behaviour

9.1   When reporting individual suicide cases, do not refer to them as such, except when the public figure or public interest tests apply.

9.2   Avoid reporting details of suicide methods.

9.3   Take particular care when reporting youth suicide trends not to imply that suicide is an acceptable means of resolving problems.

9.4   Avoid reports of extortion threats, such as bombs, poisoned food etc., except when justified by public safety or the public interest.

9.5   Avoid reporting descriptive details of drug manufacture, distribution and usage, except when justified by public safety or the public interest.

9.6   Take particular care to avoid implying that illegal drug usage or the misuse of legal drugs is an acceptable means of resolving problems.

9.7   Avoid reporting descriptive details of the manufacture or usage of firearms, crossbows, booby traps or any other life-threatening device.

10.0 Children

10.1   You should not normally interview or photograph children under the age of 16 on subjects involving the personal welfare of the child in the absence of, and without the consent of, a parent or other adult responsible for the child.

10.2   Children should not be interviewed about their parents or siblings when the parents or siblings are the subject of any story except in the presence of, and with the consent of, a parent or other adult responsible for the child.

10.3   No inducement should be offered to a child to cooperate in an interview.

10.4   Children should not be approached or photographed while at school without the permission of the principal or principal's delegated representative.

11.0 Payment for Information

11.1   As a general principle, payment or offers of payment or any other inducement for stories, pictures or information should be avoided unless publication is demonstrably in the public interest and there is no alternative to payment.

11.2   Payment or offers of payment for stories, pictures or information should not be made to witnesses or potential witnesses in current criminal proceedings or to people engaged in crime or to their associates (including family, friends, neighbours and colleagues) except where the material concerned ought to be published in the public interest and where there is no alternative to payment.

11.3   When payment for any story, picture or information has been made, the readers should ideally be informed of the fact of payment, but the disclosure is at the discretion of the editor.

11.4   Any payment must be authorised by the editor.

12.0 Conflict of Interest

12.1   Staff have the right to join and participate in any political or community organisation and activity but should be aware that such participation may create a conflict of interest and reflect on the credibility of the paper and the staff member.

12.2   If you sign petitions, participate in demonstrations, or serve in decision-making or fund-raising capacities in organisations that do, or potentially can, generate news, you must inform your supervisor/s.

12.3   You should always inform your supervisor/s, in advance, of any real or potential conflict of interest that may affect your impartiality or be seen to affect your impartiality when covering a story directly or indirectly connected to an individual or organisation with which you, your close friends or family have personal dealings.

12.4   You should tell your editorial supervisor/s, in advance, of any paid or unpaid work that you undertake for any individual or organisation that may constitute a real or perceived conflict of interest.

12.5   Editorial supervisors have the right to assign a reporter to cover a story in which he or she has a real or potential conflict of interest, but the story must carry an acknowledgment to that effect.

12.6   You should not contribute to outside publications/ companies, either by name or nom-de-plume, without the prior and express approval of the editor.

12.7   You should not participate in interviews or debates for other media outlets without the prior approval of a supervisor or the editor.

12.8   Tell your editorial supervisor/s when you are offered, or given, any inducement such as money, products, subsidised or free travel, accommodation, tickets and special discounts.

12.9   If a supervisor believes any gift may put the reporter's or the paper's integrity at risk, the gift should be returned with a polite explanatory note.

12.10   The editor, section editors or other supervising staff are the only people authorised to accept offers of free or subsidised travel, accommodation, tickets etc. on behalf of the paper. They have the right to assign staff to cover any resulting story as they see fit, even if the original offer was made directly to an individual journalist.

12.11   Acceptance of an offer of trip or accommodation is conditional on the paper being free to assign staff independently, to publish adverse material or not to publish at all; these conditions should be made in writing to the person or individual making the offer.

12.12   Any story generated from free travel or other benefit should carry a tag acknowledgment.

12.13   Supervising staff have a duty to find out whether any contributor, who has been commissioned or who offers material for publication, has a real or potential pecuniary or general conflict of interest, although this responsibility does not absolve the contributor from declaring any such conflict.

12.14   Where there is no other suitably qualified person available to contribute material in which conflict of interest
may arise, the material may be commissioned and published but readers should be told of the potential conflict
either in the body or at the end of the story.

12.15   Failure to advise a real or potential conflict of interest will
result in immediate suspension.

12.16   Contributors who are not full-time journalists employed
by the Herald and Weekly Times should make any
potentional conflicts of interest known to the editor. Any
association or activity which might have, or be deemed to
have, a bearing on their views should be identified with
the published material.

13.0 Financial Reporting

13.1   You should not use financial information you receive in
advance of general publication for your own profit nor
should you pass on such information to others in advance
of publication.

13.2   You should not write about shares, securities or companies
in whose performance you know that you, your close
friends or your immediate family has a significant financial
interest without disclosing that interest to the finance
editor or editor.

13.3   You should not buy or sell, either directly or through
nominees or agents, shares or securities about which you
have written recently or about which you intend to write
in the near future.

14.0 Advertising

14.1   Any editorial material that is generated as a condition of
the placement of an advertisement must be labelled as an
advertising feature.

14.2   Wherever possible stories that are critical of, or adversely
affect, an advertiser should not be carried on the same
page as that advertiser's advertisement.

15.0 Plagiarism

15.1   Plagiarism or the unsourced reproduction of other people's
work, including the work of public relations and publicity
officers, is unacceptable.

15.2   All material for publication that is supplied by an external source should be fully acknowledged, either in the body of the story or in a tag statement.

15.3   No story or illustration should carry the by-line of staff journalists or contributors unless it is substantially their own work.

15.4   Reporters and contributors have a responsibility to identify to their supervisor/s any stories which are ostensibly retyping of publicity material.

16.0 Image Manipulation

16.1   It is the prime responsibility of photographers to produce work which is a true and accurate representation of events.

16.2   Reasonable touch-up to improve picture reproduction quality is acceptable.

16.3   Only with the approval of the editor should elements of a photograph be deleted or altered to avoid causing offence.

16.4   Under no circumstances may the basic elements of a photograph be manipulated to produce better composition, nor shall the appearance of any element be altered or the image unduly cropped so that the representation is distorted.

16.5   Computerised images and photo illustrations that have been altered must carry an appropriate credit line to ensure readers are not misled into believing they are accurate representations.

16.6   All computerised images or photo illustrations sent interstate or overseas must carry an appropriate and clear advisory that the image has been electronically generated or altered.

17.0 Interviews

17.1   While cooperation in inquiries by police and other authorities is urged, any employee who is asked to give information or an interview to an authority such as police or to give evidence in a matter related to their profession etc. should refer the request to their editor/supervisor.

17.2   Staff cannot have their work published elsewhere without the prior permission of the editor.

18.0 Other

18.1   No employee or contributor should give an undertaking to anyone, whether a complainant or subject of an article, that commits themselves or the company to anything that is written or published, particularly in relation to corrections, apologies etc., without reference to an editor/supervisor.

Endnotes

Introduction

1. Sam Lipski, in Bruce Stannard, 'Why our media are on the nose', *The Bulletin*, 14 November 1989.
2. Ibid, *passim*.
3. John Elliott, ibid.
4. Padriac McGuinness, ibid.
5. *Time Australia*, 24 May 1993.
6. Morgan Gallup Poll May 1988, cited in Julianne Schultz, *Accuracy in Australian Newspapers, Australian Centre for Independent Journalism Working Paper No. 1*, University of Technology, Sydney, 1990, p. 5.
7. Schultz, ibid., p. 11.
8. Loc. cit.
9. Ibid., p. 10.
10. Clem Lloyd, *Profession: Journalist, A History of the Australian Journalists' Association*, Hale & Iremonger, Sydney 1985, p. 19.
11. Loc. cit.
12. Ibid., p. 227.
13. Ibid., p. 229.
14. Ibid., p. 295.
15. Ibid., p. 227.

Chapter 1

1. John L. Hulteng, *The Messenger's Motives: Ethical Problems of the News Media*, 2nd edition, Prentice-Hall Inc., New Jersey, 1985, p. 13.
2. Fred Feldman, *Introductory Ethics*, Prentice-Hall Inc., New Jersey, 1978, p. 1.
3. Sally A. White (ed.), *Values and Communications: Selected Proceedings of the 11th Public Relations World Congress 1988*, Longman Professional, Melbourne, 1989, p. 8.
4. Feldman, op. cit., p. 13.
5. Henry Mayer, *The Press in Australia*, Lansdowne Press, Melbourne, 1964, p. 48.
6. Ibid., p. 49.
7. John C. Merrill, *The Imperative of Freedom: A Philosophy of Journalistic Autonomy*, Hastings House, New York, 1974, p. 171.
8. Clifford G. Christians, Kim B. Rotzoll & Mark Fackler, *Media Ethics: Cases and Moral Reasoning*, Longman Inc., New York, 1983, p. 2.
9. Ibid., pp. 6–7.
10. Ibid., introduction, *passim*.
11. Michael D. Bayles and Keith Henley (eds), *Right Conduct, Theories and Applications*, Random House, New York, 1983, p. 15.
12. Loc. cit.
13. Ibid., p. 4.
14. Ibid., p. 5.
15. Loc. cit.
16. Ibid., p. 6.
17. D. W. Hamlyn, *The Penguin History of Western Philosophy*, Penguin Books, London, 1990, p. 177.
18. Bayles and Henley, op. cit., p. 9.
19. Christians, Rotzoll & Fackler, op. cit., p. 110.
20. Feldman, op. cit., p. 19.
21. Bayles and Henley, op. cit., p. 14.
22. Ibid., p. 15.
23. Ibid., p. 20.
24. Hamlyn, op. cit., p. 236.
25. Bayles and Henley, op. cit., p. 86.
26. Feldman, op. cit., p. 16.
27. Everette E. Dennis and John C. Merrill, *Media Debates: Issues in Mass Communication*, Longman, New York, 1991, p. 46.
28. Australian Press Council, *Aims, Principles, Constitution and Complaints Procedure*, Booklet No. 4, 1989. David Bowman (in his foreword to *The Captive Press*, Penguin, Melbourne, 1988) says the public interest 'is a wonderfully elastic phrase that can be cheerfully stretched in opposite directions . . . The public interest is a political and social question, the answers to which depend often on one's view of society'.

29. British Press Complaints Commission, *Code of Practice*, adopted in January 1991.

30. Australian Press Council, Submission to the House of Representatives Standing Committee on Legal and Constitutional Affairs on Protection of Confidential Personal and Commercial Information, published as an insert to *Australian Press Council News*, Vol. 4, No. 3, August 1992.

31. Peter Costigan, 'Placing a price on the head of press freedom', *The Sunday Herald*, 10 December 1989.

32. John Avieson, 'The AJA — arbiter of ethics' in *Strands of Media Criticism: Reader*, Deakin University, Geelong, 1988, p. 7.

33. AJA code of ethics. For the full text, see Appendix 1.

34. House of Representatives Select Committee on the Print Media (Michael Lee, chairman), *News & Fair Facts: The Australian Print Media Industry*, Australian Government Publishing Service Canberra, 1992, p. xxxii.

35. Australian Press Council, *Australian Press Council News*, Vol. 5, No. 1, February 1993, p. 16.

36. Loc. cit.

37. Australian Press Council, *Annual Report No. 16*, June 1992, p. 59.

38. Federation of Australian Commercial Television Stations (FACTS), *Draft Industry Codes of Practice*, explanatory notes, February 1993, p. 3. For the text of relevant codes of practice, see Appendix 5.

39. Ibid., p. 2.

40. FACTS, *Draft Code on the Handling of Complaints to Licensees*, February 1993, p. 3.

41. Paul Chadwick, *Deregulation and Broadcasting: How Can We Strike an Acceptable Balance?*, RMIT Annual Communications Lecture, 20 October 1992.

42 Federation of Australian Radio Broadcasters (FARB), *Code of Practice 2*, 1993. For the text of relevant codes of practice, see Appendix 4.

43. FARB, *Code of Practice 5*, 1993.

44. Australian Broadcasting Corporation, *Manual of Operation*, Sydney, 1992, p. 57. For the text of the relevant codes, see Appendix 3.

Chapter 2

1. C. P. Scott, quoted in Anthony Smith, *The Newspaper: An International History*, Thames and Hudson, London, 1979, p. 130.

2. James Cameron, quoted in Nicholas Bagnall, *Newspaper Language*, Focal Press, Oxford, 1993, p. 120.

3. Syd Deamer, quoted in Don Whitington, *Strive to Be Fair: An Unfinished Autobiography*, Australian National University Press, Canberra, 1977, p. 73.

4. Alan Barth, quoted in Everette E. Dennis and John C. Merrill, *Media Debates: Issues in Communication*, Longman, New York, 1991.

5. Ibid., p. 110.

6. Ibid., pp. 116–22.
7. John Avieson, *Journalism 2 Study Guide*, Deakin University, Geelong, 1980, p. 7.
8. Patricia Edgar, *The Politics of the Press*, Sun Books, Melbourne, 1979, pp. 8–9.
9. Harry Holgate, in David Turbayne (ed.), *The Media and Politics in Australia*, University of Tasmania, 1980, p. 84.
10. Edith Efron, *The News Twisters*, Nash Publishing, Los Angeles, 1971, p. 1.
11. Michael Courtney, in Turbayne, op. cit., p. 66.
12. Among the many analyses of specific or general bias are Edgar, op. cit., and Keith and Elizabeth Windschuttle (eds), *Fixing the News*, Cassell, Sydney, 1981.
13. Edgar, op. cit., p. 110.
14. Quoted in Ronald Perry, 'Politics and the media 1975–1985', *Strands of Media Criticism: Reader*, Deakin University, Victoria, 1988, p. 69.
15. Edgar, op.cit., p. 8.
16. Ibid., p. 124.
17. Australian Press Council, *Annual Report No. 4*, 31 August, 1980, p. 20.
18. Loc. cit.
19. Ibid., p. 21.
20. Ibid., p. 23.
21. Loc. cit.
22. Ibid., p. 25.
23. *The News*, 24 August 1979.
24. Australian Press Council, *Annual Report No. 4*, p. 26.
25. Australian Press Council, *Annual Report No. 2*, 31 August 1978, p. 31.
26. House of Representatives Select Committee on the Print Media (Michael Lee, chairman), *News & Fair Facts: The Australian Print Media Industry*, Australian Government Publishing Service, Canberra, 1992, p. 278.
27. *The Bulletin*, 25 February 1992.
28. *Herald Sun*, 19 February 1992.
29. *Herald Sun*, 15 June 1992.
30. *The Sydney Morning Herald*, 30 November 1992.
31. Loc. cit.
32. For discussion of the implications of concentration in media ownership see Paul Chadwick, *Media Mates*, Macmillan, Melbourne 1989; David Bowman, *The Captive Press*, Penguin, Melbourne 1988; Les Carlyon, *Paper Chase: The Press Under Examination*, The Herald and Weekly Times Limited, Melbourne, 1982; House of Representatives Select Committee on the Print Media, *News & Fair Facts*, op. cit.
33. Jack Clancy, 'Bias?: A case study of coverage of RMIT in *The Age*', *Australian Journalism Review*, Vol. 14, January–June 1992, pp. 51–7.
34. Ibid., p. 54.

35. Australian Press Council, *Annual Report No. 15*, June 1991, p. 61.
36. Australian Press Council, *Annual Report No. 2*, August 1978, p. 22.
37. Loc. cit.
38. Ibid., p. 23.
39. Australian Press Council, *Annual Report No. 5*, June 1981, p. 28.
40. Courtney, op. cit.
41. Australian Press Council, *Annual Report No. 1*, August 1977, p. 17.
42. Loc. cit.
43. Ibid., p. 18.
44. Bowman, op. cit., p. xiii.
45. Australian Press Council, *Annual Report No. 2*, August 1978, p. 31.
46. Australian Press Council, *Annual Report No. 3*, August 1979, p. 23.
47. Ibid., pp. 22–3.
48. Ibid., p. 23.
49. Australian Press Council, *Annual Report No. 11*, June 1987, p. 39.
50. Jim Macnamara, *Public Relations & the Media: A New Influence in 'Agenda-Setting' and Content*, M.A. thesis, Deakin University, 1993.
51. Ibid., p. 90.
52. Ibid., p. 91.
53. *The Age*, 6 September 1991.
54. 'Smark resigns from The Age over plagiarism row', *The Australian*, 6 September 1991.

Chapter 3

1. Australian Press Council, *Booklet No. 4*, 31 August 1989, p. 4.
2. The 18-point professional practice policy at the Herald and Weekly Times was initiated by the editor-in-chief, Steve Harris, and introduced officially on 15 November 1993. Its preamble says that 'the professional activities of all editorial staff shall be guided by the principles of openness, fairness and commitment to accuracy and truth'. The policy applies to all editorial staff, whether permanent, casual or contributing and to editorial management of the company's four titles: *Herald Sun, Sunday Herald Sun, The Weekly Times* and *Sporting Globe*.
3. Australian Press Council, *Annual Report No. 16*, 30 June 1992, p. 18.
4. Ibid., p. 14.
5. Australian Press Council, *Annual Report No. 14*, 30 June 1990, p. 28.
6. Australian Press Council, *Annual Report No. 10*, 30 June 1986, p. 77.
7. National Working Party on the Portrayal of Women in the Media, *Women and Media*, Australian Government Printing Service, Canberra, July 1993.
8. *The Sydney Morning Herald*, 2 July 1993.
9. Tony Branigan, quoted in *The Australian*, 1 July 1993.
10. B. Stoddart, *Women, Sport and the Media*, University of Canberra, 1993, cited in *Women and Media*, op. cit. pp. 13–14.

11. Ibid., p. 14.
12. Murray Masterton, 'A new approach to what makes news news', *Australian Journalism Review*, Vol. 14 (No. 1), 1992, p. 22.
13. Loc. cit.
14. Mary Delahunty, quoted in 'The "male" approach to news', *Off The Record*, Victorian branch of the AJA, November 1991.
15. John Hurst, 'Kirner and the media', *Australian Journalism Review*, Vol. 15 (No. 1), 1993, p. 131.
16. Joan Kirner, quoted in 'The healing premiers', *The Age*, 18 August 1990.
17. *The Sunday Sun*, 12 August 1990.
18. 'The healing premiers', op. cit.
19. *People*, 4 March 1992.
20. *Australian Press Council News*, Vol. 4, No. 4, November 1992, p. 11.
21. Marlene Goldsmith, 'Pornography and the Press Council', *Australian Press Council News*, Vol. 5, No. 1, 1993, p. 4.
22. Ibid., p. 5.
23. David Flint, 'Offensiveness and erotica in the press', *Australian Press Council News*, Vol. 4, No. 4, November 1992, p. 4.
24. Australian Press Council, *Annual Report No. 11*, 30 June 1987, pp. 29–30.
25. Ibid., p. 30.
26. Loc. cit.
27. Richard Walsh, quoted in Goldsmith, op. cit. p. 5.
28. *Communications Update*, October 1992, p. 17.
29. Clifford G. Christians, Kim B. Rotzoll and Mark Fackler, *Media Ethics: Cases and Moral Reasoning*, Longman Inc., New York, 1983, pp. 218-20.
30. Australian Press Council, *Annual Report No. 14*, p. 77.
31. Loc. cit.
32. Australian Press Council, *Annual Report No. 15*, 30 June 1991, pp. 93-4.
33. Australian Press Council, *Annual Report No. 16*, pp. 83–4.
34. Figures based on the Australian Bureau of Statistics 1986 census.
35. Australian Press Council , *Annual Report No. 14*, p. 30.
36. Pamphlet issued by the Victorian Commissioner for Equal Opportunity, 1992.
37. George Blaikie, *Remember Smith's Weekly*, Rigby Limited, Adelaide, 1966, p. 228.
38. *Moreton Bay Courier*, May 1860, in Raymond Evans, 'The owl and the eagle — the significance of race in colonial Queensland', *Social Alternatives*, Vol. 5, No. 4, 1986, and quoted by Michael Meadows in 'People power: reporting or racism?', *Australian Journalism Review*, Vol. 9, Nos 1 & 2, 1987, p. 102.
39. Australian Press Council, *Annual Report No. 1*, 25 August 1977.
40. Australian Press Council, *Annual Report No. 10*, p. 6.

41. Australian Press Council, *Annual Report No. 16*, p. 58.
42. *The Australian*, 14 September 1993.
43. Australian Press Council, *Booklet No. 4*, p. 4.
44. Australian Press Council, *Annual Report No. 2*, 31 August 1978, p. 20.
45. Australian Press Council, *Annual Report No. 10*, p. 39.
46. Australian Press Council, *Annual Report No. 9*, 30 June 1985, p. 49.
47. Loc. cit.
48. Australian Press Council, *Annual Report No. 11*, p. 39.
49. Human Rights and Equal Opportunity Commission, *Racist Violence: Report of the National Inquiry into Racist Violence in Australia*, Australian Government Publishing Service, Canberra, 1991, p. 161.
50. Loc. cit.
51. Ibid., p. 162.
52. Loc. cit.
53. Peter Dossor, 'White stereotypes of the Aborigines', *Identity*, 1975, quoted in Janelle Miles, 'Changes in a newspaper's coverage of Aborigines', *Australian Journalism Review*, Vol. 7, January–December 1985, p. 36.
54. Janelle Miles, ibid., p. 37.
55. Ibid., p. 39.
56. John Hurst, 'Media coverage of Aborigines: a positive view?', *Australian Journalism Review*, Vol. 12, January–December 1990, p. 113.
57. Loc. cit.
58. Michael Meadows, 'People power: reporting or racism?', *Australian Journalism Review*, Vol. 9, January–December 1987, p. 104.
59. Loc. cit.
60. Australian Press Council, *Annual Report No. 11*, p. 46.
61. Loc. cit. Timms was later cleared of misconduct by the internal police inquiry to which the council referred in its adjudication.
62. Australian Press Council, *Annual Report No. 10*, p. 63.
63. Lester Bostock, *The Greater Perspective: Guidelines for the Production of Television and Film about Aborigines and Torres Strait Islanders*, Special Broadcasting Service, Canberra, 1990.
64. Royal Commission recommendation cited in the Australian Broadcasting Tribunal's *Inquiry to Review Radio and Television Program Standards Relating to Discriminatory Broadcasts, Decision and Reasons*, September 1992.
65. For the text of the Media, Entertainment and Arts Alliance guidelines, see Appendix 6.
66. Quoted in Muriel Snow and Grant Noble, 'Urban Aboriginal self images and the mass media', *Media Information Australia*, No. 42, November 1986, p. 47.
67. Mark Pearson, 'Interviewing Aborigines: a cross-cultural dilemma', *Australian Journalism Review*, Vol. 9, *passim*.

68. Quoted by the federal Minister for Aboriginal Affairs, Robert Tickner, at the *Reporting Cultural Diversity* seminar, Sydney, June 1991, and reported in *Communications Update*, July 1991, p. 4.
69. Australian Press Council, *Annual Report No. 10*, p. 6.
70. Australian Press Council, *Annual Report No. 6*, 30 June 1982, p. 53.
71. Australian Press Council, *Annual Report No. 9*, p. 29.
72. Ibid., p. 30.
73. Australian Press Council, *Annual Report No. 11*, p. 32.
74. Australian Press Council, *Annual Report No. 10*, p. 56.
75. *Racist Violence*, op. cit., p. 145.
76. Ibid., pp. 365–6.

Chapter 4

1. *The Bulletin*, 20 June 1989, quoted in Henry Mayer, *The Press in Australia*, Lansdowne Press, Melbourne, 1964, p. 22.
2. Peter Grabosky and Paul Wilson, *Journalism and Justice: How Crime is Reported*, Pluto Press, Sydney, 1989, p. 9.
3. Ibid., p. 13.
4. Ibid., p. 12.
5. Australian Press Council, *Booklet No. 4*, July 1989, p. 20.
6. Superintendent Norm Hazzard, quoted in *Australian Press Council News*, Vol. 5, No. 3, August 1993, p. 6.
7. Loc. cit.
8. Interview with Jane Munday, 17 September 1993.
9. Media release, issued jointly by the six state police commissioners, 31 March 1993.
10. 'Two hurled off cliff, court told', *Herald Sun*, 1 April 1993.
11. Graham Reilly, 'Guns and Words', *The Age*, 3 April 1993.
12. *The Age*, 1 April 1993.
13. Police commissioners' release, op. cit.
14. Loc. cit.
15. Reilly, op. cit.
16. *Herald-Sun*, 2 April 1993.
17. Australian Broadcasting Authority, personal communication, 9 December 1993.
18. 'Ratings report', *The Age* Green Guide, 7 April 1993.
19. Senator Reynolds, quoted in Reilly, op. cit.
20. Jock Rankin, quoted in 'Head to head', *Herald Sun*, 2 April 1992.
21. Grabosky and Wilson, op. cit., p. 121.
22. Ibid., pp. 121–3. The ABC news code of practice specifically mentions coverage of suicide. The Herald and Weekly Times' professional practice policy includes guidelines on reporting details of suicide, particularly youth suicide, and the manufacture and use of illegal drugs, firearms, booby traps and other life-threatening devices.
23. Ibid., p. 124.

24. *Herald-Sun,* 1 April 1993.
25. Tim Watson-Munro, quoted in *Herald Sun,* 1 April 1993, p. 3.
26. Tim Watson-Munro, 'Crime in the prime-time', *Herald Sun,* 1 April 1993, p. 13.
27. Transcript, compiled from media telephone interviews with Leonard Leabetter, *Herald-Sun,* 31 March 1993.
28. Grabosky and Wilson, op. cit., p. 44.
29. Advice on contempt of court law issued to Victorian police officers, November 1992.
30. For a view of journalists' attitudes to contempt laws, see Grabosky and Wilson, op. cit., Chapter 4.
31. Reilly, op. cit.
32. Grabosky and Wilson, op. cit., pp. 26–32.
33. Ibid., p. 32.
34. *Herald Sun,* 31 March 1993.
35. AGB–McNair figures, prepared for the Radio Marketing Bureau, estimated 87 per cent of Australian households had three or more radios in 1993. The estimate of total radios for 1992 was 29.1 million. AGB–McNair, personal communication, 9 November 1993.
36. ABC Radio, 30 March 1993.
37. Tim Watson-Munro, 'Crime in prime-time', op. cit.
38. Michael Willesee, interviewed by Iain Gillespie in *Fear or Favour,* SBS Television, 21 September 1993.
39. Reilly, op. cit.
40. Jane Munday, op. cit.
41. Interview with Graham Coddington, 1 April 1993.
42. *Geelong Advertiser,* 15 September 1984.
43. *The Sun News-Pictorial,* 15 September 1984.
44. Bill D'Arcy, *The Sunday Observer,* 30 September 1984.
45. *The Herald,* 15 September 1984.
46. David Bowman, 'The Geelong conundrum', *Australian Society,* November 1984.
47. Victoria Police media briefing notes, 29 June 1989.
48. Derryn Hinch, quoted in *The Age,* 30 June 1989.
49. Trevor Barr, quoted in Reilly, op. cit.
50. Richard Pyle, *Schwarzkopf: The Man, the Mission, the Triumph,* Mandarin, London, 1991, p. 129.
51. Coddington, op. cit.
52. 'Live hostage coverage: what do you report?', *The Rundown,* Vol. X, No. 42, p. 319.
53. Ibid., p. 325.
54. Ibid., p. 324.
55. Ibid., p. 319.
56. Inspector Bruce Knight to a meeting of the Victoria Police Media Liasion Committee, December 1992.
57. *The Rundown,* op. cit., p. 320.

58. Police commissioners' release, op. cit. The Canadian code also forbids conducting interviews with victims or offenders during the course of a siege.
59. Coddington, op. cit.
60. Professor Brent Waters on *A Current Affair*, quoted in the *Herald Sun*, 1 April 1993.
61. *A Current Affair*, 30 March 1993.
62. Dr Janet Hall, quoted in the *Herald Sun*, 1 April 1993.
63. Editorial, *Herald Sun*, 2 April 1993.
64. *A Current Affair*, 31 March 1993.
65. John O'Neill, 'A family under siege', *The Independent Monthly*, July 1993.
66. Loc. cit.
67. Loc. cit.
68. Loc. cit.
69. A classic case of children being subjected to intense media scrutiny over the actions of their parents was that of Adain Chamberlain, son of Lindy and Michael Chamberlain.
70. *The Sun News-Pictorial*, *The Australian*, *The Age*, 18 April 1984.
71. *The Age*, 8 October 1984.
72. *The Age*, 24 August 1987.
73. *The Age*, 21 August 1987. The demands also included a list of prison reforms.
74. *The Sunday Herald*, 24 February 1991.
75. *The Age*, 21 August 1987.
76. *The Age*, 24 August 1987.
77. Dr Jim Cairns, quoted in *The Age*, ibid.
78. *The Age*, 1 February 1990.
79. *The Age*, 10 May 1989.
80. *The Sunday Age*, 18 February 1990.
81. Telephone interview with Sally Gluyas, 16 September 1993.
82. *The Age*, 11 May 1989.
83. Sally Gluyas, op. cit.
84. Interview with Alan Kohler, 13 September 1993.
85. *The Sunday Age*, op. cit.
86. *The Age*, 7 April 1992.
87. Michael Smith, editor of *The Age*, quoted in 'A question of intervention', *The Age*, 8 April 1992.
88. Loc. cit.
89. 'Clampdown on terrorist attacks', *The Australian*, 29 April 1992.
90. Letters to the Editor, *The Age*, 8 April 1992.
91. *The Australian*, 20 April 1992.
92. Paul Chadwick, quoted in 'A question of intervention', op. cit.
93. *The Age* Green Guide, 16 April 1992.
94. Loc. cit.
95. Letters to the Editor, *The Age*, 9 April 1992.

Chapter 5

1. See annual reports of the Australian Press Council (1977–1992), which include many complaints of invasion of personal privacy or intrusion into grief; also the Australian Broadcasting Tribunal report, *Violence on Television*, ABT, Sydney, 1990.

2. Kenneth Morgan, 'Press, politicians and privacy', *Australian Press Council News*, Vol. 3, No. 4, November 1991, pp. 1–3.

3. Australian Law Reform Commission, *Report No. 11: Unfair Publication: Defamation and Privacy*, AGPS Canberra 1979, p. 121.

4. Ibid.

5. Discussion on privacy, *The Couchman Show*, ABC Television, 18 April 1990.

6. Ibid.

7. Ibid.

8. See, for instance, the article by John Sylvester, 'Knocking on doors shouldn't be banned', in *Off The Record*, journal of the Victorian branch of the Australian Journalists Association, September 1986, p. 5; and also Peter Grabosky and Paul Wilson, *Journalism and Justice: How Crime is Reported*, Pluto Press, Sydney, 1989, p. 117.

9. Grabosky and Wilson, op. cit., p. 118.

10. Father Dennis Vanderwolf, 'A mining community grieves', in *NALAG Newsletter*, February 1990.

11. John Harrison, 'Deathknocks: the media come to grief', in John Henningham (ed.), *Issues in Australian Journalism*, Longman Cheshire, Melbourne, 1990, pp. 83–4.

12. Harrison, op. cit., p. 81.

13. Ibid., p. 87.

14. Australian Press Council, *Annual Report No. 11*, June 1987, pp. 28–9. See also the following adjudication, pp. 29–30.

15. John Sylvester, op. cit., p. 5.

16. Grabosky and Wilson, op. cit., p. 120.

17. John Geraint and David Willcock, 'Grief Observed', *The Listener*, 11 August 1988.

18. Grabosky and Wilson, op. cit., p. 117.

19. Ibid., p. 127.

20. Australian Law Reform Commission, *Report No. 11*, op. cit., p. 126.

21. Interview with John Gibson, Channel Seven, 14 July 1992.

22. Greg Thom and Glenn Conley, 'Lane human fireball shock for rescuers', *Herald-Sun*, 29 May 1992.

23. Interview with John Gibson, Channel Seven, 14 July 1992.

24. John Hurst, *The Walkley Awards: Australia's Best Journalists in Action*, John Kerr, Melbourne, 1988, pp. 175–6 and pp. 221–2.

25. John Hurst, 'Invasion of privacy and the public right to know', *Strands of Media Criticism: Study Guide*, Deakin University, Victoria, 1988, pp. 22–3.

26. J. Masterton, Letters to the Editor, *The Age*, 7 October 1986.
27. Philip Patterson and Lee Wilkins (eds), *Media Ethics: Issues and Cases*, Wm. C. Brown Publishers, 1991, p. 171.
28. R. P. Handley, 'Trespass to land as a remedy for unlawful intrusion on privacy', *Australian Law Journal*, Vol. 62, No. 3, March 1988, pp. 216–22.
29. J. M. Aberdeen, 'Media "walk-ins": privacy invasion or public interest?', *Australian Current Law*, August 1986, 36057–60.
30. Australian Law Reform Commission, *Report No. 22: Privacy*, Vol. 1 (background), AGPS, Canberra, 1983, p. 25.
31. Ibid., pp. 117–18.
32. Clem Lloyd, *Profession: Journalist*, Hale & Iremonger, Sydney, 1985, pp. 235–6.
33. Australian Law Reform Commission, *Report No. 11*, op. cit., p. 121.
34. Australian Press Council, *Annual Report No. 2*, August 1978, p. 6.
35. Ibid., p. 7.
36. Australian Press Council, *Annual Report No. 1*, August 1977, pp. 41–2.
37. Australian Press Council, *Annual Report No. 4*, August 1980, p. 29.
38. Australian Press Council, *Annual Report No. 2*, op. cit., pp. 28–9.
39. Australian Press Council, *Annual Report No. 3*, August 1979, p. 11.
40. Australian Press Council, *Annual Report No. 4*, op. cit., p. 17. See also comment by Ric Lucas, 'The Press Council, guarding the fourth estate,' *Legal Service Bulletin*, February 1986, pp. 17–19.
41. Australian Press Council, *Annual Report No. 6*, August 1982, p. 45.
42. Australian Press Council, *Annual Report No. 1*, op. cit., pp. 41–2.
43. Ibid., p. 13.
44. Australian Law Reform Commission, *Report No. 11*, op. cit., p. 120.
45. David Flint, 'A healthy division', edited version of speech to National Press Club, Canberra, on 27 November 1991, in *Australian Press Council News*, Vol. 4, No. 1, February 1992, p. 6.
46. Ibid.
47. Australian Press Council, *Annual Report No. 15*, June 1991, pp. 86–7.
48. Australian Press Council, *Annual Report No. 5*, June 1981, pp. 29–31.
49. Speech by Ian Sinclair, Minister for Communications, to a seminar entitled 'The Politics of Information' at the University of Sydney Law School, 20 May 1981, reproduced in the *Commonwealth Record*, 18–24 May 1981.
50. Rod Usher, 'The scoop that sank', *The Age Weekend Review*, 9 May 1981, and also the editorial, 'Why publish the stuff', *The Age*, 11 May 1981.
51. Australian Press Council, *Annual Report No. 5*, op. cit., pp. 30–1.
52. 'The Prince Charles tapes', *Sunday Observer*, 10 May 1981.
53. Australian Press Council, *Annual Report No. 5*, op. cit., pp. 29–30.
54. Helen Ballard, 'Tape shock: Kennett/Peacock in late night call', *The Sun News-Pictorial*, 23 March 1987.

55. Nikki Savva, 'Sack backlash', *The Sun News-Pictorial*, 24 March 1987.
56. 'Expletives deleted', *The Sun News-Pictorial*, 24 March 1987.
57. Geoffrey Russell, 'Privacy in modern Australia', radio tape, Deakin University, 18 May 1987; also *The Sun News-Pictorial*, 24 March 1987.
58. Gary Tippet, 'Lib leader "warned of phone tap"', *The Sun News-Pictorial*, 24 March 1987.
59. Russell, op. cit.
60. Russell, op. cit.
61. Ibid.
62. Ibid.
63. Australian Press Council, *Annual Report No. 11*, June 1987, pp. 76–7.
64. *Australian Press Council News*, August 1992, pp. 11–12.
65. Ibid.
66. Ibid.
67. Interview with Daryl McLure, 21 August 1992.
68. Ibid.
69. John Hurst, 'Invasion of privacy and the public's right to know', op. cit., p. 21.
70. Stuart Robertson, interviewed by Phillip Adams on *Late Night Live*, ABC Radio, 9 September 1991.
71. Muriel Cooper, 'A good nose for tell-tale rubbish', *The Herald*, Melbourne, '17 September 1990; also 'Rap for TV over Ita's rubbish', *The Sun News-Pictorial*, Melbourne, 13 September 1990.
72. Ibid.
73. Derryn Hinch, 'Here is the news . . . that we think you should watch', *The Sun News-Pictorial*, May 1990.
74. Ibid.
75. 'The American public figure concept', Appendix 'F', in Australian Law Reform Commission, *Report No. 11*, op. cit., p. 251.
76. Ibid.
77. Philip Patterson and Lee Wilkins, op. cit., p. 111.
78. Ibid.

Chapter 6

1. Australian Press Council, *Annual Report No. 12*, June 1988, p. 21.
2. Australian Press Council, *Annual Report No. 10*, June 1986, p. 79
3. Australian Press Council, *Annual Report No. 6*, June 1982, p. 63.
4. Australian Press Council, *Annual Report No. 12*, p. 21.
5. Australian Press Council, *Aims, Principles, Constitution and Complaints Procedure*, Booklet No. 4, 1989, p. 7.
6. Australian Press Council, *Annual Report No. 14*, June 1990, pp. 77–8.
7. Peter R. Young, Submission to the Senate Standing Committee on Legal and Constitutional Affairs on 'The Rights and Obligations of the Media in Time of War and Limited Conflict', 3 September 1993.
8. Australian Press Council, *Annual Report No. 10*, op. cit., pp. 65–6.

9. Australian Press Council, *Annual Report No. 16*, op. cit., pp. 97–8.
10. 'Violence and the media', *Media Information Australia*, No. 54, November 1989, p. 158.
11. Peter Grabosky and Paul Wilson, *Journalism and Justice: How Crime is Reported*, Pluto Press, Sydney, 1989, p. 15.
12. Richard Glover, 'Farewell to polite society', *The Sunday Age*, 13 September 1992.
13. Australian Press Council, *Annual Report No. 5*, June 1981, p. 28.
14. Australian Press Council, *Annual Report No. 15*, June 1991, pp. 80–1.
15. Australian Press Council, *Annual Report No. 16*, June 1992, p. 107.
16. Ibid., pp. 106–7.
17. Ibid., pp. 116–17.
18. Australian Press Council, *Annual Report No. 13*, June 1989, p. 57.
19. Australian Press Council, *Annual Report No. 15*, op. cit., p. 73.
20. Australian Press Council, *Annual Report No. 12*, op. cit., pp. 66–7.
21. Australian Press Council, *Annual Report No. 9*, June 1985, p. 55.
22. Australian Press Council, *Annual Report No. 11*, June 1987, pp. 73–4.

Chapter 7

1. 'News man jailed for seven days', *The Sun News-Pictorial*, 13 December 1989. See also 'Jail term rage', in *The Journalist*, January 1990.
2. Jan Mayman, 'Journalist gets $10 000 fine', *The Sun News-Pictorial*, 8 September 1990.
3. 'Journalist jailed over silence', *The Age*, 21 March 1992.
4. Ibid.
5. 'Journalist jailed for withholding source', *The Age*, 20 April 1993.
6. See Appendix 1, clause 3.
7. Western Australian Law Reform Commission, *Report on Privilege for Journalists*, 1980, pp. 26–7.
8. Ibid., p. 8.
9. Ibid., pp. 24–5.
10. Ibid., pp. 24–5.
11. Western Australian Law Reform Commission, *Working Paper: Privilege for Journalists*, 1977, p. 20.
12. Op. cit., pp. 1–3.
13. *McGuinness* v. *Attorney-General of Victoria* (1940), 63 CLR 73, pp. 102–3.
14. John Doogue, *The Writer and the Law*, Deakin University Press, Victoria, 1982, pp. 248–51.
15. Op. cit., p. 251.
16. Western Australian Law Reform Commission, *Working Paper*, op. cit., pp. 5–6; see also ACT Law Reports, 1977–78, *Hewitt* v. *West Australian Newspapers Ltd*, 17 ACTR 15, pp. 15–29.
17. J.G. Starke, 'Non-disclosure by a journalist of the identity of his source

of information', *Australian Law Journal*, Vol. 63, No. 1, January 1989, pp. 9–11.

18. Press release, 'Disclosure of sources', in Australian Press Council, *Annual Report No. 13*, 30 June 1989, pp. 38–40.

19. J.G. Starke, loc. cit.

20. David Bowman, 'Can nine judges be wrong?', *Australian Society*, December 1988/January 1989.

21. Ibid.

22. Grant Hattam and Stephen Maloney, 'The newspaper rule', *Law Institute Journal*, Vol. 63, June 1989, pp. 468–9.

23. 'Reporters ordered to name source', *The Advertiser*, Adelaide, 21 September 1988.

24. 'Sources stay secret', *Australian Press Council News*, November 1989, p. 3.

25. Western Australian Law Reform Commission, *Report on Privilege for Journalists*, op. cit., pp. 7–8; also Western Australian Reform Commission *Working Paper*, op. cit., pp. 6–7.

26. Telephone interview with Richard Hall, 28 January 1993.

27. 'Contempt law held in contempt', *The Journalist*, July 1984.

28. Australian Press Council, *Annual Report No. 13*, June 1989, p. 40.

29. Simon Lloyd, 'Alleged HLC leak sparks raid on Financial Review', *The Australian Financial Review*, 6 July 1990.

30. Australian Press Council, *Annual Report No. 15*, June 1991, pp. 13–14.

31. Lloyd, op. cit.

32. Jack Waterford, 'Police raids and press freedom', and Greg Ellis, 'Management of public information', *Australian Press Council News*, November 1992, pp. 2–3.

33. David Elias and Michael Magazanik, 'Court acts on Age raid', *The Age*, 28 January 1993.

34. 'Confidential sources', *Australian Press Council News*, November 1992, p. 8.

35. Doogue, op. cit., p. 241.

36. Australian Press Council submission to the Western Australian Law Reform Commission's discussion paper on professional privilege for confidential communications, 12 March 1992, paras 2.7 and 2.8.

37. Australian Press Council, *Annual Report No. 10*, June 1986, p. 21.

38. Ibid.

39. Ibid., pp. 28–30.

40. Ibid.

41. Rodney Tiffen, 'Confidential sources in the news: conventions and contortions', *Australian Journalism Review*, Vol. 10, 1988, p. 24.

42. Ibid., p. 23.

43. Ibid., p. 26.

44. Ibid., p. 25.

45. Western Australian Law Reform Commission, *Working Paper No. 53*, 1977, p. 19.

46. Richard Cunningham, 'Should reporters reveal sources to editors?', *The Quill*, October 1988, *passim*.

47. Telephone interview with Don Woolford, 27 January 1993.

48. Telephone interview with Greg Turnbull, 6 January 1993.

Chapter 8

1. Pauline Turner, 'A word ruffles Willesee feathers', *The Sydney Morning Herald*, 7 April 1988.

2. Ibid.

3. Tom Rood, 'The ethical values of US and Australian journalists', *Australian Journalism Review*, Vol. 7, Nos 1 & 2, January–December 1985, pp. 19–21.

4. John Hulteng, *The Messenger's Motives: Ethical Problems of the News Media*, Prentice-Hall, Englewood Cliffs, New Jersey, 1985, p. 82.

5. David Anderson and Peter Benjaminson, *Investigative Reporting*, Indiana University Press, Bloomington, Indiana, 1976, pp. 6–7.

6. See Appendix 1.

7. Report of the AJA Code of Ethics Review Committee to the federal council of the AJA, 12 July 1984.

8. Australian Press Council, *Aims, Principles, Constitution and Complaints Procedure*, Booklet No. 4, July 1989, pp. 3–4.

9. Australian Press Council, *Annual Report No. 7*, June 1983, pp. 43–46.

10. Ibid.

11. Ibid.

12. John Avieson, 'The AJA — arbiter of ethics', in John Hurst (ed.), *Strands of Media Criticism*, Deakin University Press, Victoria, 1988, p. 9.

13. 'School investigation was a tawdry exercise, says Metherell', *The Sydney Morning Herald*, 16 September 1988.

14. Ibid.

15. 'The editor-in-chief replies', *The Sydney Morning Herald*, 16 September 1988; see also 'Metherell accuses Herald of breach of ethics', loc. cit.

16. See Lawrence Apps, 'Journalism, ethics and ideology', in John Henningham (ed.), *Issues in Australian Journalism*, Longman Cheshire, Melbourne, 1990, pp. 74–5.

17. John Hurst, *The Walkley Awards: Australia's Best Journalists in Action*, John Kerr, Melbourne 1988, pp. 155–7.

18. Ethics and the Media, videotape, Deakin University, 1988.

19. Transcript of Hinch program segment on Radio 3AW, Melbourne, 25 February 1983.

20. Report of AJA South Australian branch judiciary committee, 12 May 1983, and also Maurice Dunlevy's letter to the committee on 18 April 1983.

21. Report by AJA South Australian branch judiciary committee to AJA federal council, 1983.

22. Alan R. Ginsberg, 'Secret taping: a no-no for Nixon but okay for reporters?', *Columbia Journalism Review*, July–August 1984, pp. 16–19.

23. Theodore L. Glasser, 'On the morality of secretly taped interviews', *Nieman Reports*, Spring 1985, pp. 17–20.

24. Ginsberg, op. cit., p. 16.

25. Elizabeth S. Bird, 'Newspaper editors' attitudes reflect doubt on surreptitious recording', *Journalism Quarterly*, Summer 1985, pp. 284–95. For a comparative study of the attitudes of Australian and American editors see the study by Tom Rood mentioned earlier.

26. See, for instance, Australian Law Reform Commission, *Unfair Publication: Defamation and Privacy*, Report No. 11, AGPS, 1979, p. 119.

27. Peter Putnis, 'Television journalism and image ethics', *Australian Journalism Review*, Vol. 14, No. 2, July–December 1992, pp. 12–13.

28. Australian Press Council, *Annual Report No. 1*, August 1977, pp. 14–15.

29. John Hurst, *The Walkley Awards*, op. cit., p. 174.

30. Australian Press Council, *Annual Report No. 7*, June 1983, p .27.

31. Ibid.

32. Putnis, op. cit., p. 2.

33. S. Wright, 'Camera gets issue in sharp focus', *The Sun News-Pictorial*, 4 August 1990.

34. Telephone interview with Laurie Oakes, 14 September 1992.

35. Edward Klein, editor of *The New York Times*, quoted in Philip Patterson and Lee Wilkins (eds), *Media Ethics*, Wm C. Brown Publishers, Dubuque, Iowa, p. 174.

36. Patterson and Wilkins, ibid.

37. J. D. Lassica, 'Photographs that lie, the ethical dilemma of digital retouching', *Washington Journalism Review*, June 1989, p. 22.

38. Interview with Steve Harris, 20 October 1993.

39. Lassica, op. cit., p. 23.

40. S. Reaves, 'Digital retouching: is there a place for it in newspaper photography?', *Journal of Mass Media Ethics*, Spring–Summer 1985, pp. 40–8.

41. Lassica, op. cit., p. 25.

42. Ibid.

43. Hulteng, op. cit., p. 67.

44. Ibid., p. 68.

45. 'A debate about ethics code', *Editor and Publisher*, 9 October 1993.

46. Australian Press Council, *Annual Report No. 3*, August 1979, p. 21.

47. *The Age*, 6 March 1987.

48. 'ABC inquiry criticises Pilger–PM interview', *The Age*, 16 March 1987.

49. 'PM tops Pilger's rude politician list', *The Sun News-Pictorial*, 10 March 1987.

50. 'How a Hawke interview was "Pilgerised"', *The Bulletin*, 24 March 1987.

51. Ibid.
52. Ibid.
53. John Pilger, 'Hawke manipulation', *Australian Journalism Review*, Vol. 9, January–December 1987, p. 16.

Chapter 9

1. Telephone interview with Bruce Guthrie, 5 October 1993.
2. Ibid.
3. Iain Gillespie, *Fear or Favour*, SBS Television, 21 September 1993.
4. Danielle Cook, 'Chequebook journalism widespread: media chief', *The Age*, 7 October 1991, p. 3. Walsh later qualified his remarks by saying it was mainly magazines who were involved in chequebook journalism.
5. Ibid.
6. Telephone interview with Steve Harris, 1 October 1993.
7. Guthrie, op. cit.
8. Ibid.
9. Ibid.
10. *See Woman's Day*, 8 September 1992.
11. Telephone interview with Richard Walsh, 12 October 1993.
12. Ibid.
13. British Press Council, *Press Conduct in the Sutcliffe Case*, Booklet No. 7, 1982, pp. 93–4.
14. Ibid., pp. 173–4.
15. Ibid., p. 82.
16. Ibid., p. 83.
17. Ibid., p. 82.
18. Ibid., p. 193.
19. Bruce McDougall, 'Outrage over TV drugs interview fee', *Daily Telegraph*, 5 May 1989.
20. John Avieson, 'Chequebook journalism: A question of ethics', *Australian Journalism Review*, Vol. 14, No. 1, January–June 1992, pp. 49–50.
21. Bruce McDougall, '$12,000 paid for story of Hayward jail saga', *Daily Telegraph*, 4 May 1989.
22. Peter Luck, 'Fifth column', *The Sydney Morning Herald* Guide, 8–14 May 1989.
23. John Avieson, op. cit., p. 49.
24. Ibid., p. 50.
25. British Press Council, op. cit., pp. 96–7.
26. Ranald Macdonald, 'Chequebook journalism', *Australian Press Council News*, Vol. 1, No. 3, August 1989, pp. 1–2.
27. British Press Council, op. cit., p. 83.
28. Avieson, op. cit., p. 47.
29. Walsh, op. cit.
30. British Press Council, op. cit., pp. 155–8.

31. 'Bowled over', picture caption in *The Sunday Age*, 17 May 1993.
32. British Press Council, op. cit., p. 80.
33. Guthrie, op. cit.
34. John Hurst, *The Walkley Awards: Australia's Best Journalists in Action*, John Kerr, Melbourne, 1988, pp. 47–53.
35. Ibid., pp. 282–3.
36. Telephone interview with Max Markson, 13 September 1993.
37. Ibid.
38. Ibid.
39. Telephone interview with David Emerson, 13 September 1993.
40. Greg Roberts, 'Lewis in deal with Murdoch paper', *The Sydney Morning Herald*, 9 May 1989.
41. Avieson, op. cit., p. 48.
42. Macdonald, op. cit., p. 2.
43. Guthrie, op. cit.
44. Professional Practice Policy, Herald and Weekly Times Limited, 15 November 1993.

Chapter 10

1. Margaret Simons, 'Junkets: Choking on a free trip', *Off The Record*, April 1986, pp. 6–7
2. Ronald Perry, 'Politics and the media, 1975–1985', Edward Wilson Memorial Lecturer, Deakin University, 1985, reproduced in *Strands of Media Criticism*, Deakin University, Victoria, 1987.
3. Ibid.
4. Ed Avis, 'Have subsidy, will travel', *The Quill*, Vol. 79, No. 2, March 1991, p. 24.
5. Jane Cadzow, 'The well kept secrets of men of taste', *The Age Good Weekend*, 20 May 1989.
6. Ibid.
7. Ibid.
8. Ibid.
9. Ibid.
10. Ibid.
11. Ibid.
12. Ibid.
13. Interview with Ben Hills, 12 March 1990.
14. 'Rothman's used funds to influence media, court told', *The Sydney Morning Herald*, 10 February 1990; and also *The Sydney Morning Herald*, 13 February 1990.
15. John L. Hulteng, *The Messenger's Motives: Ethical Problems for the News Media* (2nd edn), Prentice-Hall, Inc., New Jersey, 1985, p. 85.
16. Simons, op. cit., p. 6.
17. Ibid., pp. 6–7.
18. Ibid., p. 7.

19. Jim Sibbison, 'Pushing new drugs — can the press kick the habit?', *Columbia Journalism Review*, July–August 1985, pp. 52–4.
20. Ibid.
21. Ibid.
22. Peter Laud, 'Freebie path full of pitfalls', *The Journalist*, February 1988, p. 7.
23. Ibid.
24. Ibid.
25. Stuart Littlemore, *Media Watch*, ABC Television, 29 March 1993.
26. Julianne Schultz (ed.), *Reporting Business*, Australian Centre for Independent Journalism, University of Technology, Sydney, 1993, p. 3.
27. Peter Grabosky and Paul Wilson, *Journalism and Justice: How Crime is Reported*, Pluto Press, Sydney, p. 95.
28. Schultz, op. cit., pp. 2-3.
29. Schultz, op. cit., pp. 23 and 24.
30. Ibid.
31. Australian Press Council, *Annual Report No. 15*, June 1991, p. 103.
32. Karen Schneider and Marc Gunther, 'Those newsroom ethics codes', *Columbia Journalism Review*, July–August 1985, pp. 55–7.
33. Ibid.
34. Hulteng, op. cit., pp. 33–4.

Chapter 11

1. House of Representatives Select Committee on the Print Media (Michael Lee, chairman), *News & Fair Facts: The Australian Print Media Industry*, Australian Government Publishing Service, Canberra, 1992, p. 290.
2. Ranald Macdonald, *David Syme*, Vantage House, Melbourne, 1982, p. 25.
3. Peter Cole-Adams, 'Censorship and self-censorship in the press', *Australian Press Council News*, November 1992, p. 7.
4. Ibid.
5. Australian Press Council, *Annual Report No. 9*, June 1985, pp. 10–11.
6. Tony Wells, quoted by Georgina Griffin, *Re-inventing Journalistic Ethics for the 90s: A Study of the Effects of the Recession on Advertiser Pressure and Freebies in the Victorian Media*, Bachelor of Arts final year research project, Royal Melbourne Institute of Technology, 1993, p. 8.
7. Griffin, ibid., p. 10.
8. Loc. cit.
9. R. B. Walker, *Yesterday's News: A History of the Newspaper Press in New South Wales from 1920 to 1945*, Sydney University Press, Sydney, 1980, p. 186.
10. *Media Watch*, ABC Television, 27 September 1993.

11. *Media Watch*, ABC Television, 29 March 1993.

12. Australian Press Council, *Annual Report No. 3*, August 1980, p. 14.

13. Australian Press Council, *Annual Report No. 9*, pp. 12–13.

14. Griffin, op. cit., p. 12.

15. Ian Needham, quoted in Griffin, ibid., p. 12.

16. Adrian Deamer, 'Self-censorship', in Keith and Elizabeth Windschuttle (eds), *Fixing the News: Critical perspectives on the Australian media*, Cassell Australia, Sydney, 1981, p. 42.

17. Griffin, op. cit., p. 12.

18. *The Australian*, 11 October 1993.

19. Australian Press Council, *Annual Report No.9*, p. 44.

20. Ibid., p. 45.

21. Loc. cit.

22. Creighton Burns, 'Not much power and very little glory', Hugo Wolfsohn Memorial Lecture, LaTrobe University, 13 September 1988.

23. Julianne Schultz (ed.), *Reporting Business: A Report into the Attitudes, Values and Practice of Business, Finance and Economics Journalism in Australian*, Australian Centre for Independent Journalism, Sydney, 1993, p. 25.

24. House of Representatives Select Committee on the Print Media, *News & Fair Facts*, op. cit., p. 267.

25. Ibid., p. 268.

26. Loc. cit.

27. Ibid., p. 269.

28. Ibid., p. 270.

29. Loc. cit.

30. Ibid., p. 271.

31. 'Editor rejects claim papers are owners' propaganda tools', *The Australian*, 28 October 1993.

Chapter 12

1. Michelle Edmunds, *The Journalists' Code of Ethics in Practice: How Melbourne Journalists Use the Code*, Bachelor of Arts final year research project, Royal Melbourne Institute of Technology, 1993. Edmunds in her study of Melbourne print journalists found that the reason behind 21 of 61 admitted breaches of the code was 'pressure from superiors'.

2. Ibid. Seven per cent of the respondents to Edmund's survey said they used the code in day-to-day decision making; 22 per cent said they never used it.

3. Letter to the Victorian branch committee of the AJA from Maclaren Gordon, chairman of the branch judiciary committee, 6 March 1992.

4. Maclaren Gordon, letter of resignation to the AJA Victorian branch committee secretary, Michael Sutherland, 24 July 1992.

5. For an outline of the inadequacy of the tribunal's operation on ethical

issues, see submissions No. 16 and 17 to the Australian Broadcasting Tribunal, *Inquiry to Review Radio and Television Program Standards Relating to Discriminatory Broadcasts (RPS 3 & TPS 2(b)): Decision and Reasons*, 1992, pp. 26–30.

6. Examples of possible models are ABC Radio's *The Media Report*, and ABC Television's *Media Watch* and *Backchat*.

7. See 'SMH editor-in-chief rejects ombudsman's suggestion', *PANPA Bulletin*, June 1990.

Index

The exercises have not been indexed. The word *bis* following a page number indicates the topic appears separately twice on that page, and *passim* after a range of numbers indicates that the topic appears in scattered passages on each of those pages. Words beginning with Mc are listed as if they were spelt Mac.

Potter, Andrew   109
Potter, Ralph: and the Potter Box
    7
prejudice   *see* bias
Press Complaints Commission
    (UK)   15
    see also predecessor British Press
    Council
press releases   *see* media
    releases
privacy   3, 10, 22, 111–38
    of documents   130–2
    justification of invasions of
        115–20
    and nakedness   118–19, 123
    of public figures   111, 123–5,
        136–7
    in public places   111, 122
    and telephone calls   125–30
    see also grief, death, news
        values, pictures,
        Telecommunication
        (Interception) Act
Privacy Committee (NSW)   122,
    124, 134–5, 182
public interest   15–18, 57, 66,
    253
    vs bad taste   140, 141–3
    vs business interests of the
        media company   237–51
    and chequebook journalism
        205
    and confidentiality of sources
        148–69
    and freebies   217
    vs honesty   173–5
    vs privacy   111–38
    vs public relations   229–30
    see also public's right to know
Public Interest Advocacy Centre
    146
public relations: 216–36
    media releases   50–2
Public Relations Institute of
    Australia   225
public's right to know   3, 10,
    14–15, 16–17, 19, 81, 91, 94–7
    see also public interest

quotations   190–2

race   *see* ethnicity
Radio Television News
    Directors' Association of
    Canada   99
Rajhneesh Organisation   174–5
Ramsay, Alan   244–5
Ramsay, Tom   232
Rankin, Jock   87
rape: non–disclosure of victim's
    identity   115
Rawls, John   12–13
regulation   ix–x, 18–24, 54–5,
    120–5, 252–9
    see also D–notices
relativism   8–9
religion   54–7, 77–80
    see also Judaism, Islam
responsibilities   *see* duties
Reynolds, Margaret   87, 102
Richards, Ron   213
Richardson, Graham   169
right of reply   26–7, 39, 47–50
rights   9–10, 56
    see also natural rights, privacy
Robertson, Stuart   133–4
Robinson, Peter   161
Robson, Frank   74
Rogers, Ian   160–1
Rood, Tom   172
Rothmans (company)   227–8
Rotzoll, Kim B.   6–7
Royal Commission into
    Aboriginal Deaths in
    Custody   74, 75–6, 253
Royal Commissions: and
    confidentiality of sources
    158–60
Royal Melbourne Institute of
    Technology (RMIT)   42

*St. George and Sutherland Shire
    Leader*   48–9
salami questioning: and
    confidentiality of sources
    160
satire   57, 66
Saunders, Ray   118
Saxon, M.B.   160
scepticism   8
Schildberger, Michael   32